CAMBRIDGE

Brighter Thinking

The Reformation in Europe, c1500–1564

A/AS Level History for AQA
Student Book

Max von Habsburg

Series Editors: Michael Fordham and David Smith

CAMBRIDGE
UNIVERSITY PRESS

University Printing House, Cambridge CB2 8BS, United Kingdom

Cambridge University Press is part of the University of Cambridge.

It furthers the University's mission by disseminating knowledge in the pursuit of education, learning and research at the highest international levels of excellence.

www.cambridge.org

Information on this title: www.cambridge.org/ukschools/9781107573215 (Paperback)
www.cambridge.org/ukschools/9781107573222 (Cambridge Elevate-enhanced Edition)

First published 2015

A catalogue record for this publication is available from the British Library

ISBN 978-1-107-57321-5 Paperback
ISBN 978-1-107-57322-2 Cambridge Elevate-enhanced Edition

Additional resources for this publication at www.cambridge.org/ukschools

Cambridge University Press has no responsibility for the persistence or accuracy of URLs for external or third-party internet websites referred to in this publication, and does not guarantee that any content on such websites is, or will remain, accurate or appropriate. Information regarding prices, travel timetables, and other factual information given in this work is correct at the time of first printing but Cambridge University Press does not guarantee the accuracy of such information thereafter.

Message from AQA

This textbook has been approved by AQA for use with our qualification. This means that we have checked that it broadly covers the specification and we are satisfied with the overall quality. Full details of our approval process can be found on our website.

We approve textbooks because we know how important it is for teachers and students to have the right resources to support their teaching and learning. However, the publisher is ultimately responsible for the editorial control and quality of this book.

Please note that when teaching the A/AS Level History (7041, 7042) course, you must refer to AQA's specification as your definitive source of information. While this book has been written to match the specification, it cannot provide complete coverage of every aspect of the course.

A wide range of other useful resources can be found on the relevant subject pages of our website: www.aqa.org.uk

Contents

About this book

Cambridge A/AS Level History for AQA is an exciting new series designed to support students in their journey from GCSE to A Level and then on to possible further historical study. The books provide the knowledge, concepts and skills needed for the two-year AQA History A Level course, but it's our intention as series editors that students recognise that their A Level exams are just one step to a potential lifelong relationship with the discipline of history. This book has further readings, extracts from historians' works and links to wider questions and ideas that go beyond the scope of an A Level course. With this series, we have sought to ensure not only that the students are well prepared for their examinations, but also that they gain access to a wider debate that characterises historical study.

The series is designed to provide clear and effective support for students as they make the adjustment from GCSE to A Level, and also for teachers, especially those who are not familiar with teaching a two-year linear course. The student books cover the AQA specifications for both A/AS Level. They are intended to appeal to the broadest range of students, and they offer challenge to stretch the top end and additional support for those who need it. Every author in this series is an experienced historian or history teacher, and all have great skill in conveying narratives to readers and asking the kinds of questions that pull those narratives apart.

In addition to high-quality prose, this series also makes extensive use of textual primary sources, maps, diagrams and images, and offers a wide range of activities to encourage students to address historical questions of cause, consequence, change and continuity. Throughout the books there are opportunities to criticise the interpretations of other historians, and to use those interpretations in the construction of students' own accounts of the past. The series aims to ease the transition for those students who move on from A Level to undergraduate study, and the books are written in an engaging style that will encourage those who want to explore the subject further.

Icons used within this book include:

 Key terms

 Speak like a historian

 Voices from the past/Hidden voices

 Practice essay questions

 Chapter summary

About Cambridge Elevate

Cambridge Elevate is the platform which hosts a digital version of this Student Book. If you have access to this digital version you can annotate different parts of the book, send and receive messages to and from your teacher and insert weblinks, among other things.

We hope that you enjoy your AS or A Level History course, as well as this book, and wish you well for the journey ahead.

Michael Fordham and David L Smith

Series editors

1 The condition of the Church, c1500–1517

In this section we will study the structures, functions and beliefs of the pre-Reformation Church.

Specification points:

- the Church: secular power and influence; the clerical hierarchy; church courts; influence in government; influence on daily life
- the Church: religious power and influence; church doctrine, teachings and belief; the sacraments, salvation, the role of the priest and of 'good works'
- criticism of the Church; Pope Alexander VI; papal and clerical corruption; humanism: Colet, More and Erasmus; heresies and anti-clericalism
- church finances, indulgences, popular piety and the extent of demand for reform.

The Church: secular power and influence

The late medieval Church was by no means merely a spiritual entity. The Church closely resembled a political system, owing to its various administrative and bureaucratic functions. In Richard Southern's view, the medieval Church was a state. 'It had all the apparatus of the state: laws and law courts, taxes and tax collectors, and a great administrative machine.'[1] Medieval popes explicitly affirmed the Church's secular credentials. Pope Boniface VIII noted in unambiguous terms in 1302, that 'he who denies that the secular sword is in the power of Peter does not understand the words of the Lord'.[2] Not all Christians embraced this assertion. In particular, Lorenzo Valla (1407–1457) discovered that the Donation of Constantine – a document declaring that

Constantine the Great had granted Pope Sylvester I the power to govern the western Roman Empire – was a forgery. However, Valla's views were not widely supported.

While the Church's spiritual authority remained relatively uncontested, its secular powers were partly wielded by kings and princes. It has been suggested that papal power was strengthened, rather than undermined, by this delegation, for popes could theoretically dictate what was being delegated. However, in practice, this entailed many potential problems, including the competence and, more importantly, the self-interest of secular rulers. The Church lacked the authority and means to impose its will. It was thus heavily reliant on the collaboration of secular rulers throughout Christendom. The greatest weakness of the Church as a state was that it had only one sanction, namely **excommunication**. For this to be truly effective, the Church depended on the cooperation of Europe's princes.

The Church's secular power was inseparably linked to the development of the monarchical papal system. In the aftermath of the conciliarist debates in the early 1400s, the papacy emerged as a potent force in the politics of the Italian city-states, with Rome at the epicentre. The city itself and the Vatican were transformed as a result. Pope Nicholas V (1447–1455) embarked on a massive rebuilding project, making Rome worthy of being the universal Church's headquarters. In addition to being a patron of the arts and sciences, Nicholas planned to build a new basilica and palace, though the old cathedral was not destroyed until 1506 during Julius II's pontificate (1503–1513). Nicholas V's successors built on his strong legacy. Rome was restored as a major centre of learning and scholarship, embracing both the classical and Christian past. While Pius II (1458–1464) was a man of learning and a distinguished humanist, Pope Sixtus IV (1471–1484) established the Vatican library, and Alexander VI (1492–1503) contributed much to the completion of the Vatican.

On a broader front, Rome was also the capital of the Papal States, the outlying territories that surrounded the city. For that reason, popes wielded secular power directly as territorial princes. They supervised a political and fiscal administration and, on occasions, even became embroiled in military campaigns. Popes were often more focused on administering the Papal States than dealing with Church affairs. The papacy was much sought after by Italian families and remained the decisive factor in explaining the outcome of papal elections. The papacy's political identification with the Italian city-states was reinforced by the dominance of Italians at the papal court. As political rulers of the Papal States, popes regularly competed with the rulers of the Italian city-states. Rome became the centre for Italian dynastic and political factionalism, encouraging nepotism for the sake of self-advancement. The granting

Voices from the past

Lorenzo Valla, 'On the Falsely-Delivered and Forged Donation of Constantine'

I shall show that nothing was given to Sylvester by Constantine, but to an earlier Pope, and that the grants were inconsiderable, for the mere subsistence of the Pope. For the Donation is not found in any history, and it is comprised of contradictions, impossibilities, stupidities, barbarisms and absurdities ... Can we justify the principle of papal power when we perceive it to be the cause of such great crimes and of such great and

varied evils? The Pope himself makes war on peaceable people, and sows discord among states and princes. The Pope not only enriches himself at the expense of the republic, but he enriches himself at the expense of even the church and the Holy Spirit.[3]

Using the extract above and your wider reading, answer the following questions:

1. What was the Donation of Constantine and how was Valla able to prove that it was a forgery?
2. What do you think were Valla's intentions?
3. What does it tell us about the papacy in the 15th century?

of offices to family members, even to illegitimate sons, ensured greater stability and security. Many popes, and some cardinals, owned country palaces and went hunting like ordinary princes. The papacy came to be dominated by powerful Italian families; in fact, four families secured the papal office on nine occasions, with the della Roveres securing three elections. Successive popes also encountered the growing ambition of foreign rulers, who sought to exploit the wealth and vulnerability of the Italian peninsula. On account of its geographical position, the Papal States were often used as a route for armies, such as Charles VIII's march to Naples in 1494.

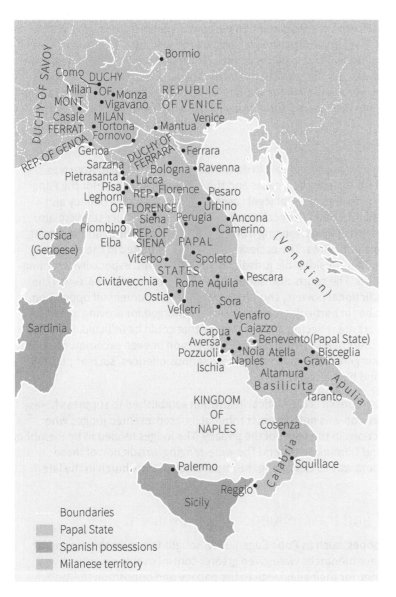

Figure 1.1: The Italian city-states, c1500

The clerical hierarchy

At the top of the clerical hierarchy was the *Curia*, or Roman court, consisting of the Vatican's numerous administrative offices.

Popes claimed the right to confer church benefices (offices) directly. The clerics appointed to senior positions within the Church (that is, cardinals, archbishops and bishops) required papal letters of confirmation for their benefice. By special agreement, secular rulers could maintain the right to nominate clergy to an episcopal

Key term

The *Curia* included the College of Cardinals, which, acting as a Senate, deliberated on all matters pertaining to the Church. The papal household, also part of the *Curia*, contained all the leading administrators, including those of the datary (which processed church revenues) and the papal chancery (which issued papal decrees).

Research the medieval Inquisition and explain how it was structured, how it functioned and where it was most prevalent. Draw up a timeline of key moments in the history of the Inquisition in the Middle Ages.

and archiepiscopal position. Outside the Italian city-states, the leading bishop in a region was the **primate**, the chief bishop of a particular state (such as the Archbishops of Toledo and Canterbury).

Cardinals, archbishops and bishops had the power to ordain priests and administer the rite of confirmation. Bishops were expected to supervise their diocese, the main territorial unit of church administration. Church (or canon) law dictated that bishops should summon annual diocesan synods (meeting of the clergy within his diocese) every year and archbishops were expected to convene provincial synods every three years. In practice, such synods took place infrequently in the late Middle Ages. At the local level, the Church was dependent on numerous parishes, the size of which varied enormously. The parish structure was well established by 1200. Parish priests supervised the parishes, while parishioners, especially churchwardens, tended to be responsible for maintaining the fabric of the local church. Churchwardens' accounts show impressive lay intervention in the church. Evidence for lay contributions is also supported by wills and the records of **religious guilds and fraternities**.

Church courts and their influence on daily life

Church courts played an important role in daily life. In Rome, the *Sacra Rota* was the Supreme Court for ecclesiastical cases and the sovereign law court for the Papal States. It dealt with a diverse range of legal cases referred to it by the papacy and from other episcopal tribunals. The ecclesiastical courts in local dioceses were also given numerous responsibilities, ranging from the approval of wills to administering dispensations from church laws. The ecclesiastical courts, situated in the episcopal palace or cathedral, had considerable jurisdiction over disputes, especially regarding matrimonial problems. The courts also supervised the payment of tithes. Given the extent of their jurisdictional powers, church courts could encounter stiff opposition. Wealthy urban families in particular resented the fees charged for proving wills. The church courts' powers are reflected in the penalties that could be inflicted on the laity. Failure to attend a court hearing might lead to suspension or even excommunication, though the latter was generally enforced for more serious offences, such as perjury, violence to clergy and heresy.

The Inquisition was a special ecclesiastical institution established to suppress heresy. The medieval Inquisition was not a distinct tribunal, but represented judges who exercised their functions in the name of the papacy. The judges tended to be members of the Franciscan and Dominican orders. The wide-ranging jurisdiction of these institutions goes some way to explaining the importance of the Church in the late Middle Ages.

Church courts and their influence in government

Fifteenth-century popes, such as Pope Eugenius IV, sought to secure the support of Europe's rulers. These monarchs were given greater control over their respective churches, in exchange for their allegiance to the papacy and opposition to conciliarism. For example, Emperor Frederick III signed a concordat with the Pope in 1448, which granted him greater control over ecclesiastical offices. The papacy had its own representatives operating in the localities; these papal legates regularly corresponded with the Vatican and invariably reinforced papal authority. Secular rulers, of course, were aware of the Church's potential and some sought to increase their share of ecclesiastical power at the expense of papal powers. These resulting tensions often focused on major Church appointments; monarchs could greatly increase their control over the Church by promoting their own servants to key offices. With powerful allies in the Church, monarchs could exploit its financial resources. Within the Holy Roman Empire, Pope Eugenius IV secured support from the princes by allowing them to collect papal taxes. In England, Henry VII did not hesitate to take

Key term

Conciliarism represented an idea, which claimed that Church authority rested primarily in the general councils of the Church, and that these councils were superior to the papacy.

some of the proceeds from the indulgences, which were being collected to fund the rebuilding of St. Peter's in Rome.

In addition to disagreements over church revenues, there were clashes over jurisdiction. The extensive jurisdiction of local church courts sometimes ran into conflict with that of the secular courts. Monarchs obviously resented any ecclesiastical interference with their own jurisdictional control. Yet the emergence of stronger national churches did not necessarily have a detrimental impact on the Church as a whole.

The Spanish Church under Ferdinand and Isabella provides a case in point. The work of Cardinal Jiménez de Cisneros, the Primate of Spain, indicates how much could be achieved by a national church, without close papal intervention. Jiménez de Cisneros embarked on an impressive programme that included the reform of religious orders. He also founded the University of Alcalá, which became a centre for the education of priests and produced the extraordinary **Complutensian Bible**. The creation of an Inquisition on the Iberian peninsula, administered by the first Grand Inquisitor, Torquemada, was also inspired by the Spanish.

The Spanish example demonstrates the benefits of a decentralised institution. The emergence of regional and local variations was equally true of forms of religious worship as it was of ecclesiastical reform. Liturgies might differ institutionally between various religious orders and geographically between dioceses and ecclesiastical provinces. There was even an evolution of different, regional theologies, which was encouraged by the foundation of numerous theological faculties in the universities. The later medieval period was an age of intellectual revolution, which saw a revival of Neoplatonism, the prevalence of Thomas Aquinas's (1225–1274) theology, and the flourishing of Augustinianism. There were noticeable tensions between the different schools of theological thought, as represented by the *via antiqua* (following Aquinas) and the *via moderna* (which stemmed from William of Ockham's writings, 1287–1347). This conflict between nominalism and realism reflected differences of opinion about what the human mind could know of God, and concerning the nature of divine revelation. With new cults and different strands of spirituality emerging throughout Europe and with the growing importance of vernacular languages reinforcing local spirituality and traditions, it is possible to speak of catholicisms rather than Catholicism.

The Church: religious power and influence

In the late Middle Ages, the Church wielded considerable religious power because it was indispensable to salvation. The importance of the visible Church was clearly stated in Pope Boniface VIII's **bull**, *Unam sanctam* (1302): 'Outside this Church there is no salvation or remission of sins.'[4] The Church comprised all baptised Christians, whether they were living or dead. While the Church Militant represented living Christians, the Church Dormant designated those who had died, and were awaiting judgement, and the Church Triumphant consisted of the saints.

The religious authority of the papacy dominated the Church. Popes were empowered by Christ's identification of St Peter as the rock on which the Church would be built and who was granted the power of the keys (as indicated in Matthew's Gospel, chapter 16, verses 18–19). The Bishop of Rome claimed direct spiritual descent from St Peter and, therefore, supremacy within western Christendom. The papacy thereby held spiritual pre-eminence, though the precise nature of papal authority was never fully agreed. The popes were not considered to be infallible and no individual pope had exclusive rights to determine the evolution of doctrine. The precise locus of supreme doctrinal authority on earth remained undetermined, though papal spiritual headship was rarely contested. In the late Middle Ages, the **Great Schism** (1378–1417) profoundly

ACTIVITY 1.2

Research the following theologians and explain the significance of their writings in a late medieval context: Thomas Aquinas; William of Ockham; St Augustine of Hippo. Research and define the following terms: Neoplatonism; Augustinianism; Nominalism; Realism. On the basis of your wider reading, how important were these developments in preparing the ground for theological challenges to the established Church?

Key term

The **Great Schism** emerged in 1378 with the rival papal elections of Urban VI and Clement VII and ended with the election of Martin V at the Council of Constance in 1417. The followers of the two popes were divided principally along national lines. One of the proposals for ending the Schism came with the growth of the conciliar movement, placing greater authority in general councils, an alternative that the rival popes rejected.

affected the western Church; rival popes in Avignon and Rome each claimed spiritual ascendancy.

Although the Schism was largely resolved by the Council of Constance, in which Emperor Sigismund encouraged unity, underlying tensions between popes and Councils remained. Papal authority was challenged by conciliarism, a cause that was promoted by two key conciliar decrees: *Haec Sancta* (1415) declared that Church councils held authority from God alone, to which even popes had to submit; and *Frequens* (1417) noted that popes were expected to summon Councils regularly, at least once every ten years. Conciliarism peaked between 1380 and 1450, when the Councils of Pisa (1409), Constance (1414–1418) and Basle (1431–1437) all tried to limit papal authority. After Basle, a Council would never again challenge papal authority so rigorously, though successive popes remained deeply suspicious of summoning Councils. As Bruce Gordon has reminded us, 'the rise of the Renaissance papacy was itself a pyrrhic victory, for despite its triumph over the Council of Basle its authority was confined to the Italian peninsula'.[5] This would make it more difficult to undertake comprehensive reform of the Church. Papal centralisation, characterised by nepotism and political intervention, was becoming increasingly discredited. Whereas previously reformers had looked to the papacy, and later would look to kings, in the late Middle Ages they looked to a general council – this debate would continue in the 16th century.

List of popes

Sixtus IV: August 1471–August 1484

Innocent VIII: August 1484–July 1492

Alexander VI: August 1492–August 1503

Pius III: September 1503–October 1503

Julius II: November 1503–February 1513

Leo X: March 1513–December 1521

Church doctrines, teachings and belief

The doctrines of the Church were clearly central because Christianity claimed to represent truth. Central to these beliefs was the doctrine of the Holy Trinity. In addition to the Holy Spirit, Christians believed in a paternal God, Creator of mankind, who sent His Son Jesus Christ to endure the Passion and the Crucifixion in order to redeem humanity. The fundamental tenets of Christian teachings were outlined in the Church's key **creedal statements**. The Apostles' Creed summarised the essential elements of Christianity, while the more detailed Nicene Creed devoted greater attention to the complex relationship between the Persons of the Trinity.

Underpinning these creedal statements was the prominence of the Bible as a key text in the late medieval period. The Bible was the first work to be printed by Johannes Gutenberg's new press. At the leading universities, doctors of theology lectured on the Bible; and Nicholas of Lyra's commentaries on the Bible became a bestseller. For educated Christians, the Latin Bible was an essential text and the most printed book in the 15th century. In the German-speaking lands, there were a large number of Bible translations, though in other countries vernacular editions were viewed with suspicion, if not hostility. In England the circulation and possession of vernacular Bibles was prohibited. Widening access might lead readers untrained in theology to misinterpret the Scriptures and challenge Church teachings. More specifically, the Bible's precise standing remained ill defined. While its authority was derived from the Church, which was responsible for identifying its canonicity, some biblical scholars raised the question of whether the Bible authorised the Church. It was also potentially problematic that the official Latin text of the Bible, the Vulgate, was not the original version. The relative absence of vernacular translations until approximately 1500 meant that the actual text was less accessible.

Ordinary Christians rarely encountered the full version of the Bible, but that is not to say that they were ignorant of its key messages. Most people encountered biblical extracts and stories in a liturgical context. The Missal (the book used by priests to celebrate the Mass) contained selected biblical readings, so that the liturgical year provided a comprehensive insight into the different Books, Letters and Gospels of the Bible. Excerpts from the Bible appeared in numerous liturgical and para-liturgical forms, including the Psalter, sermons and Books of Hours. Church liturgy included a series of daily prayers, known as the Divine Office, in which the annual cycle commemorated Christ's life and ministry, while the weekly cycle focused on the principal theme for the coming Sunday. Biblical stories were retold in Passion and Mystery Plays throughout western Europe and beyond. The dramatisation of the Christian story in plays and informal sermons were particularly appealing to the illiterate, and those who could not afford Bibles.

Another feature of late medieval Christianity was the role of the Virgin Mary and the saints. Mary's compassion and the example of the saints convinced Christian believers that Mary and the saints could intercede with Christ on their behalf. The saints' extraordinary lives were retold in countless biographies and **hagiographies**, with the most popular being Jacobus de Voragine's *Golden Legend*, a compendium of saints' lives. Many were labelled as saints without papal approval, and assumed responsibility for guarding against wide-ranging ailments. For example, St Sebastian and St Roch were nominated protectors against the plague. As a result, devotion to the saints was common, with images and statues found in homes, on street corners and in churches. Once **canonised**, individual saints were recognised for their exemplary holiness, and their bones became relics warranting veneration. Saints could assist on earth by performing miracles and, as a result, saints' shrines and pilgrimage sites flourished throughout western Christendom.

Sacraments

According to Church teaching, Christ instituted the sacramental system. The Church believed that Christ instituted the seven sacraments – the exact number was defined only at the end of the 12th century – which were baptism, confirmation, communion, matrimony, ordination, confession and extreme unction. The sacraments were interpreted as a sign of God's grace and a conduit for it. They told the story of the Christian life, demonstrated and confirmed membership of the Church, and marked specific stages in each individual's spiritual development. Baptism was the means by which individuals entered the Church and accepted Christ's offer of salvation; it could be administered in emergency by anyone. Any person in similar circumstances could also administer extreme unction. Confirmation represented an individual's formal affirmation of their baptism and, like ordination, was a sacrament that could only be performed by a bishop. Interestingly, matrimony did not require priestly participation, for the freely willed consent of both husband and wife was sufficient. Priestly mediation was more prominent in the sacraments of confession and communion. Regarding the former, penitents could only be absolved of their sins by priestly absolution, though this required the sinner's **contrition**, confession and **satisfaction**. A mere acknowledgement of sins was insufficient. Confession was indispensable for receiving communion and the Fourth Lateran Council of 1215 demanded that all Christians should receive both on an annual basis at the very least, preferably at Easter. It is difficult to ascertain whether annual communion was the norm.

Communion, or the Mass as it is better known, was the most important liturgical celebration, in which Christ's self-sacrifice was commemorated and re-enacted. By the Middle Ages, the Church had formulated the doctrine of transubstantiation.

Figure 1.2: Albrecht Dürer's *Praying Hands*

Key term

After death, a person who has led a remarkable life can be **canonised** and become a saint. The process is complicated, requires the authentification of miracles associated with the person, and involves much discussion and then approval by the highest Church authorities. Sometimes a person is not canonised until several hundred years after their death.

Key terms

Sinners were expected to show **contrition** to a priest, meaning that they were supposed to show displeasure and remorse for any sins that they had committed. Having confessed to a priest in the sacrament of confession, they were expected to do penance (**satisfaction**). Following the sinner's confession, the priest would indicate what penances the penitent should undertake.

This teaching was formalised at the Fourth Lateran Council: 'His body and blood are truly contained in the sacrament of the altar under the forms of bread and wine, the bread and wine having been changed in substance, by God's power, into his body and blood.'[6] This led to the reservation of consecrated hosts in tabernacles and meant that they could be processed through the streets. By 1300, only priests received both the bread and wine, further reinforcing their power as spiritual intermediaries. The climax of the Mass was the consecration of the bread and wine, which was reserved for the priest. It is worth noting that consecration was dependent on the correct performance of the rite (*ex opera operato*) rather than on the qualities and virtues of the human performer (*ex opere operantis*). More frequent communion was usually a sign of special devotion, but there were moves towards more frequent reception, especially among reform movements such as the Beguines and the Devotio Moderna.

Given the relative infrequency of receiving communion, Mass was as much a spectator event for the laity. The elevation of the Host and the chalice took on ever-increasing importance in the 13th century, and the intensification of Eucharistic devotion culminated in the feast of **Corpus Christi**. The Mass was considered to represent a semi-magical force, which could produce miracles and favourable harvests.

Salvation and good works

Until 1200, Christians had a clear choice of avenue at the end of their lives: Heaven or Hell. From the 13th century, the doctrine of **purgatory** gradually evolved. It was only at the Council of Florence in 1437 that the existence of purgatory was decreed an article of faith. Purgatory emerged to facilitate the atonement of all sins; only God could determine if there had been sufficient satisfaction in the sacrament of confession. While admission to purgatory secured entry into Heaven, it was believed that the fires of Hell brought dreadful suffering to those in purgatory. The possibility of purging sins after death provided new incentives to prepare for the afterlife. The intercessory prayers and charitable deeds of the living, as well as Mass celebrated by priests, could reduce the number of days in purgatory. This led to a plethora of chantries, which were institutions where Masses for the dead could be celebrated for a period of years, or in perpetuity. Priests, who were attached to a chantry, might also be expected to distribute alms and do good works on behalf of the dead. With the development of purgatory, life became a preparation for death and this largely explains why the *ars moriendi* tradition was so strong in the later medieval period. Hell, on the other hand, was reserved for irredeemable sinners and heretics.

Priests and the 'mixed life'

The nature of late medieval religion meant that the clergy were vital instruments in the Church's daily life. Priests were expected to pray the canonical hours, to be literate, to administer the sacraments, and to celebrate the Mass by heart. The mystery of transubstantiation, which could be effected only by a duly ordained priest, did much to elevate the priesthood. Priests were crucial intermediaries of divine power and provided protection for the laity. At times, they fulfilled purely spiritual functions, especially via the sacraments. On a more mundane level, priests could be called upon to bless crops and say prayers for good weather. Ultimately, priests were the guardians of truth in the localities and late medieval instructional manuals assisted them in their duties as preachers, teachers, confessors and pastors. Interestingly, the primary function of late medieval sermons was not to spread doctrine, but to convey the broader message of Christian morality through exhortation, tales of saints and reports of miracles.

To these ends, parish priests were helped and supported by the mendicant friars, the Dominicans and Franciscans. Famed for their sermons, the friars loaned books to local clergy, provided essential training grounds for preaching and undertook countless charitable deeds. The 12th century had seen a transformation in monasticism,

Key term

Perceptions of death and the everlasting life were an important feature of late medieval religion. Sermons, devotional works and worship frequently emphasised death, judgement and the pains of Hell or purgatory, with the intention of encouraging the laity to repent and do good works. The 'art of dying' or *ars moriendi* tradition was at its most pronounced for those who were at the threshold of death.

including the formation of the rule of St Augustine and subsequent foundation of Augustinian canons, as well as the proliferation of **regular and contemplative orders** like the Cistercians and the Carthusians.

By the late Middle Ages, there was a growing tendency towards pursuing a pious life within the world, rather than withdrawing into a cloistered existence. The Beguines, for example, who were based in the Netherlands and western parts of the Holy Roman Empire, adopted a life of voluntary renunciation and prayer, though not total poverty. The movement spread rapidly, with a notable presence in Cologne by 1250. The movement had passed its peak by 1388, the date of their last foundation. Their principal difficulty lay in their status, since they were neither fully 'regular' (following a monastic rule, *Regula*) nor lay. When the laity sought to practise their piety outside the Church's formal structures, they were often viewed with suspicion. This highlights one of the problems of contemplative devotion, especially when mystics claimed that their spirit was sufficiently liberated to be incapable of sin. In some cases, such as the heresy of the Free Spirit, they were condemned. Unsurprisingly, Beguine communities were pressurised to move into cloisters and become regular – such as the renowned mystic, Mechtild of Magdeburg.

Devotio Moderna

Another, albeit far more influential, group to undertake the *via mixta* was the Devotio Moderna. Based in the Low Countries and flourishing in the mid- to late 14th and early 15th centuries, the movement was inspired by Geert Groote of Deventer (1340–1384). Although laymen took the lead, characterised by the Brothers and Sisters of Common Life, who did not take vows, priests and monks quickly joined them. The lay component of the movement lived in religious communities, without taking monastic vows. They were situated in towns and had links with schools, for which they provided spiritual guidance. They emphasised rigorous prayer, meditation and spiritual note-taking (known as *rapiaria*). The Brothers and Sisters of Common Life quickly expanded, centred mainly on the northern Netherlands but also extending to the Holy Roman Empire.

In due course, they developed a monastic component, known as the Windesheim Congregation. One of its members was Thomas à Kempis, author of the bestseller, the *Imitatio Christi*, which called on its readers to follow Christ's example through disciplined prayer. Both components of the Devotio Moderna encouraged a reforming type of spirituality, with a strong emphasis on the Bible and Christ. They strikingly encouraged restraint where devotional practices were practised to excess (such as pilgrimages, miracle-seeking and the veneration of relics).

Criticisms of the Church

By the end of the 15th century, Church corruption was widely criticised. There was widespread dissatisfaction because key individuals, cardinals and bishops, who were supposed to be the most responsible figures in the Church tended to be the most fraudulent. Instead of setting an example as the highest spiritual authority, the papacy was arguably the most corrupt force within the Church. There was thus an absence of spiritual leadership and direction. Although popes were responsible for Church reform, they avoided convening Councils, the principal instrument for reform, because of their conciliarist fears.

The Church was in constant need of reform, yet the impetus was half-hearted. Rather than being role models, bishops and cardinals often exploited their positions of authority to pursue their own careers and to enrich themselves. Popes and cardinals endorsed candidates on the basis of nepotism (favouritism that benefited members of their own family). Promotion through the ecclesiastical hierarchy was not necessarily achieved by merit. Senior clerics could secure high positions by buying their way into

ACTIVITY 1.3

Research the *Imitatio Christi*, the famous bestseller by Thomas à Kempis and consider the following questions:

1. What were the origins of the text?
2. Why did it become a bestseller?

Make sure that you also consider the transition from manuscript to printed book.

Read chapters 15–19 of Machiavelli's *The Prince* and consider the following questions:

1. What necessary qualities does Machiavelli identify?

2. How consistent are these characteristics with what you know of the Renaissance papacy?

3. What was the historical context in which Machiavelli wrote *The Prince*?

power via simony. The buying and selling of ecclesiastical offices led to an increase in the degree of pluralism, the holding of more than one ecclesiastical office. Pluralism inevitably culminated in absenteeism. Bishops and cardinals who held numerous ecclesiastical offices were unable to reside in all their dioceses and abbeys. An absentee office-holder would neglect their ecclesiastical duties and responsibilities. Some members of the clergy also broke their vows of celibacy and fathered illegitimate children.

Pope Alexander VI

The life and career of Rodrigo Borgia (1431–1503), who later became Pope Alexander VI, provides a useful insight into the nature of the Renaissance papacy. Rodrigo's mother was Isabella Borgia, sister of Cardinal Alfonso Borgia, who was elected Pope Callixtus III in 1455. Rodrigo's career undoubtedly benefited from nepotism, as his uncle granted him wealthy benefices, including: Cardinal Deacon of St Nicolo in Carcerre; Cardinal Bishop of Albano and of Porto; Dean of the Sacred College; and after 1457, Vice-Chancellor of the Roman Church. Despite his unethical rise to power, Rodrigo's work in the papal chancery gained him a reputation for competence and administrative experience. The Renaissance historian Francesco Guicciardini (1483–1540), who was by no means a devotee, described Rodrigo's competence and prudence. Rodrigo used his talents to accumulate more archbishoprics, bishoprics and abbacies. Although ordained a priest in 1468, two years later he started having sexual relations with Vanozza Catanei, the mother of his four children (Juan, Cesare, Lucrezia and Jofre).

On 11 August 1492, Rodrigo was elected Pope Alexander VI, a post that he most likely obtained through bribery and simony. For all his notoriety, once he was pope, he sought to stop the lawlessness in Rome by dividing the city into four districts and appointing a magistrate for each. He also transformed Emperor Hadrian's mausoleum into a fortress for defensive purposes, and rebuilt Rome's university and the magnificent via Alessandrina, which became a key thoroughfare to St Peter's Basilica. Further afield, Alexander VI drew an important line of demarcation between the Spanish and Portuguese empires, as declared in the 1494 Treaty of Tordesillas.

Figure 1.3: A portrait of Pope Alexander VI

As pope, Alexander maintained a strong parental affection for his children. Cesare was chosen as the key ecclesiastical representative of the Borgias; he was appointed Bishop of Pamplona and Archbishop of Valencia without ever visiting Spain. Cesare's own notoriety was such that his character formed the basis for Machiavelli's *The Prince*. Nepotism was further evident during Alexander's pontificate and he appointed his nephew, Cardinal Giovanni Borgia, as his personal representative in the Sacred College. Alexander was more interested in factional struggles than Church reform. He resisted attempts by the Della Rovere family to overthrow him, even though they had secured an alliance with the French King Charles VIII. Alexander subsequently targeted the various noble families who had allied with the della Roveres, most notably the Orsinis. In many ways, Alexander VI's career resembled that of a Renaissance prince rather than the spiritual leader of western Christendom. Yet in that pursuit, Alexander was very much the product of his times.

Papal and clerical corruption

The type of example set by Alexander VI might explain the existence of anti-papal sentiment in Rome, within the Italian city-states and beyond. Unsurprisingly, the Renaissance papacy did not have many enthusiastic advocates. Despite the criticisms of the papacy, few rejected the Pope's spiritual authority. Popes continued to be an indispensable part of the Church. It should also be borne in mind that the extent of papal corruption is better known to modern historians than it was to contemporaries. Only a very small minority had any direct contact with the popes. Even in those countries that had asserted greater ecclesiastical independence, popes retained a spiritual influence. For example, following Charles VII's Pragmatic Sanction of Bourges, which represented a powerful assertion of Gallican liberties and ecclesiastical autonomy, the French certainly did not abandon Eugenius IV as Pope. French **Gallicanism** did not represent a denial of the Pope's spiritual authority.

Humanism: Colet, More and Erasmus

One of the most important intellectual developments in the late medieval Church was humanism, a movement that drew attention to papal abuses. Humanists returned *ad fontes*, to the original sources of classical antiquity. However thoroughgoing it was supposed to be, the revival of antiquity was not intended as a substitute for Christianity. To that effect, Raphael's frescoes in the Vatican juxtaposed classical themes with the central tenets of Christian belief. Despite their fixation with classical culture, humanist scholars were devout Christians, including one of the movement's founding fathers, Francesco Petrarch (1304–1374). Some of its leading protagonists, Leon Alberti (1404–1472), Lorenzo Valla (1407–1457) and Marsilio Ficino (1433–1499), were priests. Alberti and Valla had both worked for the papacy, though the latter had of course, exposed the Donation of Constantine as a forgery. Aeneas Silvius Piccolomini was an influential humanist and was later elected Pope Pius II (r1458–1464).

The Northern Renaissance

A parallel development north of the Alps followed the pattern of the Renaissance in Italy, focusing on classical civilisation. Humanist scholars such as Willibald Pirckheimer, Konrad Peutinger and Sebastian Brant, also edited classical texts. Rudolph Agricola (c1444–1485) was one of the earliest northern scholars to work in Greek and Hebrew. Emperor Maximilian I (1493–1519) invited humanist scholars to his court and the rediscovery of Tacitus' *Germania* contributed to the emergence of a more distinctive German culture. While northern humanists owed much to their Italian counterparts, they were also determined to research and expound on a northern claim to antiquity. This is closely related to another distinctive feature of the Northern Renaissance: its impact on the development of vernacular languages. In 1400, people spoke a variety of regional dialects. By the end of the Renaissance, the German language had achieved greater use and standardisation, largely thanks to the printing industry. Added to this technological dimension was the use of German, instead of Latin, for administrative purposes.

The religious dimension of the Renaissance is better known as Christian humanism. Humanists sought to apply the better understanding of classical languages to biblical scholarship in order to restore Christianity to its essence. The platform for this reform programme was founded on the revision of the Bible. By referencing the text in its original languages (Hebrew for the Old and Greek for the New Testaments), scholars worked on producing a more authentic biblical text. **Desiderius** Erasmus published Valla's *Annotations on the New Testament* in which the latter had demonstrated how frequently Latin versions of the New Testament differed from the original Greek. Reformers could then base their programmes on an accurate version of the Bible. The **Vulgate** (the official, medieval Latin version of Bible) had helped to shape much of late medieval Catholic theology, so when the text was revised, it suddenly put into question some key Catholic doctrines. For example, Erasmus insisted that *metanoeite* should be translated as 'repent' rather than 'do penance', which had significant implications for the sacrament of confession. In addition to retranslating and reinterpreting the Bible, Christian humanists focused on ridding the Church of clerical and monastic corruption.

The Dutch humanist Erasmus (c1466–1536), the Northern Renaissance's leading advocate, was a prolific author and renowned biblical scholar, as well as an outspoken critic of Church abuses. Erasmus spent time in Italy, where he learnt Hebrew and befriended the Venetian printer Aldus Manutius. When he returned, Johannes Froben

Key term

Gallicanism represented some key characteristics of the French Catholic Church, including superiority of a general council of the Church over the Pope and a desire to limit the intervention of the Pope within the French kingdom.

ACTIVITY 1.5

German humanism

Research the following figures: Willibald Pirckheimer, Konrad Peutinger, Rudolph Agricola and Sebastian Brant. Identify the key characteristics of German humanism. What were the similarities and differences between the Northern and Italian Renaissance?

ACTIVITY 1.6

Draw up a timeline of Desiderius Erasmus's key works. Using your wider reading, explain Erasmus's significance during the period 1500–1520.

Figure 1.4: Holbein's portrait of Thomas More

printed Erasmus's *Novum Instrumentum* (a Greek edition of the New Testament begun in 1512) in 1516 in Basle, with a Latin translation and extensive notes and commentary. Luther later used it as a basis for his own scholarship, in particular his German translation of the Bible.

In addition to the strong presence of humanism in Spain, especially as promoted by Jiménez de Cisneros in Alcalá, the movement was also prominent in England. The leading humanists in England included John Colet (1467–1519) and Thomas More (1478–1535). Educated at Oxford and in Italy, Colet was influenced by the Italian humanist Marsilio Ficino. From 1496, Colet lectured at Oxford on the New Testament according to humanist principles. In 1505, he was appointed Dean of St Paul's, London, and is best known for his sermon to the Convocation of the Clergy in 1512, in which he denounced contemporary abuses and emphasised the desperate need for clerical reform. Colet's close associate in England was Thomas More, who was also educated at Oxford, where he first encountered humanism. Both More and Colet were friends of Erasmus, who came to visit them on several occasions. More was the author of numerous works, including *Utopia* (first printed in 1516), a classic of the Northern Renaissance.

Heresy

The late medieval Church is best characterised by its multiplicity of practices and traditions. Medieval Latin Christianity 'was not a monolith, spiritually regimented and strongly controlled, with all of western Christendom subscribing to an identical set of beliefs and engaging in identical religious activities'.[7] Yet most beliefs could be aligned to what was perceived to be orthodox teaching. So frustrated were some reformers with the state of the Church that they made increasingly radical demands. They did not merely call for an end to abuses, but directly challenged Church teachings. The rejection of Church doctrines was infrequent and confined to specific regions. These threats to the Church's authority inevitably led to accusations and, on occasions, condemnation of heresy. As Thomas Aquinas explained, heretical ideas were a grave threat to society: 'heresy is a sin which merits not only excommunication but also death, for it is worse to corrupt the Faith which is the life of the soul than to issue counterfeit coins which minister to the secular life'.[8] Some of the apparently heretical beliefs stemmed from reactions to uncertainties about Christian teachings, while others originated in denial of key Catholic beliefs.

The Waldensians
Some, such as John Wyclif (1329–1384) in England, Jan Hus (1369–1415) in Bohemia, and the Waldensians in the Alpine valleys, proposed more radical alternatives to the Church's teachings. Existing in Germany and central Europe, and as the Vaudois in southern France and northern Italy, the Waldensians principally attacked Church corruption rather than key doctrines, though more radical strands emerged. In particular, some of their members sought separation from official Catholic worship to increasingly private Scripture reading.

John Wyclif
John Wyclif presented several complaints, notably a critique of indulgences. Yet more radical was his scathing attack on monasticism, for which, in his view, there was no scriptural warrant. He also rejected scholastic theology, asserted that the Bible should be the only source of authority and promoted vernacular Bibles. He argued that incompetent bishops and priests should be lawfully deprived of their positions. Wyclif also opposed the Catholic teaching on the Eucharist.

Jan Hus
Jan Hus was strongly influenced by Wyclif, similarly emphasised the Scriptures as the key source of authority and was highly critical of Church corruption. He also criticised

aspects of the Mass and encouraged the reception of Communion in both kinds for the laity. In fact, the adoption of **Utraquism** made the lay chalice the movement's most potent symbol. Hus was eventually found guilty of heresy and, despite being granted a safe conduct, he was burned at the Council of Constance in 1415. The Hussite movement that followed posed a serious threat to the Church, as the Hussites created their own church organisation. Although the Hussites provoked civil wars in Bohemia during 1419–1436, they were eventually reconciled with the Catholic Church. In the end, the Hussites were deeply divided between the moderate Utraquists (mainly nobles and academics) and Taborites (who were more **apocalyptic** and militant), and their fragmentation proved too damaging for the movement. The Compacta of Basle of 1436, which reintegrated the moderate Hussites, nullified the Hussite challenge. While communion in both kinds was conceded, the movement's doctrines were virtually ignored.

Anti-clericalism

Anti-clericalism was rife in the late medieval Church, though the term carries various connotations. Definitions range from simple resentment towards individual clerics to the more extreme rejection of the priestly office. Robert Scribner has highlighted different types of anti-clericalism. In some cases, it was political – resentment of the clergy's secular power – because nobles monopolised the higher offices. In others, it was economic, where people opposed the numerous church taxes – the tithe, mortuary dues and other fees for services rendered – and the pressure to buy indulgences. In yet others, it was legal, reflecting lay frustration with clerical exemptions from secular law, and growing opposition to Church courts. Some were anti-clerical on sexual grounds, objecting to the hypocrisy of clerical misdemeanours; others on social grounds, because some clerics were drunk and disorderly. Most importantly, there were religious grounds for anti-clericalism: some neglected their pastoral supervision or, worse still, did not administer the sacraments (leaving infants unbaptised or Masses uncelebrated).[9] The key concern was that the priest should be available when required and should be properly trained. John Colet's sermon to the Canterbury Convocation typifies the anti-clericalism of the time, which sought to improve the Church. Far from rejecting the clergy's power, most anti-clerical sentiment aimed to strengthen priests as intermediaries between God and lay believers.

Church finances

The Chamber, the papal court's key financial institution, processed Church finances centrally. The chamberlain, the pope's financial secretary supervised it. He was also responsible for the appointments of officials in the Papal States and delegated powers to the vice-chamberlain and apostolic treasurer: the latter audited and approved the Chamber's accounts. Receipts came from both spiritual incomes, such as annates, and temporal incomes. The latter included taxes from the Papal States, notably on salt. In addition to the Chamber, the datary was established to receive revenues from venal offices within the papal bureaucracy, as well as payments for special papal dispensations. Venal offices included the positions in the papacy's legal and financial bureaucracy that were put up for sale. Payments were made in gold and sent directly to the datary, which could borrow money on the strength of the expected income.

Indulgences

Linked to the matter of finances was the Church's promotion of indulgences. The granting of papal indulgences dated back to 1095, when Pope Urban II declared that participation in the Crusades was considered an acceptable substitute for all other penances. Pope Clement VI elaborated on the idea in 1343 and presented a fuller statement on the papal theory of indulgences. As he noted, 'out of the abundant superfluity of Christ's sacrifice there has come a treasure that is to be used for the full

ACTIVITY 1.7

Using your wider reading, write short biographies of Jan Hus and John Wyclif. In what ways did they challenge the Roman Catholic Church and how serious was the threat posed by their ideas and the movements that promoted them?

Speak like a historian

Robert N. Swanson

Even in the individual accusations made before the church courts or during visitation proceedings, the hope was that a remedy would be provided, the recalcitrant cleric be reprimanded and forced to amend his ways. In that sense, most apparently 'anti'-clericalism is nothing of the sort: it is rather a contribution to the disciplinary process, seeking to chastise the errant to enforce true clericalism. Far from denying clerical status, if anything it elevates the clergy's role as mediators between God and Man.[10]

A.G. Dickens

At the other end of the scale a parish priest in a poor living or the incumbent of a chantry might receive little more than the wage of an unskilled labourer. The former could count himself fortunate if he still had a glebe to plough on weekdays. His tasks were hardly conducive to study or self-improvement; his Latin usually extended to the correct celebration of Mass, but far less often to reading Augustine or Erasmus. Everywhere in Europe angry voices were raised against clerical ignorance and against the superfluous ordinations of candidates ill-qualified by learning. Needless to add, many of these mundane priests failed to observe the law of celibacy.[11]

Using the extracts above and your wider reading, identify any evidence for anti-clericalism during this period.

1. What does that evidence tell us about the state of the pre-Reformation Church?
2. Was the late medieval Church in a state of terminal decline?

or partial remission of the temporal punishments of the sins of the faithful who have repented and confessed'.[12] Indulgences were certifications which could be granted to remit the punishment in purgatory of those who had confessed and been absolved.

Indulgences became a major feature of the economics of salvation in late medieval Europe. The practice was closely associated with pilgrimages, monasteries, Masses, chantries and fraternities. Most indulgences were not actually bought, but earned by actions that were either devotional (attending sermons, visiting churches on feast days) or charitable (assisting the poor, funding churches). Many leading churchmen, including Pope Boniface IX (1389–1404) condemned the abuse of the practice, but as a profitable source of revenue, even senior churchmen found it hard to resist.

Indulgences attracted growing criticism owing to countless innovations. Remissions were offered for innumerable issues, allowing individuals to gather enormous accumulations of time off purgatory. The multiplication of indulgences, and the increasingly excessive periods gained, had a detrimental impact on how they were perceived by the laity. An ever-growing number of indulgence sellers subordinated penitential activity to the payment of a sum to reduce time in purgatory. The sheer scale of the demand for indulgences is unmistakable. In 1498, a Barcelona printer was commissioned to print 18 000 copies of indulgences for the Benedictine abbey of Montserrat. On the evidence of printed indulgences, it would seem that the Italian city-states provided much less of a market than the Holy Roman Empire. By the time the papacy launched a major indulgences' campaign in order to fund the rebuilding of St Peter's, there was much opposition to the practice. This increased as it came to light that Archbishop Albrecht of Mainz spent money from the indulgences campaign to repay the debts he owed the **Fuggers**, loans that had enabled him to acquire the wealthy Archbishopric of Mainz.

Popular piety

In spite of the growing disapproval of the abuses surrounding indulgences, many lay Christians continued to buy them. This reflected one dimension of a broader and striking popular piety in the late Middle Ages. Prayer formed an integral part of lay devotion, for which the key prayers of the Apostles' Creed, Lord's Prayer and *Ave Maria* were widely known.

The increasing number of feasts and devotions focusing on Christ and the Eucharist showed the primacy of the Mass and Christ-centred piety. This included devotions to the Five Wounds of Christ and to the Sacred Heart of Jesus, most of which had localised beginnings. The emphasis on Christ's Passion was matched by the devotion to the Cross. The literate had access to Books of Hours, which were an important link between the Church's liturgy and private devotion. Books of Hours and many other devotional practices highlighted the popularity of Marian devotion. The Virgin Mary had no equal among the saints, for she merited a different kind of veneration (known as *hyperdulia*). What secured her status was the relationship with her Son, and Marian feasts were littered across the liturgical calendar. Saints formed a vital part of piety, as indicated by sermons, prayer books and the numerous saints' lives. Saints had various functions within popular piety, ranging from working miracles and healing the sick to finding lost property. They were considered to be spiritual protectors and religious intercessors. Like Mary, they had the power to intercede with Christ on behalf of the faithful.

Piety was popularised by various means, especially via printing. With cheaper paper, reprinting was possible, facilitating the wider availability of Latin and vernacular works. Printed books complemented and enriched oral culture, and certainly did not act as a substitute. Sermons were vital to the nurturing of popular piety. Bernardino of Siena (1380–1444) clearly articulated how significant they were in the 15th century: 'if between these two things – either to hear Mass rather than the sermon – you can only do one, you must miss Mass rather than the sermon; there is less danger to your soul in not hearing Mass [than] the sermon'.[13]

The devotional messages conveyed in sermons were complemented by religious drama. Plays contributed to people's understanding of the biblical story and drama helped to popularise the Christmas crib in the 13th century. In a society that was predominantly illiterate, popular piety was enhanced by the visual aspects of religion. Elaborate processions on feast days and the use of images, statues and altarpieces as instructional aids reinforced the message conveyed in sermons and books. Church interiors provided simple images, books for the unlearned, while the printing press combined text with illustrations, representing the tradition of **Biblia pauperum** – Bibles for the poor – which were illustrated books addressed to the illiterate. Popular piety is also indicated by the numerous lay offerings to churches, such as altar cloths, clerical vestments and altarpieces.

Religion dominated society to the point that popular piety extended well beyond the confines of the local church and graveyard. Towns and the countryside were steeped with religious symbols, including roadside shrines, holy wells, statues and crosses, and small chapels. Popular piety contributed to the growing practice of pilgrimages. Shrines at Aachen and St Wolfgang of Salzkammergut attracted numerous devotees. Surviving pilgrim badges indicate the scale and distance of pilgrimages. In Munich, 60 000 pilgrims were recorded in a single week in 1392. In Einsiedeln, 130 000 pilgrim

ACTIVITY 1.8

Using this section and your wider reading, how did individual believers express their devotion and piety in the late medieval period? Consider, in particular, the vast majority of people, who were illiterate.

badges were sold within a fortnight in 1496. Some shrines acquired international renown, such as Santiago di Compostela, Canterbury, Wilsnack, and the many sites in Rome.

Pilgrimages were inseparably linked to the cult of saints, the search for miracles and the veneration of relics. Pilgrims sought to burn candles and offer prayers at particular shrines, as well as hearing Mass. The ultimate destination was the Holy Land to meditate on the events of Jesus' life. Many of the laity expressed their devotion within the framework of religious organisations, such as guilds or fraternities. Some were linked with specific devotions, like Corpus Christi. Geneva listed as many as 38 fraternities in 1487, while Florence had at least 100. Many of these fraternities became major social forces within their respective communities; they could fund and administer almshouses, provide education and pay pensions.

At times, popular piety could verge towards superstition, especially in rural regions. The illiterate were more susceptible to the use of spells and even sources of magic. There is evidence of peasants using the consecrated Host to ward off insects from growing vegetables. Yet these more practical uses were considered complementary to the spiritual devotion to the Host. Eamon Duffy has insisted that many of these folklore practices did not constitute 'paganism, but lay Christianity'.[14]

The extent of the demand for reform

Any assessment of the late medieval Church requires an understanding of the nature and extent of the demand for reform. Bruce Gordon has suggested that 'the true character of Christianity on the eve of the Reformation will never be found in a narrative of irredeemable decay, or in a celebration of a lost golden age. There was something of both, and no single perspective suffices.'[15] Robert Swanson has also provided a nuanced interpretation of the late medieval Church, though his perception is that the Church was not in dire need of reform and that only a minority presented serious opposition to the Church's structures and doctrines. In the main, the late medieval Church was in a relatively healthy state. As Swanson noted, 'does that mean that "the Reformation" was unforeseeable in 1515? Probably. Does it mean that pre-Reformation religion was in fact vital and progressing rather than decadent and ready to fall? Almost certainly.'

Clearly, there were tensions within the Church and powerful advocates for reform. Yet the vast majority of these reforms sought to improve the Church from within, not establish a brand new Church. The invention of the printing press revitalised religious debates and gave reformers an additional means of being more assertive. The majority were willing collaborators in the late medieval Church, as indicated in the churchwardens' accounts, wills and records of guilds and **confraternities**. As Swanson argued, 'there is little sign of any decline in people's commitment or investment – often the reverse'.[16] Yet at its highest levels, the late medieval Church did not reform itself effectively. There was little impetus and will to do so, as popes and cardinals were reluctant to undermine their own status. The key to substantive reform lay in Church councils, but the popes hesitated to exploit this channel for personal reasons. For that reason, it may well be true that the Fifth Lateran Council (1512–1517) was a missed opportunity. While the Church did not lack dynamic individuals and appropriate schemes for reform, the ability and the will to implement them from the top was lacking. This would make all the difference in the period of Luther's revolt from 1517 onwards.

Practice essay question

With reference to these sources and your understanding of the historical context, assess the value of these three sources to an historian studying the condition of the pre-Reformation Church.

Extract A: Savonarola on the Renovation of the Church, 1495

O Italy, O princes of Italy, O prelates of the Church, the wrath of God is over you, and you will not have any cure unless you mend your ways! Do penance while the sword is not out of its sheath and while it is not stained with blood! Flee from Rome! O Florence! Flee from Florence, that is, flee in order to do penance for your sins, and flee from wicked men! [17]

Extract B: Colet's Convocation Sermon, 1512

I am about to exhort you, reverend fathers, to endeavour to reform the condition of the Church. Nothing has so disfigured the face of the Church as the secular and worldly way of living on the part of the clergy. We are troubled in these days too also by heretics, but this heresy of theirs is not so pestilential and pernicious to us and the people as the vicious and depraved lives of the clergy. [18]

Extract C: Erasmus's *Sileni Alcibiadis*, 1515

Who should the pontiffs portray in their lives, if not those whom they portray on their seals, whose titles they bear, whose places they occupy? Which models are more suitable for imitation by the vicar of Christ – the Juliuses, Alexanders, Croesus, and Xerxes, nothing but robbers on the grand scale, or Christ himself, 'the only leader and emperor of the Church?' Whom could the successors of the Apostles more properly strive to copy, than the prince of the Apostles? [19]

Chapter summary

By the end of this chapter you should understand:

- the secular powers and structures of the pre-Reformation Church
- the religious, doctrinal and spiritual roles of the late medieval Church
- the nature and extent of criticisms directed towards the pre-Reformation Church
- the evidence for popular piety and the demand for reform.

Endnotes

1   R.W. Southern, *Western Society and the Church in the Middle Ages*. London, Penguin, 1970, p. 18.

2   Cited in Southern, *Western Society*, p. 143.

3   Cited in Peter Elmer, Nick Webb and Roberta Wood (eds), *The Renaissance in Europe: An Anthology*. New Haven and London, Yale University Press, 2000, pp. 24, 27.

4   Cited in R.N. Swanson, *Religion and Devotion in Europe, c1215–c1515*. Cambridge University Press, 1995, p. 1.

5   Gordon, 'Conciliarism', p. 44.

6   Cited in Swanson, *Religion and Devotion*, pp. 21–22.

7   Swanson, *Religion and Devotion*, p. 8.

8   Cited in Southern, *Western Society*, p. 17.

9   See R.W. Scribner, *Popular Culture and Popular Movements in Reformation Germany*. London, Continuum, 1988.

10   Swanson, *Religion and Devotion*, p. 252.

11   A.G. Dickens, *Reformation and Society in Sixteenth-Century Europe*. London, Thames & Hudson, 1970, p. 40.

12   Southern, Western Society, pp. 138–139.

13   Bruce Gordon, 'Late Medieval Christianity', in Peter Marshall (ed.), *The Oxford Illustrated History of the Reformation*. Oxford University Press, 2015, p. 22.

14   Eamon Duffy, *The Stripping of the Altars: Traditional Religion in England,1400–1580*. London and New Haven, Yale University Press, 1992, p. 283.

15   Gordon, 'Late Medieval Christianity', p. 1.

16   R.N. Swanson, 'The Pre-Reformation Church', in Pettegree, *Reformation World*, p. 29.

17   John Olin, *The Catholic Reformation: Savonarola to Ignatius Loyola*. New York, Fordham University Press, 1992, pp. 14–15.

18   Olin, *The Catholic Reformation*, pp. 32, 35.

19   Olin, *The Catholic Reformation*, pp. 83–84.

2 The challenge of Luther, 1517–1521

Doctor ⟨...⟩nat Argen⟨...⟩em.   Doctor bock Emſer Lipſn   Leo papa.r. Antichriſt   Doctor Eckius. Ingelſtatenſis   Doctor Lemp. Tübingenſis

In this section, we will examine the political and social conditions of the Holy Roman Empire, as well as the early life, career and revolt of Martin Luther until 1521.

Specification points:

- the Holy Roman Empire, its government, condition and social composition: emperor, princes, knights, towns and electors; urban workers and peasants
- Martin Luther: influences on early life; the content and impact of the 95 Theses
- disputations; the development of Lutheran thought; publications and the influence of printing
- excommunication and Diet of Worms: attitude of Catholic Church hierarchy; Emperor and Princes; the imperial edict and the protection of Frederick the Wise.

The Holy Roman Empire

Imperial governance

The Holy Roman Empire was not a unified kingdom, but a federation of disparate powers, ranging from larger princely states to small duchies and imperial cities, with 85 per cent of the population living in the countryside. The German territories tended to be larger in the east (such as Bavaria, Brandenburg and Saxony) with smaller lordships, prelacies and imperial cities in the west. Despite the prestige that was attached to being Emperor, the fragmented nature of the Holy Roman Empire

Key term

Throughout Maximilian I and Charles V's reigns, the **Imperial Diet** remained the principal forum for political affairs, though its powers were largely confined to the granting and withholding of taxes and providing military aid. The Diet consisted of the seven electors, spiritual and secular rulers, and the imperial cities, yet it struggled to govern effectively.

meant that it was very difficult to govern effectively. In theory, the Emperor was meant to dictate imperial policies, but he was very much constrained by the political framework in which he operated. By the end of the 15th century, the Imperial Estates (*Reichsstände*) included a diverse range of imperial subjects, who were permitted to sit and vote at the **Imperial Diet**. By tradition, the Emperor ruled only with the consent of that assembly.

The Imperial Diet's numerous representatives and their multiplicity of interests led to procrastination and indecision. In practice, the workings of the Empire highlighted the Emperor's limited powers and ensured that the German-speaking lands remained a composite of different territorial powers rather than a monarchy under the sway of a single ruler.

In the 1490s, Emperor Maximilian I embarked on various reforms within the Empire. Archbishop Berthold of Henneberg (1441–1504), the Elector of Mainz, introduced the changes. Maximilian gained the approval for an imperial court to resolve disputes between territories, but the majority of judges were named by the Imperial Diet not the Emperor, illustrating the limits of his authority. Maximilian also established a system of imperial circles (*Reichskreise*), which was intended to provide greater regional control by dividing the Empire into administrative districts. By 1512, there were ten circles: Austrian, Burgundian, electoral Rhenish, Franconian, Bavarian, Swabian, Upper Rhenish, Lower Rhenish-Westphalian, Upper Saxon and Lower Saxon.

Figure 2.1: The Holy Roman Empire

Yet again, this came under princely supervision, though the circles were invaluable for collecting taxes, recruiting troops and nominating judges to the imperial court. The new imperial tax, the Common Penny, was also controlled by the Diet, not the Emperor. Maximilian's reforms barely affected the decentralised nature of the Empire. Nor did the changes allow the Emperor to gain an ascendancy over the princes. The Holy Roman Empire remained fragmented and displayed 'a durability and a resistance to centralisation that present a dramatic contrast to contemporary developments in Europe's western kingdoms'.[1]

The condition of the Empire

The 15th and early 16th centuries were characterised by a developing sense of German identity, as articulated by humanist scholars. This was partly fabricated, representing the self-serving fictions of princely and even the imperial courts. Since German identity was such a vague concept and so underdeveloped, German nationalism tended to be defined by what it was opposed to. It was aggressively xenophobic, especially against the French, the Italians and, above all, the papacy. Germans particularly resented the extent of papal control over the German Church 'since Germany's prince-bishops were in the unique position of passing the burdens of papal taxation on to the subjects whom they ruled as temporal princes, the flow of revenues to Rome became a political issue here as nowhere else'.[2]

Numerous scholars of the period carried out research on German history, literature and culture. In 1501, Abbot Trithemius wrote *On the Fame of Germany* and edited Tacitus's *Germania*, which was one of the period's foundational texts. Celtis, who wrote exclusively in Latin, claimed that Germans were far more eloquent and civilised than the southerners in the Italian city-states. In certain cases, such as in Ulrich von Hutten's (1488–1523) works, the anti-Italian element was pronounced. Thomas Brady noted that, 'for Hutten, to be German is to be anti-Roman, to hate in the same breath the ancient Romans as ancient Germans' oppressors and papal Rome as a tyranny over the Germans and their churches'.[3]

Unsurprisingly, the Northern Renaissance represented more than a simple imitation of its Italian counterpart. A distinct type of intellectual movement evolved, with German cities at the heart of a culture as advanced as any in Europe. These intellectual and cultural developments benefited enormously from the spread of printing within the Holy Roman Empire; by 1500, over 60 cities had printing presses. Maximilian I had helped to foster this intellectual climate at his own court, to which he had invited Celtis. After all, the official designation of the Empire was the Holy Roman Empire of the German nation, implying that the Emperor's powers were confined to the German lands. However, German nationalism could be directed against the Emperors. It was well known that the Habsburgs considered the interests of the German lands to be secondary to their broader conception of Empire and dynasticism.

Emperor, electors, princes and knights

Holy Roman emperors had to possess substantial wealth to be even considered for the imperial office. A powerful territorial base was a necessary prerequisite for prospective candidates. By the early 16th century, the Habsburgs were the pre-eminent dynasty within the Holy Roman Empire. As the most powerful family in Europe, they had secured a massive territorial inheritance. In addition to the Austrian hereditary lands, Maximilian's marriage to the duchess of Burgundy in 1477 had secured the Burgundian lands. In 1516, his grandson Charles inherited Castile and Aragon, which granted access to parts of the New World, as well as Sardinia, Sicily and Naples.

Although the Habsburgs possessed the largest empire in Europe, its size made it difficult to control. Financial and military resources were often overstretched, forcing successive emperors to prioritise. During this period, the Habsburgs were threatened

Figure 2.2: Portrait of Emperor Maximilian I, by Albrecht Dürer

ACTIVITY 2.1

Using the section 'Imperial governance' and your wider reading, explain the nature of Emperor Maximilian I's imperial reforms and assess how effective they were.

ACTIVITY 2.2

Research Abbot Trithemius, Conrad Celtis and Ulrich von Hutten, and draw up a biographical timeline. For each individual, explain what they contributed to German humanism. Identify any similarities or differences between the three figures. What does this tell us about the movement?

Key terms

The **electors** were the most powerful nobles within the Empire and included the Margrave of Brandenburg, the Count Palatine, the King of Bohemia, the Elector of Saxony and the archbishops of Cologne, Mainz and Trier. These secular and ecclesiastical princes had the right to elect the Holy Roman Emperor.

The **imperial knights** were lesser nobles, located mainly in the southwest and west, especially Swabia, Franconia and the Rhine valley. By the turn of the 16th century, the imperial knights were no longer central to the Empire's military affairs and political developments.

by the French Valois dynasty and by the Ottoman Turks, both of whom were seeking to expand their territory and influence. Luther's revolt presented a challenge to the unity of Christendom within the Empire for which the Habsburgs, as emperors, were supposed to be the main secular defenders.

The nobility were the most powerful group within the Empire, yet they were far from unified and quite diverse. The noble ranks ranged from leading princes (**electors**, dukes) to the lesser nobility, such as the **imperial knights**, who had experienced a gradual loss of prestige. After the Emperor, the electors were without doubt the most influential figures within the Empire. The ability to elect a new Emperor allowed them to wield enormous power. The electors were able to extract election pledges (*Wahlkapitulationen*) from candidates, promises that the Emperor was expected to fulfil. Maximilian I's determination to secure the imperial office for his grandson, Charles, meant that he spent his final years courting the seven electors.

When Maximilian died and Charles was elected as Holy Roman Emperor, the latter was indebted to the princes and found it virtually impossible to dictate policies to them. The princes, in turn, feared the growing power and ascendancy of the Habsburgs and, as a result, they hesitated to give their full support to the young, inexperienced Emperor. Political disharmony within the Empire ensured that the Emperor rarely secured unanimous backing for his policies. There were frequent conflicts of interest between the Emperor and the German estates; the princes were in constant fear that their traditional liberties might be undermined, especially if imperial resources were used to meet dynastic ends. This 'princely particularism' was a serious threat to Habsburg power in the Empire.

Nobles were expected to participate in imperial governance in order to justify their princely status. In return, they gained territory and control over regional governance, taxation and defence. Before Luther's revolt, German princes were also strengthening their hold over the Church: 'the extension of secular rule to the ecclesiastical realm began centuries before the Reformation'.[4] In Saxony, a series of political alliances were signed by bishops and princes, resulting in the former being eclipsed as weaker partners. In some secular territories, it is possible to speak of a princely Reformation before the 16th century. For example, Duke Eberhard the Bearded oversaw religious reform in Württemberg well before the posting of the 95 Theses. In this way, the long-term process of state formation had already weakened the Catholic Church and the Reformation was not in fact 'a radical break with the past'.[5]

The gradual accumulation of these lands and property had given rise to extremely powerful lords. Yet the demographic catastrophe created by the Black Death had greatly reduced the revenues of lesser nobles by lowering rents and property values, while increasing wages. Some of the less powerful princes worked as military contractors out of financial necessity. In the decades leading up to Luther's early revolt, the changes in late medieval society and economy had had a damaging impact on the fate of the imperial knights. The majority represented a dying class of medieval knights determined to fight wars, largely financed by robbery.

Towns

Towns formed an integral part of the Holy Roman Empire's political culture and later provided the Lutheran movement with its 'pace-makers'.[6] There were approximately 3000 towns in the German lands, 88 within the Swiss Confederacy, and 180 in the Austrian lands. The majority of these urban communes had populations of less than 2000, while the larger cities, including Nuremberg, Augsburg and Cologne, had populations of between 20 000 and 30 000 inhabitants. In 1500, only 27 cities had a population larger than 10 000 people. Inevitably, urban policies were mainly influenced by their economic priorities. Nuremberg and Augsburg were dominant in the southern part of the Empire, Strasbourg and Cologne were the leading cities on the

Rhine and Magdeburg was an important economic centre in the heart of the Empire. Numerous towns and cities had acquired a degree of independence because they had won rights from the nobility in return for fees and loans. Their most significant privileges included the right of trade, to administer justice and to impose taxation. For that reason, city governments could exercise almost unlimited sovereignty over their local populations.

One should distinguish between **territorial cities** and **imperial cities**. In both cases, the relationship between the lord and the city defined the nature of the commune. In the territorial cities, of which there were over 2000, local lords were more powerful, and urban communes were at their weakest. The urban community was thus subject to legal, political and economic manipulation by nobles. In the 60 to 70 imperial cities, including Nuremberg, Ulm and Augsburg, there was no immediate overlord. Each imperial city derived its rights and privileges directly from the Emperor in return for a promise of allegiance.

Long before Luther's revolt, the urban elites had been securing greater control of their local churches. Throughout the late medieval period, urban governments had chipped away at the local bishop's powers. Many communes had acquired rights of patronage over parish churches, and councils openly criticised unsuitable clergy. This served to reinforce the idea of a religious community, which was a key feature of town life. Urban culture was unique because it represented such a variety of different social groups, all of which tended to be sophisticated forms of social organisation, such as parish churches, humanist groups, and artisan guilds.

The countryside

In the late middle Ages, the average German village contained approximately 12 households and 70 people, who were connected to each other through ties of kinship, employment and membership of the local community. The wealth and standing of farmers varied enormously; the most powerful were able both to hire labourers and sell their crops for profit. At the lower end were the landless peasants who rented their house and supplemented farming with other work. Local governance was increasingly controlled by the village commune (*Gemeinde*) and in the 15th century village leaders sought to establish greater control over their parish church at the expense of the existing clergy. This was encouraged by the fact that some pastors ignored village customs, such as the provision of common land.

Owing to the pressures of population growth and price inflation, the rural economy was greatly weakened by the early 1500s. Landowners exerted additional pressure by restricting inheritance and by imposing new taxes in order to compensate for their own economic pressures. The frustration of peasants expressed itself in localised peasant unrest that became increasingly common and exploded in the Peasants' War of 1525.

Martin Luther

Influences on Luther's early life

Luther received a strict and well-disciplined upbringing. His father, Hans, rose from being a labourer to own a small mine. His mother Margarethe also had a peasant background (albeit a wealthier one) and both parents were eager for Luther to study law. Luther received an excellent education at Eisleben, with the Brethren of Common Life at Magdeburg, and at Eisenach. In 1501, he moved to the University of Erfurt, where he secured a Bachelor and Master of Arts, the first of his family to do so, and embarked on a law degree in 1505. That summer, he changed his mind and vowed to become a monk, against his father's will. It may be that his decision to enter a monastery was provoked by a thunderstorm that he experienced; decades later in

Key terms

Imperial cities were more independent because they owed their allegiance to an Emperor who remained distant throughout much of his reign. Robert Scribner has described them as 'those with no immediate overlord other than the Emperor'.[7]

Territorial cities were generally controlled by the local aristocratic lord, who could interfere in a wide range of affairs and dictate to the city's inhabitants.

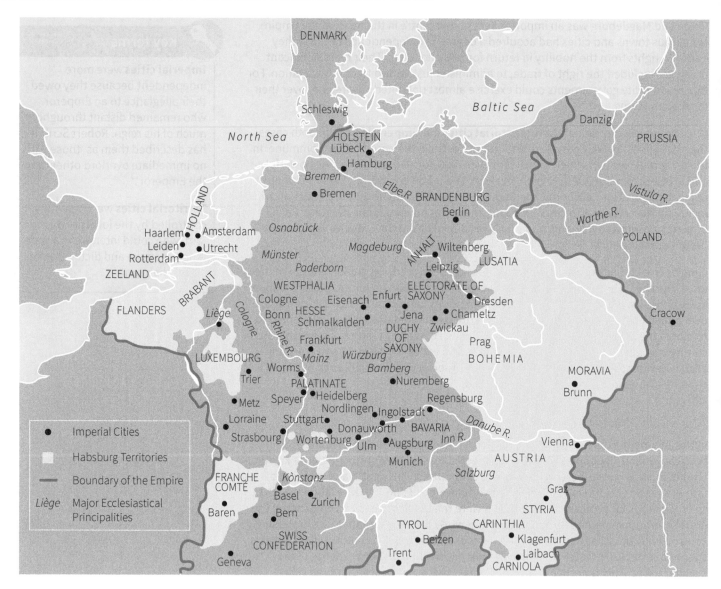

Figure 2.3: Key towns in the Holy Roman Empire

July 1539, Luther reminisced that he had made a vow to St Anne, the patron saint of miners, that he would join a monastery if he survived that storm.

He joined the community of the reformed Augustinian Hermits in Erfurt, where he gained the reputation for excessive rigour in his monastic practices. Despite his extraordinary efforts, he felt increasingly fragile and vulnerable, and that he could not satisfy the high standards expected of him. Luther received some comfort from his spiritual mentor, Johannes von Staupitz (1468–1524), the vicar-general of the German Augustinians. As a monk, Luther studied theology and had a range of academic influences, with St Augustine's (354–430) writings vital to his theological development. Nominalist theologians, who believed that God could only be known as a matter of faith, not by reason, also inspired him; he had been introduced to William of Ockham's (c1287–1347) works at the University of Erfurt. Having been profoundly influenced by the Augustinians at Erfurt, it was not long before Luther was ordained a priest in 1507.

After receiving his doctorate in theology, Luther was invited to lecture at the newly established University of Wittenberg, founded by the Elector of Saxony Frederick the Wise (1463–1525), and where Staupitz was Dean and Professor of Biblical Theology. In 1512, Luther was appointed superior of the reformed Augustinian friars in Wittenberg and in the same year he also joined the university's theological faculty. He began lecturing in biblical studies a year later and replaced his mentor Staupitz as Professor in Biblical Theology. Luther sought to replace the study of Aristotle and **scholastic theology** with that of the Bible and the **Church Fathers**. He devoted much attention to St Paul's epistles. Around 1516, the university embarked on reforms that aimed to remove Aristotle from the curriculum, and to devote greater attention to **biblical exegesis**. Luther himself influenced the promotion of new professors, hence the appointment of lecturers in Greek (including Philip Melanchthon) and Hebrew. In addition to lecturing at the University, from 1514 Luther also preached regularly at Frederick the Wise's castle church; it was unusual to combine the two roles at this time.

Timeline: Luther's early life

1501	Entered University of Erfurt
1502	Gained Bachelor of Arts
1505	Obtained Master of Arts (both at Erfurt); joined Augustinian order
1507	Ordained a priest
1510	Visited Rome
1511	Transferred to Wittenberg
1512	Appointed Superior of the reformed Augustinian friars in Wittenberg; joined University's theological faculty and began teaching
1513–1517	Lectures on the Psalms and St Paul's letters
1517	Posting of 95 Theses

The origins of the 95 Theses

The 95 theses originated in Luther's opposition to indulgences. Prior to posting the theses in October 1517, Luther had already preached against indulgences and clerical failings. The payment of money, normally adjustable to the buyer's means, in order to secure the pardoning of sins and to reduce time in purgatory, was a common late medieval practice. In the mid-1510s, Pope Leo X introduced a major indulgences campaign to fund the rebuilding of St Peter's. Johann Tetzel, a Dominican friar, was appointed to sell indulgences within the German-speaking lands, especially in ducal Saxony, which bordered electoral Saxony where Luther resided. As the town was close to ducal Saxony, some Wittenberg inhabitants went to buy indulgences with their hard-earned savings. There was growing criticism of these indulgence sellers, who were resented for believing that salvation could be exchanged for money. On 31 October 1517, Luther wrote a letter of complaint to the Archbishop of Mainz, which was ignored. The virulent nature of the opposition to indulgences was also provoked by the corruption that surrounded the practice. Albrecht of Brandenburg, Archbishop of Mainz, who supervised Tetzel, had siphoned funds from the indulgences campaign to pay for the archbishopric of Mainz; he had acquired the post in 1514 via simony. His position as Archbishop of Mainz had entitled Albrecht to be one of the seven electors of the Holy Roman Empire, hence his desperation to raise substantial sums.

Shortly afterwards, Luther nailed his 95 Theses to the castle church door in Wittenberg in order to denounce what he considered to be an unjustifiable practice. Written by Luther in his capacity as Professor of Biblical Studies, the theses questioned the legitimacy of indulgences. It was standard practice for theologians to pin theses on

Figure 2.4: Martin Luther as an Augustinian friar

Key term

Disputations were a typical form of academic debates, normally reserved for university scholars.

the castle church door to give advanced warning of academic **disputations**; it was the recognised bulletin board for the University.

The contents of the 95 Theses

The 95 Theses were primarily concerned with the theology and practice of indulgences. Luther justified his attack on the grounds that the Bible did not support them. Throughout his early (as well as his later) works, Luther repeatedly extolled the authority of the Bible.

In the theses, Luther extended his attack to a critique of the Pope's wealth. Germans resented the papacy because their money was being used to rebuild St Peter's in distant Rome. As Luther lamented in the theses, 'Christians should be taught that if the Pope knew the exactions of the preachers of indulgences, he would rather have the basilica of St Peter reduced to ashes than built with the skin, flesh and bones of his sheep.'[8] Luther did not only attack the financial corruption of indulgences, but also targeted the teachings that underpinned them. He discredited indulgences, arguing that they did not have the power either to release souls or to bring salvation. As he said in his letter to the Archbishop of Mainz: 'these unfortunate souls seemingly believe they are assured of their salvation as soon as they purchase letters of indulgence. They also believe the souls leave purgatory as soon as they put the money into the chest.'[9] Luther's criticisms represented a partial rejection of the system of indulgences, relics and pilgrimages. The papacy's support for indulgences suggested to Luther that the Pope was not fulfilling his proper spiritual role.

Despite this, in their contents and in the author's intentions, the theses did not represent a radical programme to overthrow the established Church. 'The last thing on Luther's mind was reform of the entire Church'.[10] The theses were composed in Latin, not intended for public discussion and Luther still refused to dismiss indulgences completely. It was not his aim either to provoke a revolution or even to reject papal authority.

The impact of the 95 Theses

The message of the 95 Theses quickly spread beyond the narrow circles of Wittenberg University, although the intention had been only to prompt academic debate. Yet Luther had chosen his date carefully, as the Theses were posted on 31 October for maximum effect. The following day, All Saints' Day, Frederick the Wise's massive relic collection was displayed, with pilgrims travelling from afar to gain the indulgences that the relics guaranteed. Interestingly, Luther's colleague Andreas Carlstadt had posted 151 theses for disputation on 26 April 1517, the eve of the day on which the relics had previously been displayed.

Luther's 95 Theses rapidly became a public manifesto when they were printed in numerous towns such as Magdeburg, Basle and Leipzig. By December, German translations of the Theses had appeared in Nuremberg. The success of the Theses owed much to their simple tone and their clarity, rendering them accessible to those unversed in theology. As Michael Mullett has written, they 'turned into a sensational printed artefact, precipitated fully into the public domain, to be a manifesto for change, against Papal Rome in a country seething with a mixture of religious, political and financial grievances against the Roman Church'.[12] They were also well received due to their apparent nationalist tone, which humanists such as Ulrich von Hutten effectively exploited; his works reflected a patriotic German tone and played on anti-papal sentiments.

Given the Pope's remoteness, the major targets of these diatribes were the senior German clerics, especially when their political authority exceeded their spiritual role. Equally important to posting the theses in Wittenberg was that Luther sent them to the bishop of Magdeburg and Albrecht of Mainz, who readily passed them on to Rome. The angry reaction of the Archbishop of Mainz and Tetzel helped to escalate the affair. The 95 Theses laid the foundations for a more radical theological programme, since the Augsburg (1518) and Leipzig disputations (1519) that followed saw an increasing separation between Luther and the Pope. Yet, as Mullett reminds us, 'in October 1517 the protester against indulgences was far from being the Protestant leader of later years and the full theology of the Reformation was to emerge from, not to give rise to, the 95 Theses'.[13]

The disputations

As an Augustinian friar, Luther was initially summoned to a meeting of the leading figures of the Augustinian Order in Heidelberg, but he refused to change his opinions about indulgences. Pope Leo X wanted Luther to be questioned in Rome, but this was resisted by Elector Frederick the Wise. This partly explains why Leo X sent Cardinal Tommaso de Vio (d. 1534), known as Cajetan, to question Luther and ensure that he retract his views. In 1518, Cajetan and Luther encountered each other at the Augsburg disputation, a scholarly debate that was not open to the public. Cajetan pointed out that Luther's rejection of a treasury of merit as the source of indulgences contradicted a papal decree. He also challenged Luther's view that popes had no power to assert that souls were released from purgatory. In response, Luther declared that he would only renounce his views if the Bible disproved them. Luther was indirectly and implicitly denying papal supremacy; as the leading representatives in the Catholic Church, popes claimed to be the authoritative interpreters of the Bible. The resulting impasse further strengthened the divide between Luther and Rome. Luther's stern resistance increased both his notoriety and the ever-widening gap between him and the Pope. His survival owed much to Cajetan's inability to encourage Frederick the Wise to withdraw his protection.

After the failure of the Augsburg disputation, the Church was determined to put an end to the 'Luther affair'. At the Leipzig disputation of 1519, Luther was attacked by Johannes Eck. A Dominican friar and professor at the University of Ingolstadt, Eck was a much more formidable theologian and opponent than Cajetan. Initially, the two main protagonists at the Leipzig disputation were Eck and Luther's Wittenberg colleague Andreas Carlstadt, but Luther soon took centre stage. Eck sought to discredit Luther and succeed where Cajetan had failed. Luther continued to defend himself by referring to the Bible, which Luther regarded as the only true source of Christian truth. Eck managed to persuade Luther to admit that he shared Jan Hus's view that communion should be given in both kinds (bread and wine). Hus had been condemned as a heretic and burnt at the stake at the Council of Constance. This

ACTIVITY 2.3

Using the sections on the 95 Theses and your broader reading, answer the following questions:

1. What lay at the heart of Luther's critique of indulgences?
2. How radical was Luther's attack of the Church in the 95 Theses?
3. Why was Luther's attack on indulgences so widely welcomed in the German lands?
4. On what basis did he challenge the practice of indulgences?

Voices from the past

Excerpts of the 95 Theses

6. The pope can remit no guilt, but only declare and confirm that it has been remitted by God …

21. Hence the preachers of indulgences are wrong when they say that a person is absolved from every penalty by the pope's indulgence.

27. There is no divine authority for preaching that the soul flies out of purgatory as soon as the money clinks in the collecting box.

35. It is not Christian teaching to preach that those who buy off souls or purchase confessional licences have no need to repent of their own sins.

50. Christians should be taught that if the pope knew the exactions of the preachers of indulgences, he would rather have the basilica of St Peter reduced to ashes than built with the skin, flesh and bones of his sheep.[11]

associated Luther with heresy, separated him from the Roman Church, and arguably represented a point of no return. Luther summarised his own response in a report dated 20 July 1519: 'Here I publicly asserted that some articles were condemned at the Council of Constance in a godless manner, since they were taught openly and clearly by Augustine, Paul and even Christ himself.'[14]

Yet Eck had struck a resonant chord because ducal Saxony (where Leipzig was situated) was not far from the Bohemian lands. There was a strong anti-Hussite tradition in Saxony, where the rulers, the Wettins, had been granted lands because of their loyalty to the Emperor during the Hussite wars. Hus's reformation had also led to the expulsion of Germans from Prague and its university, which culminated in the foundation of the University of Leipzig. Although Eck had managed to link Luther's ideas with those of a previously condemned heretic, this was ultimately counter-productive as it gave the latter even greater publicity. The condemnation of Luther as a heretic only counted if it led to his arrest by the secular authorities. The failure of the Church to secure Luther's arrest highlighted the papacy's powerlessness.

Figure 2.5: Woodcut of Luther, Hus and Christ

The impact of the disputations

The debates at Augsburg and Leipzig contributed much to the development of Luther's challenge. The fact that Luther was given a platform provided him with a tremendous opportunity. His performances in the respective debates illustrated his resilience as an orator and a theologian. This was particularly impressive given the standing of his formidable opponents. The debates also highlighted the failure of the Catholic authorities to deal effectively with Luther. He was not contained by his own religious order, the Augustinian friars, some of whom were actually sympathetic. Even the Pope's own representative, Cardinal Cajetan, could not handle the situation.

This encouraged Luther to develop his ideas further and to consider the broader theological implications of his attack on indulgences. Luther felt that the Church had not bothered to answer his queries, at least to his satisfaction. It convinced him that real authority in the Church had to be located somewhere other than the papacy, encouraging him to develop a more radical theological programme. Such was Luther's growing disaffection with the papacy that even before his excommunication, Luther openly identified with Hus and started to attack the Catholic Church.

First, the indulgences controversy highlighted apparent flaws in the Church's teachings. The practice of indulgences appeared to offer salvation in exchange for a sum; by paying money, one's sins could be pardoned. Luther was not convinced that individuals could do anything to contribute to their salvation, and therefore dismissed the view that good works had a central role to play. This culminated in an attack on purgatory and an acceptance of **predestination**. Luther's abandonment of indulgences developed into the more revolutionary teaching on justification by faith alone. The concentration on papal abuses and clerical misconduct reflected one of the Church's fundamental problems. As Luther intensified his attack, he quickly realised that papal authority would have to be rejected. Similarly, the frustration with clerical corruption culminated in a rejection of the sacramental system and the priestly power that it represented. The source of authority, on which Luther based his ideas, was of course the Bible. Having defended himself on biblical grounds during the early revolt, he made the Bible central to his theology. The number of sacraments was defined purely by their justification in the Bible. The Roman Catholic Church's monopoly on religious authority was thereby called into question.

Luther's publications

Luther's rise to prominence owed much to the quality of his writing. He took full advantage of the Church's apparent reluctance to eradicate abuses; its inertia suggested that reform would not be forthcoming. In response, Luther believed that it was time to dismantle the apparently rotten edifice and restore the purity of the Church's purity. Luther was convinced that believers required neither the institution of the Roman Church nor the mediation of priests to receive salvation. By the late 1510s, he had concluded that the key to salvation lay in the personal relationship between God and the believer. Martin Brecht has remarked that 'almost all of Luther's writings between 1518 and 1520 dealt with their subject matter in a novel, often revolutionary way'.[15]

He soon discarded the Church's old rituals, believing that no earthly institution should stand between God and the believer. In 1520, Luther published three key works that were integral to his theology. The *Address to the Christian Nobility of the German Nation,* written in German, appealed to the Holy Roman Empire's secular rulers to reform the Church. *On the Babylonian Captivity of the Church*, written in Latin, challenged the Catholic Church's fundamental teachings, especially the sacraments and the emphasis on priestly mediation. Finally, *On the Freedom of a Christian*, composed in Latin, elaborated on his doctrine of salvation by faith. In these works, Luther explicitly rejected the Catholic Church's authority, hierarchy and doctrines.

Luther targeted the papacy as the principal source of corruption. Its failure to remove abuses meant that it had perverted true Christianity. Such was the degree of corruption that papal authority had to be rejected. Luther dismissed the papacy as an arbiter in doctrinal matters and scriptural interpretation. He asserted that revenues should not be directed to Rome and that believers should discontinue all pilgrimages, especially to Rome. He advocated that the Pope had no authority over the Emperor and that the German princes should instigate reform.

The call for a German council struck a powerful chord within the German lands. Luther also denounced the entire ecclesiastical hierarchy, including priests. The

ACTIVITY 2.4

Using the sections 'Martin Luther' and 'The disputations', and your broader reading, draw up three columns, one for the 95 Theses, and one each for the Augsburg and Leipzig disputations, and note down in bullet points the ways in which Luther challenged the Catholic Church. On completion of this task, explain how Luther's theology and ideas developed in the crucial years of his early revolt.

clergy dominated access to the Bible and enjoyed a spiritual monopoly through the administration of the sacraments. For Luther, it made no sense to empower priests when so many failed to conduct themselves properly.

Luther identified the Bible as the sole authoritative text for the formulation of Christian teaching, hence the phrase *Sola Scriptura*. As a consequence, he abandoned Church tradition as a valid source of authority; henceforth, any doctrinal statements formulated in Church Councils and the writings of the early Christian Church were accepted only if they accorded with the Bible. In Luther's view, the late medieval Church had lost its sense of purpose, largely because it had neglected the Bible.

The Catholic Church had retained one centrally controlled biblical text, known as the Vulgate. The fact that it was in Latin ensured that few among the laity had access to it, justified on the basis that lay people untrained in theology could be prevented from misinterpreting it. Given its centrality, Luther wanted to make the Bible more accessible via translation and preaching. Church reform had to be inspired by drawing out biblical messages. To that end, Luther benefited from his monastic training: 'he adapted the tools of monastic spirituality for the study of Scripture and recommended them in place of his own writings'.[16] Only by reference to Scripture alone could each person learn for themselves whether they had faith and were among the Elect. The Lutheran stress on individual reflection, using a vernacular Bible, helped to undermine priestly power. Luther instead advocated the **Priesthood of all Believers**: all men were considered equal and had the potential to have individual access to God.

Initially, Luther reduced the number of sacraments from seven to three, arguing that the others were not justified in the New Testament. He retained baptism, communion and confession, but later abandoned the sacrament of confession for the same reason. These ideas are forcefully presented in his work entitled *On the Babylonian Captivity*. He explicitly challenged priestly superiority. Ordination was abandoned as a sacrament because it had justified treating priests as an elite group; this was consistent with the Priesthood of all Believers. The abandonment of confession was motivated by the belief that forgiveness of sins should be a private matter between God and the believer and should not depend on a priest. He was critical of the Mass because it symbolised priestly monopoly of spiritual and sacramental power. For that reason, he promoted the taking of communion in both kinds for the laity, not just priests, and transformed the Latin liturgy into a vernacular service. However Luther did not scrap the sacramental system altogether; he still believed in the need for a visible and an institutional Church.

Luther's doctrine of *sola fide* was essential to his theology. Lutherans and Catholics agreed that to enter Heaven, a soul had to justify itself before God, which was not straightforward owing to 'original sin'. Both agreed that Christ's death created a store of grace which God used to save people. Yet they disagreed on how God chose to use that grace. Catholics believed that individuals could access the store of grace and do good works that contributed to their salvation. Luther's *sola fide*, justification by faith alone, taught that believers were saved and justified by faith alone. It was neither possible to do good by oneself nor to earn merit towards one's salvation; good works could only be a product of faith.

This theology was liberating for Luther because it was no longer possible to earn grace through good works, such as fasting, saying prayers or hearing masses, but only via God's gift of grace. This had a dramatic impact on the Church's penitential system (the Catholic system of penance) by undermining the role of priests. It also led to the abandonment of indulgences, Masses for the dead and even purgatory. No amount of good works could change the fate that God had already decreed for mankind. Each individual was predestined to go either to Heaven or Hell.

Key term

Sola Scriptura represents Luther's belief that the Bible provided the only true source of authority for all Christian teachings. While he did not completely disregard other texts, they had to be consistent with biblical teachings to be considered legitimate.

Key term

Luther's doctrine of *sola fide* (justification by faith alone) had its roots in Luther's early revolt, but reached its mature form in his 1520 theological works. The theological consequences of *sola fide* led Luther to challenge and reject the fundamental theological tenets of the Roman Catholic Church.

Luther's contribution to the Reformation

Luther's contribution during the early years of the Reformation was invaluable. He provided the key impetus because he was a gifted theologian. His 95 Theses were well received because he was able to capture the mood of dissatisfaction with the German Church. Crucially, Luther identified with various role models, including prophets, biblical commentators and, more dangerously, Jan Hus. As Ulinka Rublack has written, 'this relativised the novelty of his teachings, legitimised his actions for many of those who were already critically minded and at least implicitly served to demand similar devotion in his diverse audiences'. [17] He was also remarkable because of the way in which he developed his 1517 ideas into a more comprehensive theological programme. Luther not only possessed the key ideas of the Reformation, but he was also able to articulate them persuasively on paper and verbally. His three major works in 1520 accommodated a learned readership, but he also published numerous other works for a readership not trained in theology. He was brilliant at simplifying his complex ideas and reducing his major works to the bare essentials. The quality of Luther's scholarship is also revealed in his translation of the New Testament and Complete Bible, published in 1522 and 1534 respectively. In the short term, the translation strengthened his credibility as a reformer, especially his increasing monopoly over scriptural interpretation. In the longer term, it meant that the East Middle Saxon version of German provided the roots for modern German.

In addition to being a prolific author, Luther was a highly competent preacher, which helped to communicate his ideas in what remained a predominantly oral culture. Luther's Reformation has been described as a powerful preaching revival. During the early revolt, Luther also showed tremendous courage and determination, manifest in his forceful stances at the disputations, in addition to his willingness to attend the imperial summons at Worms in 1521. He was well aware that, a century before, Jan Hus had also received a safe-conduct from an emperor, which had been ignored, thereby leading to his execution.

A final strength in Luther's character was his pragmatism. He quickly realised that he would need to court the German nobility, given their political standing within the Holy Roman Empire. In the words of Ulinka Rublack: 'Luther presented his cause as a key moment in the battle for German sovereignty against Rome, and he used all the jargon of German liberty and honour which characterised a fervent patriotic rhetoric among noblemen, knights, princes and humanists.'[18] He did this to great effect by targeting the princes in his *Address to the Christian nobility* and later by condemning the peasantry during the Peasants' War of 1525. Luther's strategy appeased the German princes and safeguarded his movement in the process.

Based on the priesthood of all believers, Luther also pointed out that the Bible made no distinction between secular and spiritual estates; all people were consecrated priests through baptism and, as a consequence, the laity could intervene in Church affairs. Luther's doctrine of the Two Kingdoms decreed that secular rule was ordained by God to keep order and peace on earth; princes had a responsibility to secure Christian worship within their territories. Having previously rejected the structures and personnel of the Roman Catholic Church, Luther realised that the Reformation would not survive without the security of an institutional framework. Inevitably, he called upon the Holy Roman Empire's secular officials to support his endeavours.

The influence of printing

Printing originated in the German lands. Johannes Gutenberg (c1400–c1467) established the first press in Mainz, and printing quickly spread to other parts of the Empire. In spite of his courage and the dynamism of his theological revolution, Luther would have struggled to succeed without the assistance of the printing industry and yet he exploited it to its full potential. The printed word had increased the size of the academic audience and Luther crucially wrote in German, as well as in Latin. The new technology and medium of print were the 'most important reason why Luther did not meet with Hus's fate'.[19]

Luther composed numerous works, including memorable sermons for his followers to copy. Such was Luther's productivity that he was responsible for 20 per cent of all that was printed on the German presses between 1500 and 1530. The *Address to the Christian Nobility* had an initial print run of 4000 copies, which sold out in five days and the work rapidly went into 16 further editions. In addition to theological works, Luther cornered the pamphlet market. His propaganda campaign was also undertaken with the assistance of visual aids. Some of the early Reformation's most striking works combined text and images, and engaged different levels of readership. The famous *Passional of Christ and Antichrist*, composed by Melanchthon and illustrated by Lucas Cranach, indicates just how effectively they used the printing press. Rather than dwelling on complex theological differences, the *Passional* contains a series of 13 simple contrasts between scenes from Christ's life (emphasising his humility) and a related image of the Pope's excessive wealth.

Figures 2.6 and 2.7: Image from Passional of Christ, Lutheran-inspired anti-papal propaganda. Jesus drives the money-lenders from the temple, whereas the Pope welcomes them into the Church.

Luther's relationship with the Emperor

In the two years preceding Emperor Maximilian I's death in 1519, the gravity of Luther's revolt had not yet made itself felt. Maximilian underestimated the threat posed by Luther. In his view, it was a minor inconvenience, which the proper religious authorities would handle with relative ease. During the years 1517–1519, Luther's theses developed into a very public and widely known manifesto. Maximilian's inertia towards the early revolt also facilitated the radicalisation of Luther's religious agenda, particularly regarding the criticisms of the Pope. Maximilian's principal concern was dynastic, namely securing the imperial succession for the Habsburgs. It was thought that Luther was just another heretic who would eventually be condemned; this was scarcely a new problem, or so it seemed at the time. For those reasons, Maximilian was unwilling to dictate to Frederick the Wise, for the latter's vote was crucial to the outcome of the imperial election.

The imperial election was by no means a foregone conclusion, and yet no internal candidate had sufficient power to be a serious contender, though Frederick the Wise was briefly considered. Charles's major rival for the imperial title was Francis I, King of France and from the Valois dynasty, against whom the Habsburgs had been fighting since 1494. This represented a struggle between Europe's two most powerful rulers. After substantial bribery of the seven electors by both candidates, Charles's indispensable support from the Fuggers, the merchant banking family in Augsburg, led him to be elected unanimously: the Fuggers provided 500 000 florins, over half of the total cost of the campaign. Given that the Habsburgs controlled the German-speaking Austrian hereditary lands, Charles was perceived to be the best choice for the German lands.

The implications of Charles's victory require careful qualification. The Habsburgs had successfully prevented the Valois dynasty from securing the throne. Yet holding the imperial title did not automatically strengthen the Habsburgs; the sheer scale of the Empire and its considerable political and linguistic disunity made it almost ungovernable. The unanimity of the election result did not mean that the electors and princes wholeheartedly supported the Habsburgs thereafter. Habsburg domination remained a cause of concern for the electors and princes, who were determined to maintain the Empire's fragmentary nature. Some princes also hoped that Charles V would restrict Rome's interference in German Church affairs. As James Tracy has noted, 'many hoped the new Habsburg emperor would defend the empire against papal domination as well as French aggression'. Yet in truth, if tensions did emerge between the Pope and the Emperor, they would never have convinced Charles either to embrace Luther's revolt or to oppose the papacy in the longer term.

The Emperor's priorities

In any case, Charles was more interested in pursuing his broader dynastic objectives, especially against the French. Charles saw himself as a Renaissance monarch, for whom the reputation of being a warrior king was vital. Status and honour were critical to his conception of monarchy. The warmongering style of Charles V's rule was encouraged by the Habsburg–Valois rivalry that pre-existed his accession to power. The conflict was intensified as both powers sought to gain access to the Italian city-states; this is hardly surprising given the wealth of the city-states. The wars had broken out in 1494, when Charles VIII of France had invaded the Italian peninsula, inspired by the French claim to Naples. Louis XII continued to promote the French right to Naples, and added a claim to Milan. His successor and Charles's principal rival, Francis I, retook Milan shortly after taking the throne and personally defended it at the battle of Marignano in 1515. Since Milan served as a strategic centre for the Habsburg Empire, linking Spain and southern Italy with the north, Charles could hardly ignore French pretensions. Only by securing Milan could Charles secure troop movements and communications.

The Habsburg–Valois rivalry that existed throughout the first half of the 16th century was the most expensive of all the conflicts with which the Habsburgs were faced. The tensions between the French and the Habsburgs were exacerbated by the fact that Francis I was a contender for the imperial throne. This made it impossible for Charles to focus exclusively on the German lands.

Timeline: the early Italian Wars

1494	Charles VIII, King of France, invaded Italy
1495	French conquered Naples
1496	Naples retaken by the Neapolitan King Ferrandino
1500	French troops seized Milan; Treaty of Granada – France and Spain agreed to divide Naples between them
1503	Decisive Spanish victory against French at Garigliano; Naples under Spanish control
1509	League of Cambrai attacked Venice
1512	Battle of Ravenna
1513	French defeat at Novara
1515	Francis, King of France, defeated the Swiss at Marignano, then seized Milan

With numerous other preoccupations, Charles constantly underestimated the threat posed by Luther. Like Maximilian, Charles V prioritised in favour of his dynastic and political concerns. For many years, Charles thought that Luther's revolt could be kept in check, if not effectively reversed, through compromise and concessions. It was a political matter that required a political solution, with no capitulation on the essential articles of faith. Like his predecessor, Charles was unwilling to pressurise Frederick into handing over Luther; he was obviously indebted to Frederick the Wise for his electoral support.

Although Charles realised that Luther had betrayed the fundamental ideals of Catholicism, he opted neither to intervene directly nor to apply diplomatic pressure. Charles persisted in this vein because he lacked sufficient power in the Holy Roman Empire. Without a proper standing army, he was dependent on the princes for their financial and military support, and for their protection against foreign invaders, notably the Ottomans. Charles was also financially weaker, given that his family had spent a fortune on bribing the electors. The Habsburgs owed the Fuggers vast sums of money. Luther's princely patronage ensured that he would never be forced to attend a hearing in Rome, which would have certainly sealed his fate. Similarly, the princes feared that acting against Luther would play into Habsburg hands.

Luther's excommunication

The papal reaction to Luther's early revolt was scarcely surprising. It had never been the Church's custom to compromise over its teachings. Given Luther's ever-growing determination, reaching a consensus seemed unlikely. Academic debate was permissible but only within strict boundaries. By 1519, Luther had definitely gone too far. In practice, however, the Church authorities struggled to contend with Luther because of the considerable distance between Rome and the Empire. This was further exacerbated by the pre-existing resentment towards Rome, which focused on the Church's financial exploitation. Following the Augsburg and Leipzig disputations, Leo X arguably had little alternative but to excommunicate Luther. In June 1520, a papal bull, *Exsurge Domine*, was published giving Luther the choice of either recanting 41 specific assertions or being excommunicated. (*Exsurge Domine* is available on the Papal Encyclicals Online website.)

Once Luther had received it, several months later, he publicly rejected the bull by burning it on 10 December. Leo X officially excommunicated him in the *Decet Romanum Pontificem* bull of January 1521. This was a significant watershed: 'the papal condemnation marks the first real break in the movement for no longer was it possible to present Luther's teaching as part of a theological debate within the normal parameters of scholarly discourse'.[20]

The protection of Frederick the Wise and the Diet of Worms

During the early stages of Luther's revolt, no political figure was more important than Frederick the Wise, Elector of Saxony. As one of the electors, Frederick the Wise was the Empire's most influential prince. Throughout the early revolt, Frederick supported Luther, protecting him without adhering to his teachings. This was important because Luther resided in electoral Saxony. Luther nurtured the friendship of Georg Spalatin, Frederick the Wise's secretary, who acted as the intermediary between the Elector and Luther.

Luther and Elector Frederick never met, so Spalatin was indispensable in brokering the Elector's support. Frederick willingly defended Luther partly because he was a professor at Wittenberg University, which Frederick had recently founded. Frederick's prestige and the academic reputation of the university were at stake. Frederick also sought to exploit the revolt as a means of undermining imperial authority.

Frederick the Wise's protection of Luther was vital in practice. He saved Luther by blocking the reformer's extradition to Rome in 1518 and by insisting that he gain a fair hearing within the Holy Roman Empire, as evidenced by the Augsburg and Leipzig disputations. He became even more influential following the death of Emperor Maximilian I in 1519. He was the most powerful of the seven electors, and much had depended on the casting of his electoral vote. It explains why the new Emperor Charles V was not more determined in his actions against Luther. The fact that the imperial election coincided exactly with Luther's early revolt was crucial: 'the uncertainty [concerning the imperial election] maximised Frederick's political influence during the crucial period when policy against the heretic was being devised'.[21] Frederick's protection explains why the Pope did not immediately dispatch Luther to Rome following his excommunication in 1520.

The Diet of Worms

Luther was guaranteed a genuine and effective safe-conduct to the Diet of Worms in April 1521, thanks to Frederick's intervention. That same year, the papal legate Jerome Aleander protested against the discussion of the Luther question because the matter, in the eyes of the Church, had already been settled. But the Diet's representatives refused to act without hearing Luther's defence of his ideas. As Patrick Collinson has written, 'that Luther survived to make his historic appearance at Worms had little to do with theology and everything to do with politics'.[22] As a result, Luther became all the more determined. His sheer resilience and boldness are indicated by the defence of his works and ideas at Worms: 'If I am not overcome by the Scriptures or arguments of reason – for I believe in neither popes nor councils alone as witnesses, since they have often erred – I remain overcome by the Bible as I have explained it,'[23] Luther's presence at Worms and his defiance of the Emperor had an enormous impact on his cause.

Even at this late stage, by which time Luther had already been excommunicated, Charles V hesitated to permit Luther's immediate arrest. In this way, Charles failed to take advantage of the only opportunity he ever had to seize Luther. Immediately following the Diet of Worms, Luther was kidnapped on Frederick's orders for his own safety and was taken to the Wartburg Castle. Frederick alleged that Luther had not received a fair hearing. This arguably saved the progress of the Reformation, given that Charles V placed Luther under an imperial ban in May 1521, making him an outlaw.

At precisely this moment, Charles returned to the Iberian peninsula, delegating imperial authority to his brother Ferdinand. On 8 May, the Imperial Edict of Worms outlawed Luther and it was forbidden to print, sell or read his writings. Charles's subsequent lack of control is evident in his inability to enforce the Edict of Worms, and this failure was exacerbated by his absence from the German lands during the critical decade of the 1520s.

Practice essay question

With reference to these sources and your understanding of the historical context, assess the value of these three sources to a historian studying Luther's early revolt (1517–1521).

Extract A: Luther's protest against Tetzel's activity, letter to Archbishop Albrecht of Mainz, 31 October 1517

There is sold in the country under the protection of your illustrious name the papal indulgence for the building of St. Peter's in Rome. In this I do not complain so much about the great clamour of the indulgence sellers, whom I have not personally heard. But I am greatly concerned about the false notion existing among the common people which has become a cause of public boast. These unfortunate souls seemingly believe they are assured of their salvation as soon as they purchase letters of indulgence. They also believe the souls leave their purgatory as soon as they put the money in the chest. It is also said that those who purchase such letters of indulgence need not be contrite.[24]

Extract B: Luther's report on the Leipzig debate, 20 July 1519

The following week Eck debated with me, first of all quite sharply concerning papal primacy. Then he went to the extreme and emphasised exclusively the Council of Constance, where the articles of Hus asserting that the papacy derived its authority from the emperor had been condemned. There he stood quite boldly, as if on a battlefield, and reproached me with the Bohemians and called me publicly a heretic and a supporter of the Hussite heretics. Here I publicly asserted that some articles were condemned at the Council of Constance in a godless manner, since they were taught openly and clearly by Augustine, Paul and even Christ himself.[25]

Extract C: Papal Legate, Jerome Aleander, reports to Cardinal Medici from the city of Worms, February 1521

A little while ago in Augsburg they were selling Luther's picture with a halo; it was offered without a halo for sale here, and all the copies were gone in a thrice before I could get one. Yesterday I saw on one and the same page Luther depicted with a book and Hutten with a sword. Over them was printed in fair letters: 'To the fair champions of Christian liberty, M. Luther and U. von Hutten'.[26]

Chapter summary

By the end of this chapter you should understand:

- the social and political composition of the Holy Roman Empire
- the influence of Martin Luther, and the development of his ideas from the 1510s to 1521
- the contents and impact of the 95 Theses and the Augsburg and Leipzig disputations
- the attempts by the ecclesiastical and political authorities to condemn Luther, and the reasons for his survival.

Endnotes

1 Thomas Brady, *German Histories in the Age of Reformations, 1400–1650.* Cambridge University Press, 2009, p. 28.

2 James Tracy, *Europe's Reformations, 1450–1650.* Oxford, Rowman & Littlefield Publishers, 1999, p. 27.

3 Brady, *German Histories*, p. 139.

4 C. Scott Dixon, 'The Princely Reformation in Germany', in Andrew Pettegree (ed.), *The Reformation World.* London and New York, Routledge, 2000, p. 148.

5 C. Scott Dixon, *The Reformation in Germany.* Oxford, Blackwell Publishers, 2002, p. 117.

6 Ulinka Rublack, *Reformation Europe.* Cambridge University Press, 2005, p. 39.

7 R.W. Scribner, *The German Reformation.* London, Macmillan, 1986, p. 25.

8 Cited in Pamela Johnston and Bob Scribner (eds), *The Reformation in Germany and Switzerland.* Cambridge University Press, 1993, p. 13.

9 Cited in Johnston and Scribner, *The Reformation*, p. 12.

10 Scott Hendrix, 'Martin Luther, the reformer', in R. Po-chia Hsia (ed.), *The Cambridge History of Christianity, Vol. VI: Reform and Expansion, 1500–1660.* Cambridge University Press, 2007, p. 3.

11 Johnston and Scribner, *The Reformation*, p. 13.

12 Michael Mullett, 'Martin Luther's Ninety-Five Theses', *History Review* (September 2003), p. 49.

13 Mullett, 'Martin Luther's Ninety-Five Theses', p. 51.

14 Cited in Johnston and Scribner, *The Reformation*, p. 16.

15 Martin Brecht, 'Luther's Reformation', in Thomas Brady, Heiko Oberman and James Tracy (eds), *Handbook of European History, 1400–1600*, Vol. II. Grand Rapids, MI, William B. Eerdmans, 1995, p. 135.

16 Hendrix, 'Martin Luther', p. 6.

17 Rublack, *Reformation Europe*, p. 16.

18 Rublack, *Reformation Europe*, p. 16.

19 Lyndal Roper, 'Martin Luther', in Peter Marshall (ed.), *The Oxford Illustrated History of the Reformation.* Oxford University Press, 2015, p. 53.

20 Andrew Pettegree, 'The Early Reformation in Europe', in *The Early Reformation in Europe.* Cambridge University Press, 1992, p. 5.

21 Roper, 'Luther', p. 53.

22 Patrick Collinson, *The Reformation.* London, Weidenfeld & Nicolson, 2003, p. 51.

23 Cited in Brady, *German Histories*, p. 154

24 Johnston and Scribner, *The Reformation*, p. 12.

25 Johnston and Scribner, *The Reformation*, p. 16.

26 Johnston and Scribner, *The Reformation*, p. 24.

In this section we will study the spread of the Lutheran and radical reformations in the 1520s, as well as the Reformation in the Swiss Confederacy.

Specification points:

- the spread of the Radical Reformation: Carlstadt and the Zwickau prophets; Luther's relations with radicals and humanists
- the development of Protestant doctrine: Luther, Melanchthon and Zwingli
- The revolt of the imperial knights and the Peasants' War: causes and outcomes; part played by Lutheranism and Luther's reaction; Luther's pamphlets of 1525; Imperial Diets, princes and cities; Lutheran–Catholic negotiations including the 1530 Augsburg Confession
- the reformation in the Swiss Confederacy; the Kappel wars; support and opposition; Lutheran-Zwinglian negotiations; the state of the Church by 1531.

The spread of the Radical Reformation

Luther's vision of a reformed Church encouraged many to follow in his footsteps, though he quickly became a victim of his own success. Representatives of the Radical Reformation can be characterised by its departure from Luther's theology and ideas. Once the Pope was removed as the authoritative interpreter of the Bible, who would succeed him as the ultimate arbiter in scriptural interpretation?

Luther's early revolt and the compilation of his key works gave way to a divergence of theological opinions. Luther was faced with radical strands of thought because radicals took his teachings to what they saw as their logical conclusion. In the early years, Luther and Zwingli hesitated in their respective German and Swiss contexts over changes that they later embraced. For example, Andreas Carlstadt's (1486–1541) early radicalism was perceived by Luther to threaten his movement's survival. The willingness to resort to violence, as evidenced by the imperial knights, the peasants in the mid-1520s, some Anabaptists (see Chapter 4) and Zwingli himself formed another component of the Radical Reformation. For some radicals, Luther's theology was considered too conservative. For Zwingli, to promote the Real Presence, as Luther's consubstantiation did, was little different from the equally superstitious transubstantiation. Although Luther's theological breakthrough in 1520 was radical, this did not prevent him from being conservative.

Luther's relations with the radicals: Carlstadt and the Zwickau prophets

After the Diet of Worms, Luther was seized and taken to the Wartburg castle in April 1521 for his own protection. He remained there for close to a year, returning to Wittenberg in March 1522. While he was away, he translated the New Testament into German and learnt Hebrew in preparation for working on the Old Testament, but lost touch with events in Wittenberg.

In Luther's absence, Carlstadt introduced worship in German and permitted the reception of communion in both kinds (bread and wine) for the laity; Carlstadt celebrated the first evangelical mass. Without liaising with Luther, Carlstadt persuaded the city council to remove images from churches. Carlstadt also recommended a Church order that was adopted by the town council, even though Frederick the Wise opposed it. He also got married, thereby breaking the vows of clerical celibacy, and began dressing as a layman.

Figure 3.1: Andreas Carlstadt, Luther's colleague at the University of Wittenberg, who was eventually expelled from the town

Religious controversies continued in December 1521 when three men arrived in Wittenberg from nearby Zwickau, from which they had been expelled for disseminating radical ideas. The Zwickau prophets, as they came to be known, took refuge in Wittenberg, and their presence threatened to undermine stability. They favoured the abolition of infant baptism, claimed to have direct inspiration from God and called for the slaughter of all Catholic priests. Philip Melanchthon and other theologians at the university questioned the Zwickau prophets and remained undecided about their various propositions. The Wittenberg town council accused Carlstadt of provoking sedition and called on Luther to intervene.

On his arrival, Luther immediately regained control and reasserted his authority. His response was firm and unambiguous. He expelled the prophets and restored the Latin Mass, although a German liturgy was reintroduced four years later. Carlstadt was prohibited from publishing anything and was eventually expelled from the city. Luther rejected Carlstadt's actions because he had accelerated the reform process too quickly. Luther was not opposed to most of Carlstadt's changes per se, but wanted to retain personal control of the movement. He wanted to prevent his **evangelical movement** from alienating important aristocratic and **magisterial** patrons. In November 1521, Carlstadt had written that Christ had more authority than any Duke. While Frederick the Wise had prohibited any major reforms, Carlstadt's supporters had also indiscriminately destroyed images and statues in Wittenberg's Churches. Luther was adamant that his movement should not be associated with civil disorder. The fact that this threat emanated from Wittenberg, on the Reformation's doorstep, was of particular concern and explains Luther's speedy return from hiding.

Luther soon realised that he could not easily control the printing press. When Carlstadt left Wittenberg in 1523 intent on establishing a peasant reformation, he used a printing

Key term

Evangelical movement

In the first decade of the Reformation, it is more common to describe Luther's disciples as evangelicals, which emphasises their commitment to the Gospel. The word evangelical is derived from the Greek *evangelion*, meaning the good news of the Christian message. The evangelists are the authors of the Gospels.

ACTIVITY 3.1

Using the section 'Luther's relations with the radicals' and your wider reading, account for the significance of Andreas Carlstadt. Why was he perceived to be a threat by Luther and the Wittenberg authorities?

ACTIVITY 3.2

Using the section 'Luther's relations with the humanists' and your wider reading, draw up a table (with two columns) focusing on the similarities and differences between Luther and Erasmus. Would you agree that Erasmus 'laid the egg that Luther hatched'?

press in Jena and, in due course, published some 90 works in over 200 editions. In 1523, he moved to Orlamünde and 'gave concrete form to the priesthood of all believers by instituting democratic congregationalism' – laymen were empowered to elect their pastors.[1] In Orlamünde, images were removed from churches, infant baptism was abandoned and the Real Presence was denied. In 1524, Frederick the Wise banished Carlstadt from electoral Saxony. In September of that year, the latter went to the Swiss Confederacy and to the Upper Rhine, where he helped to inspire the early Anabaptist movement in Zurich. (See Chapter 4 for Anabaptism).

Meanwhile, Luther consolidated his position by promoting loyal supporters in important positions. Georg Spalatin was appointed court preacher, Justus Jonas was given the headship of the All Saints' Foundation and Lucas Cranach became a key publisher and illustrator. In condemning the early radicals, Luther showed his gradual and cautious approach to reform. For that reason, the laity was not offered bread and wine at communion before January 1523.

Luther's relations with the humanists

Luther's association with humanism was indefinite. Some humanists supported Luther such as Philip Melanchthon, while others turned against him, notably Erasmus. Initially, there were significant points of agreement between Erasmus and Luther. They both emphasised the Bible as the primary source for Christian teaching and were outspoken in their opposition to Church corruption. While Erasmus shared Luther's biblicism and his criticisms of Church abuses, he was essentially a reformer from within and was not as radical as Luther would become in 1520. Although many people struggled to distinguish between them particularly in the early years, the divisions became clearer owing to the publication of Luther's three key works in 1520. In the early 1520s, Erasmus strove to avoid any **polemical debate** with Luther, until he felt compelled to respond to him in the mid-1520s over the question of free will.

Despite the various points of agreement, the differences between Erasmus and Luther were ultimately far more important. In September 1524, Erasmus published a work entitled *On the Freedom of the Will*, which articulated his opposition to Luther's *sola fide*. Erasmus argued that man did have free will in matters pertaining to salvation and he opposed Luther's complete denial of free will. Erasmus asserted that the fact that God foreknows every choice human beings make does not mean that God causes us to make one choice rather than another. In response, Luther published his *On the Bondage of the Will*, which attacked Erasmus' views on justification and reaffirmed the teachings that he had outlined in 1520.

The development of Protestant doctrine

Luther

Having published his key theological works in 1520, Luther rarely left electoral Saxony and supervised the Reformation from Wittenberg. In addition to preaching and lecturing, he also produced catechisms, orders of worship and hymns. In response to Carlstadt's radicalism, Luther stressed the importance of the Christian's duty to obey political rulers in his work *On Secular Authority*. In fact, the example of Wittenberg 'signalled the ability of Lutherans to submit to the clear authority of one leader, one church, one prince and one magistrate'.[2] In 1523, Luther encouraged communities to redirect the wealth of the old Church towards poor relief, evangelical preaching and education. He had assisted the Wittenberg town's council in drafting their *Ordinance of the Common Chest*, which insisted on weekly collections for the poor.

He was also determined to educate the laity, especially children, in scriptural ideals. In 1529, he wrote a *Large Catechism* as guidance for preachers. In 1529, he also published a *Shorter Catechism* for children. Composed of carefully constructed questions and answers, it became the key text for teaching the young. In the preface to the *Shorter Catechism*, Luther wrote, 'What misery I have seen! The common man, especially in the villages, knows absolutely nothing about Christian doctrine, and unfortunately, many pastors are practically unfit and incompetent to teach … They live just like animals and unreasoning sows.'[3]

Philip Melanchthon

Philip Melanchthon (1497–1560) was a colleague of Luther's at Wittenberg University. He was educated at the universities of Heidelberg (1509–1512) and Tübingen (1512–1518). In 1518, he was appointed Professor of Greek at Wittenberg University, where Luther persuaded him to switch to lecturing on theology. Melanchthon accompanied Luther to the Leipzig disputation and became one of his closest associates. He was the author of the first **systematic statement** of Lutheran theology, published in 1521 as the *Loci Communes*. He composed guidelines for teaching and pastoral practice, facilitating the consolidation of Lutheranism; he was directly involved in the strengthening of Lutheranism in Nuremberg in the years 1525–1526. The Lutheran practice of **visitations** was initiated by the first major Saxon visitation between 1528 and 1529, and it was Melanchthon who wrote the *Instruction of the Visitors to the Pastors in the Electorate of Saxony*. In addition to supporting Luther at the Marburg Colloquy where Luther debated theology with Zwingli in 1529, Melanchthon contributed the most to the drafting of the Augsburg Confession of 1530 (see later section on Lutheran-Catholic negotiations).

Huldrych Zwingli

The Swiss theologian Zwingli launched the most important alternative to Luther's evangelical message, though they shared much common ground. Both were influenced by, and benefited from, humanism albeit to different degrees. In his first parish at Glarus in 1506, Zwingli devoted his attention to the New Testament in Greek. Both reformers started by attacking Catholic rituals and corrupt practices, notably the sale of indulgences. Both were committed to *sola fide*, though it is generally agreed that they arrived at this central theological tenet independently of each other. Zwingli had personal control of the Swiss Reformation in a way that paralleled Luther's pre-eminence within the German lands. Both determined the speed of the Reformation in their respective territories, though with varying degrees of success. In 1518, Zwingli moved to Zurich and was appointed a priest at the Great Minster, where he resided for the rest of his career.

The eating of sausages at the house of the printer Christoph Froschauer on Ash Wednesday, 9 March 1522, marked the beginning of the Zurich Reformation. This was a deliberate and symbolic gesture implying that good works such as fasting contributed nothing to salvation. Shortly afterwards, Zwingli broke the vow of celibacy and got married. Zwingli's challenge to the religious status quo attracted sufficient attention for the Zurich town council to organise a public disputation in his defence. On 29 January 1523, Zwingli's 67 religious articles were approved by the city council. On the same day, Zurich's council introduced a decree establishing evangelical preaching. Zwingli later elaborated on his articles and published them as the *Commentary on the Sixty-seven Theses*. In the same year as the disputation, Zwingli called for the abolition of the Mass, but this was achieved only later in April 1525.

Figure 3.2: Portrait of Zwingli

The differences between Luther and Zwingli became acute when the latter espoused a new understanding of the Lord's Supper. Zwingli's Eucharistic theology differed greatly from Luther's because he argued that the Words of Institution ('This is my Body') should be taken figuratively, not literally – by 'is', Zwingli understood the term 'represents'. For Zwingli the true Body of Christ was not a piece of bread, but an assembly of the faithful gathered to commemorate the Last Supper. With Luther considering this to be blasphemous, there was little room for negotiation. In 1526,

ACTIVITY 3.3

Using your wider reading, research the concept of German humanism (focusing on individuals such as von Hutten and Celtis) and make a list of its different characteristics.

Figure 3.3: Image of Luther as German Hercules

Luther accused the Swiss reformers of being inspired by the Devil. In the late 1520s, Zwingli sought to consolidate his Reformation. The funds from tithes, for example, were redirected towards poor relief and education. In contrast with Lutheran territories, church music was banned and images were removed from churches.

Revolt of the imperial knights

The imperial knights were some of Luther's earliest supporters but they quickly became a liability. They found Luther's call to unite against Rome appealing. Closer to home, they resented the German Church's wealth, especially that of clerical princes. They were determined to overthrow a hierarchical system dominated by corrupt, foreign, or at least foreign-dominated, clerics. Rather than being powerful territorial princes, the imperial knights included figures such as Franz von Sickingen, Ulrich von Hutten and Hartmut von Cronberg, mainly from the Rhineland and Franconia, who were relatively impoverished. Unsurprisingly, given their poor status, they were motivated by financial gain.

They saw Luther less as a reforming theologian than as a German hero, standing for national opposition to Rome. Given Luther's adoption of the German language, the Reformation came to be seen increasingly in cultural and nationalist terms. Luther was perceived as the defender of German liberties in the face of foreign and Roman exploitation. This was highlighted by the campaign against indulgences, since the controversy was partly provoked by opposition to the papacy raising funds for St Peter's in Rome.

This message was well received by Ulrich von Hutten (1488–1523) and by the imperial knights; von Hutten's writings, like those of his predecessor Conrad Celtis (1459–1508), had a strong patriotic German tone. Hutten's Germanness is characterised by his nationalistic resentment of a foreign pope whose authority was transmitted through senior German clerics. Opposition to the Church was stronger when the clergy's political influence seemed to exceed its spiritual role. Above all, von Sickingen and von Hutten promoted their views by the use of force, which ultimately led to their downfall. A group of pro-Lutheran and anti-Lutheran princes, including the Archbishop Elector of Trier, the Elector Palatine, Philip of Hesse and the Emperor's peacekeeping force, the Swabian League, overlooked their religious differences and overpowered the imperial knights. The knights were first and foremost seen as a serious threat to civil order.

The defeat of the imperial knights' revolt of 1523 weakened some of the early Lutheran fervour among the nobility, especially von Hutten's passionate call for an anti-clerical war. Although Luther distanced himself because of the knights' use of violence, their ultimate objectives were widely supported within the German lands. The opposition to the papacy was more appealing when placed within a nationalist context than as part of a complicated theological controversy; only a minority of Germans were well versed in theology.

The spread of the Reformation

Luther's theology was not fully understood by the majority of Germans. Its simplification and transmission to the masses via preaching, the printed and the illustrated word ensured that it was quickly adopted in urban and rural regions. The early growth of Lutheranism owed much to its emergence in an urban context. Yet it could not have developed into a mass movement without rural support.

The Reformation in the cities

Cities were more receptive to Luther's message partly because they contained a more literate population (10–30%), well above the 'national' average of 5%. Towns also possessed schools and, in some cases, universities, which explains the reception of more intricate ideas. German humanism, which flourished in many towns, nurtured an educated and stern resistance to Rome, encouraging opposition to indulgences and clerical abuses. Anti-clericalism was well established in cities, which Luther's movement certainly harnessed. Although artisans might not have grasped Luther's complicated Priesthood of all Believers, they were attracted to his anti-clerical message. Towns also obviously contained a denser population, which facilitated the distribution of ideas.

Luther's ideas spread thanks to the numerous cities that had printing centres within the Holy Roman Empire – 60 by 1500. Printing 'created a new reading public, who seized eagerly on the reformers' ideas to form a large-scale public opinion, which in turn served to spread the movement on a large scale'.[4] Between 1518 and 1529, 80% of Luther's works were printed in German and Luther was the author of 20% of the 7500 broadsheets printed between 1520 and 1526. The key printing centre was Wittenberg with over 1000 editions of Luther's works printed between 1516 and 1546. This allowed Luther and his advisers to maintain closer supervision of the Reformation's printing output. For the illiterate and semi-literate, there were also illustrated broadsheets, often with a rhyming text that could be easily sung or memorised. Lucas Cranach produced much of this early propaganda in Wittenberg itself.

Although the written word was vital to the dissemination of ideas, the success of Lutheranism also depended on oral communication. The spread of the Reformation owed much to preaching. The preaching revival pre-existed Luther's arrival on the scene, with a wave of lay-funded preacherships in the two generations before 1520. A leading preacher inspired each major town to adopt the Reformation: Luther and Melanchthon in Wittenberg; Andreas Osiander in Nuremberg; and Johannes Oecolampadius in Basle. The urban clergy were the movement's key leaders. Informal preaching enabled new ideas to bridge the cultural divide between town and country, and between the literate and the illiterate. From the sermon, evangelical ideas were transmitted to the home, the workplace, taverns and the market square. This might explain why towns without a printing industry, like Bremen, adopted the Reformation.

These factors greatly contributed to the success of the urban Reformation. But there were also political, economic and social factors at work. Recent research has revealed the complexity of urban culture within the Holy Roman Empire. It is not possible to reduce the urban Reformation to a single model of reform. Lutheranism thrived in the imperial cities, the inhabitants of which swore their allegiance to a distant emperor. Although Charles V was eager to suppress Lutheranism, his absence during the 1520s made it difficult to enforce his will. In Nuremberg, for example, the evangelical movement forced the ruling elites to ignore the Emperor's wishes. Charles had advised the city to suppress the movement, but it was too late.

The approval of Luther's movement was a form of rebellion, yet refusing to compromise with the town's citizens could be political suicide. The principal solution was for the authorities officially to obey imperial requests, such as promising to enforce censorship and to control preaching, yet in practice to permit religious reform. Ignoring the threat presented by the Reformation was a greater political risk than condemning the movement in the interests of a distant, imperial government.

Thomas Brady has summarised the dilemma with which urban authorities were confronted: 'there arose a kind of political scissors, of which one blade was the urban commons' direct pressure for religious change, and the other was Charles V's new determination to scotch the Lutheran heresy'.[5] Brady's own research on Strasbourg shows the importance of popular pressure. The political authorities were resistant to religious change because they had funded the building of chapels and altars. The elites were also dependent on tithes, monasteries and religious foundations to supplement their income. In the end, they adopted the Reformation for their own survival.

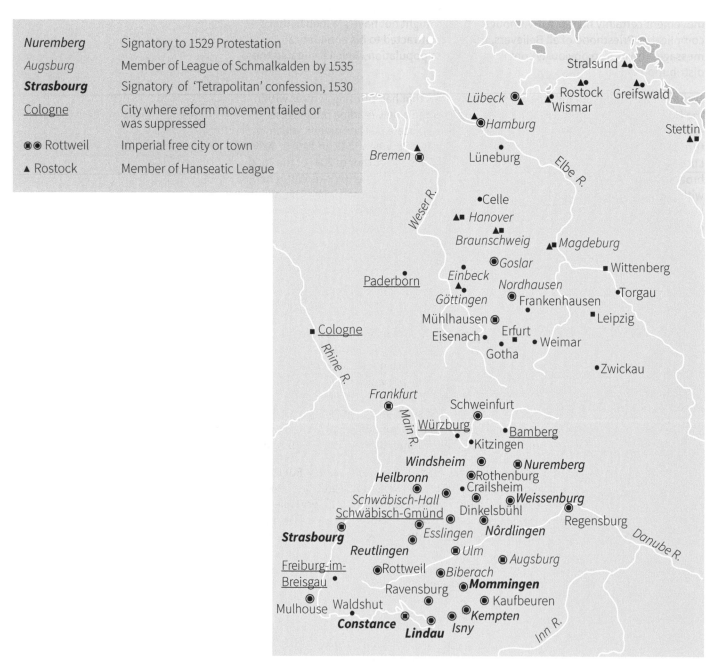

Nuremberg	Signatory to 1529 Protestation
Augsburg	Member of League of Schmalkalden by 1535
Strasbourg	Signatory of 'Tetrapolitan' confession, 1530
Cologne	City where reform movement failed or was suppressed
◉◉ Rottweil	Imperial free city or town
▲ Rostock	Member of Hanseatic League

Figure 3.4: Cities and towns of the German Reformation

The fate of the Reformation was often dictated by broader political factors. The imperial city of Rottweil favoured Catholicism, even though the evangelical movement had taken root. Rottweil was the seat of the imperial court of justice, which contributed to the town's wealth and influence. Many members of the court were also town magistrates and the town's neighbours were Ferdinand (Charles V's brother) and the powerful Catholic bishop of Constance. In contrast, Ulm adopted Lutheranism for security reasons and joined the **Schmalkaldic League** in the early 1530s.

Every urban reformation was also a magisterial reformation, for every religious settlement was secured by the intervention of secular authorities in the name of public order. In small territorial towns, the dialogue was not so much between the town authorities and the urban masses, but rather the town authorities and the urban overlord. In the northern Hanseatic towns, including the key centres of merchant wealth – Rostock, Lübeck, Hanover – the evangelical movement heightened tensions between the urban elite (who remained true to Catholicism) and the politically isolated middle classes (who were supporters of the new faith). In Lübeck, the pro-reform movement assumed control over the commune, forced through the Reformation and drove the conservative council into exile. Yet the Reformation did not give rise to the social vision of the common man, but confirmed ideas of order and governance held by the ruling elite.

Lutheranism flourished in cities with important trading interests. It survived in Augsburg because its suppression could have endangered that city's economic interests. Cities lying on trade routes benefited from the transmission of Lutheran ideas via merchants. The abolition of Catholic feast days increased the number of work days, providing Protestantism with its reputation of a distinctive work ethic. Different social classes were attracted to Luther's message, though the bulk of support came from artisans.

Trade guilds influenced the course of religious reform, such as in Basle, where over 12 guilds pressurised the town council to adopt the Reformation. In Strasbourg, the most active support came from the gardeners' guild, while in Ulm the question of religious reform was put before the guilds, fraternities and master craftsmen. In Memmingen, the guilds encouraged public action and forced the council to implement religious change. In towns such as Ulm, Strasbourg, Esslingen, Colmar and Augsburg, the urban Reformation provoked mixed responses from guilds and the ruling elites, which could lead to violent confrontation.

The rural Reformation and the causes of the Peasants' War

Towns made it possible for Lutheranism to access the countryside due to the close contacts between urban and rural communities, especially via the daily markets. The rural population provided Lutheranism with numerical support, without which it would never become a mass movement; 85% of the population lived in the countryside. The spread of Lutheranism to the countryside was partly due to the flexibility and anti-clerical tone of the message. Rural communities arguably felt the absence of proper pastoral care more strongly than urban communities. Luther's ideas found fertile soil because the common man responded to his call, creating a 'communal Reformation'.[6] The peasantry called for the preaching of the Gospel, the election of the priest by members of the community and the abolition of Church courts. Lutheranism enjoyed considerable success in the countryside because its message was combined with pre-existing socio-economic grievances.

The extent of rural dissatisfaction was such that significant unrest was a distinct possibility. The Reformation was the vehicle for this rebellion, providing the common people with a new basis of action. It allowed long-held grievances against the clergy to have much greater cohesion and sharper focus. Many firmly believed that the evangelical message provided a justification for transforming the countryside's social and economic norms. Peasant manifestos were characterised by a mixture of socio-economic and religious grievances. The Twelve Articles adopted by the Memmingen peasants clearly use Scripture as political ideology; the manifesto called for a reduction in taxes, the priest's election by his parishioners, and the protection of hunting, fishing rights, and other communal rights.

The rural Reformation encountered considerable difficulties. Lutheranism struggled to contend with the higher levels of illiteracy. The shortage of Lutheran preachers inevitable in a new movement hampered successful consolidation. In the countryside, theology played a secondary role and was measured against the socio-economic norms of the community. Catholic rituals were more deeply entrenched than in urban communities. Sacraments had represented social and cultural events, not just dry liturgical practices. Many landlords, however, were clerics or monasteries,

ACTIVITY 3.4

Using this chapter and your wider reading, research three cities from the following list and explain why the Reformation was successful in them: Nuremberg, Augsburg, Strasbourg, Bremen, Lübeck, Hanover and Ulm.

Research the cities of Rottweil and Cologne, which rejected Lutheranism and compare notes with the other cities. What best explains the spread of the urban Reformation?

so the resentment towards tithes and the Church's failings could become a critique of the relations between clerical lords and peasants. These problems explain why Lutheranism was such a divisive force within rural society.

Although Luther was determined to promote the common man – consistent with the Priesthood of all Believers – the rural population hijacked his movement. Luther distanced himself from the rural reformation when peasants resorted to force. Many peasant actions began with a call for true Christian preaching. This included uprisings motivated by challenging the traditional rights of the nobility, such as feudal dues. Peasant unrest rendered Lutheranism susceptible to the charge of sedition.

The Peasants' War and Luther's response

The Peasants' War started in the summer of 1524 in the southern part of the Black Forest and then spread throughout the Holy Roman Empire and to the Swiss Confederacy by the spring and early summer of 1525. Many smaller towns and some larger cities joined the peasantry. The rebels presented a serious military threat. Bands of armed peasant rebels roamed the countryside, sacked monasteries and captured towns with sympathetic inhabitants, such as Würzburg and Freiburg-im-Breisgau. The Peasants' War lasted more than a year largely because the nobility were caught unawares. Between 70 000 and 100 000 people were killed during the revolt. The Swabian League, the Holy Roman Empire's peacekeeping force, did not take the field until late March 1525, but in due course all rebel armies were brutally suppressed.

Interestingly, in his *Admonition to Peace* (April 1525), Luther had initially laid equal blame on rulers for oppressing the peasants and on peasants for acting as judges in their own cause. It took less than a month for Luther to become aware of the potentially disastrous consequences of the uprising. He also reacted with genuine horror to the peasantry's disregard for authority. Accordingly, in May 1525 he published his damning treatise entitled *Against the Robbing and Murdering Hordes of Other Peasants*. Luther encouraged rulers to perform their spiritual duty by offering terms to the rebels and punishing them with swift and brutal force if they refused. This reflected Luther's conservatism in the face of a crisis.

The outcome of the Peasants' War

The defeat of the peasants indicated that Luther's sympathy was with the princes, and with a more conservative vision of Reformation. It convinced Luther to enforce a significant reorientation to the movement. It put an end to the freedom of religious

Voices from the past

The Twelve Articles of Memmingen

First, we should have the power and authority for the whole community to choose and elect its own pastor, and also to have the power to depose him should he conduct himself improperly.

Although the true tithe is ordained in the Old Testament and discharged in the New, nonetheless we will gladly pay the true grain tithe, only in just measure. We wish this tithe in future to be collected and received by our churchwarden, elected by the community.

It has hitherto been the custom that no poor man has been empowered or permitted to catch game, wildfowl, or fish in flowing water, which we consider quite improper and unbrotherly, indeed selfish and contrary to the Word of God.

We are aggrieved that some have appropriated meadows or arable that once belonged to the community. We wish to restore these to common ownership, unless they have been properly purchased.[7]

Using the sources and your wider reading consider the following questions:

1. Were peasant grievances largely motivated by religious concerns?
2. Did the peasants hijack Luther's movement?
3. How serious a threat did the peasants pose to Lutheranism?

dialogue that had characterised the early years and led to a decline in the publication of pamphlets devoted to the common man. That the Reformation survived this crisis was a tribute to the firm roots that it had already put down in German soil, as well as Luther's timely and vitriolic critique of peasant radicalism.

The princely response to the Peasants' War was central to the development of Lutheranism. It was a coalition of princes, not the Emperor, who defeated the peasant armies. The princes had withstood a crisis without resorting to the Emperor's support. It encouraged them to be more assertive and less willing to compromise as the religious crisis intensified in subsequent decades. The threat posed by the Peasants' War illustrated that Lutheranism was a major force that needed to be contained and carefully manipulated. Even Catholic princes reluctantly accepted Lutheranism within their lands: 'Many Catholic princes were now persuaded that a religious order imposed by heretical governments was better than the chaos that seemed to loom on the horizon.'[8] Many princes decided to adopt the Reformation in order to control their territories more effectively.

ACTIVITY 3.5

Using your wider reading, draw up a detailed timeline of the Peasants' War to accompany Figure 3.5.

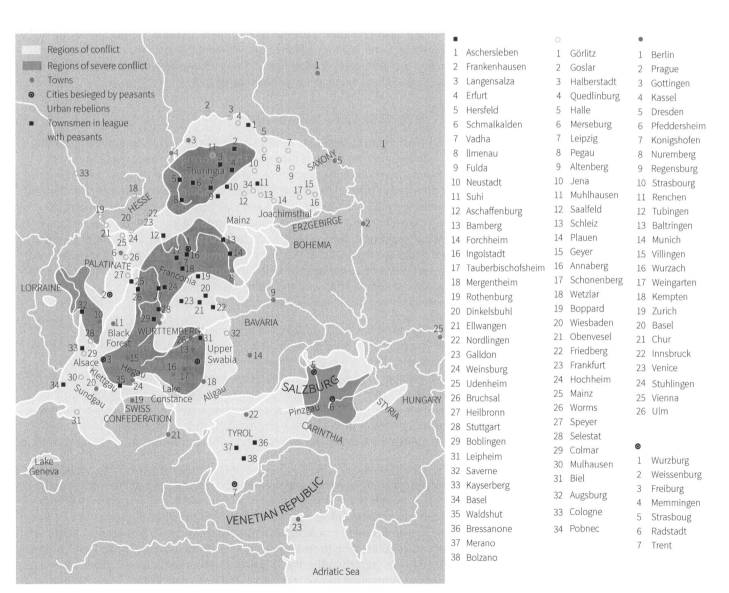

Legend:
- Regions of conflict
- Regions of severe conflict
- • Towns
- ⊙ Cities besieged by peasants
- ○ Urban rebelions
- ■ Townsmen in league with peasants

■
1 Aschersleben
2 Frankenhausen
3 Langensalza
4 Erfurt
5 Hersfeld
6 Schmalkalden
7 Vadha
8 Ilmenau
9 Fulda
10 Neustadt
11 Suhi
12 Aschaffenburg
13 Bamberg
14 Forchheim
16 Ingolstadt
17 Tauberbischofsheim
18 Mergentheim
19 Rothenburg
20 Dinkelsbuhl
21 Ellwangen
22 Nordlingen
23 Galldon
24 Weinsburg
25 Udenheim
26 Bruchsal
27 Heilbronn
28 Stuttgart
29 Boblingen
31 Leipheim
32 Saverne
33 Kayserberg
34 Basel
35 Waldshut
36 Bressanone
37 Merano
38 Bolzano

○
1 Görlitz
2 Goslar
3 Halberstadt
4 Quedlinburg
5 Halle
6 Merseburg
7 Leipzig
8 Pegau
9 Altenberg
10 Jena
11 Muhlhausen
12 Saalfeld
13 Schleiz
14 Plauen
15 Geyer
16 Annaberg
17 Schonenberg
18 Wetzlar
19 Boppard
20 Wiesbaden
21 Obenvesel
22 Friedberg
23 Frankfurt
24 Hochheim
25 Mainz
26 Worms
27 Speyer
28 Selestat
29 Colmar
30 Mulhausen
31 Biel
32 Augsburg
33 Cologne
34 Pobnec

●
1 Berlin
2 Prague
3 Gottingen
4 Kassel
5 Dresden
6 Pfeddersheim
7 Konigshofen
8 Nuremberg
9 Regensburg
10 Strasbourg
11 Renchen
12 Tubingen
13 Baltringen
14 Munich
15 Villingen
16 Wurzach
17 Weingarten
18 Kempten
19 Zurich
20 Basel
21 Chur
22 Innsbruck
23 Venice
24 Stuhlingen
25 Vienna
26 Ulm

⊙
1 Wurzburg
2 Weissenburg
3 Freiburg
4 Memmingen
5 Strasboug
6 Radstadt
7 Trent

Figure 3.5: The Peasants' War

ACTIVITY 3.6

Based on this chapter and your wider reading, draw a mind map to analyse the reasons for the successful spread of Lutheranism in the 1520s.

Early princely responses to Lutheranism

The spread of Lutheranism in the towns and countryside owed little to princely support. With the important exception of Frederick the Wise, princely backing for the Reformation was slow to develop. There were three main princely reactions to Luther's early revolt: a strong, conservative, anti-Lutheran response, certainly in a minority; a pro-evangelical and pro-Luther standpoint, also in the minority; and, finally, a majority who remained neutral. At the beginning, the anti-Lutheran princes were the most determined and active. Elector Joachim of Brandenburg forbade the circulation of Luther's works, while Duke Heinrich of Wolfenbüttel published a mandate against Luther's teachings. Similarly, while Duke George of Saxony outlawed evangelical publications, Wilhelm IV of Bavaria was eager to enforce the Edict of Worms within his territory.

Strangely, it was these secular lords, rather than the powerful prince bishops, who assumed the leadership of the Catholic response; the Bishop of Würzburg was particularly slow to act. Far more common was the policy of neutrality, favoured by the great majority of the German princes, such as Duke Casimir of Brandenburg-Kulmbach. The nobility as a group stood to lose more from a Reformation than any other social class, since church offices provided a major source of income. These considerations even played a role in those territories where Lutheranism was embraced. In Hesse, for example, Landgrave Philip was unwilling to confiscate church properties because of the potentially hostile reaction of his nobles. Crucial to Lutheranism's early survival was the fact that this majority of princes did not actively resist the movement. This was evident at the highest political level, the Imperial Diet.

The princes and the Imperial Diet

Luther's Reformation compounded the fragmentary nature of the Empire by adding religious divisions to the political disunity. The Reformation affected Charles V's relations with his subjects because it placed its followers in a religious camp that was diametrically opposed to his own. Charles, in Spain rather than the Holy Roman Empire during the 1520s, lacked control and was not able to enforce the Edict of Worms. His absence ensured that the princes increased both their power and their political self-awareness. Above all, the princes resisted the enforcement of the Edict of Worms throughout the 1520s. At the Diet of Nuremberg in 1522–23, princes declared that they were willing to enforce the Edict of Worms but only to the extent that it did not provoke rebellion. In this way, the representatives of the Diet pacified the Emperor by accepting his demands yet simultaneously reserving the right to ignore them.

In the aftermath of the Peasants' War, the princes' increasing control led to Lutheranism's most decisive stage, namely the princely Reformation. At the first Diet of Speyer in 1526, the relative absence of conservative representatives led to the adoption of a formula that allowed evangelicals an unexpected degree of freedom. The Edict of Worms was temporarily annulled, encouraging more cities to adopt Lutheranism. At that same meeting, the Imperial Diet agreed to support the magisterial right to reform (*ius reformandi*), which stated that until a general council was held, princely and urban authorities could address the question of Church reform.[9]

Princely support took on a military dimension with the emergence of the defensive League of Torgau in 1526, which was created to resist the Edict of Worms. Even with the return of a Catholic majority at the second Imperial Diet of Speyer in 1529 and its inevitable attempt to enforce the Edict of Worms, the evangelical movement was sufficiently entrenched to risk a calculated act of defiance. Six princes and 14 imperial cities signed a Protestation (from which Protestantism derives its name), which openly challenged the Emperor's authority. This was an important moment, 'the first time leaders of the evangelical movement were sufficiently conscious of their common interests to act as a body'.[10] Three days later, Hesse, electoral Saxony and the cities of

Ulm, Strasbourg and Nuremberg formed a defensive alliance to protect themselves against the Catholics. Full Protestant unity was prevented, however, by the tensions between Zwingli and Luther. This explains Philip of Hesse's support for the Colloquy of Marburg of 1529, during which Luther and Zwingli attempted to resolve their doctrinal differences.

Timeline: the main events of the 1520s and early 1530s

January–May 1521	Diet of Worms
November 1522–February 1523:	Diet of Nuremberg
1522–1523	Imperial Knights' revolt
1524–1525	Peasants' War
June–August 1526	Diet of Speyer Creation of defensive League of Torgau
March–April 1529	Second Diet of Speyer Recess of 22 April banned introduction of Zwinglianism
19 July 1529	Publication of the Protest, signed by several princes and 14 cities
October 1529	Colloquy of Marburg
April–September 1530	Diet of Augsburg Recess of Diet 22 September: required the enforcement of the edict of Worms
1531	Formation of Schmalkaldic League

Lutheran–Catholic negotiations and the Diet of Augsburg

Several princes and cities supported the presentation of a Protestant Confession of Faith at the Diet of Augsburg (1530) in the presence of the Emperor, which was a significant watershed for the Reformation. The Confession stated the Lutheran message with distinct clarity, though it also stressed possible points of agreement with Catholics, such as a belief in the Real Presence. Philip Melanchthon composed most of it, and in conciliatory fashion, he omitted references to the Catholic doctrines of purgatory and transubstantiation, as well as the Lutheran teachings on the Priesthood of all Believers. Unable to attend the Diet owing to the imperial ban, Luther followed the proceedings from Coburg Castle. He initially distanced himself from the Confession which he considered too conciliatory, but he later supported it. It granted the Protestants an identity around which they could conform. Soon afterwards, Melanchthon amended and elaborated on the Confession by incorporating his responses to the Emperor's theologians; the final text was published in 1531.

Crucially, the Confession of Augsburg had political backing because it was signed by seven princes and two cities. It became 'one of the most significant confessional writings of Protestantism and had an influence far beyond Lutheranism'.[11] The Confession of Augsburg also sought to clarify the theological boundaries between Lutheranism and Zwinglianism. In response, Martin Bucer, Wolfgang Capito and Jakob

ACTIVITY 3.7

Using this chapter and your wider reading, explain the significance of the key princely supporters of Lutheranism, Philip of Hesse and the Electors of Saxony. You may wish to consider the following themes: their relationship with Luther and the early reformers; their political position within the Holy Roman Empire (associations with other princes and especially with Charles V); the strength of their territorial bases in Hesse and electoral Saxony (political, legal and financial).

ACTIVITY 3.8

Research Charles's different preoccupations outside the Holy Roman Empire during this period. You may wish to divide your material according to the following themes: domestic problems in Spain (especially the *Comuneros* revolt); military threats from the French (in northern Spain, Netherlands, Duchy of Milan).

Sturm drafted a compromise confession in July 1530; the Tetrapolitan Confession was signed by the cities of Strasbourg, Constance, Memmingen and Lindau.

Motives for princely support for Lutheranism

Luther had deliberately targeted the nobility in his works, especially in the *Address to the Christian Nobility*. Frederick the Wise remained a critical figure in the early years of the revolt until his death, allowing Wittenberg to become the centre of the Reformation. Princes were receptive to Luther's message for various reasons. The anti-Roman stance appealed to many nobles because the papacy represented a foreign and interfering influence in the German lands. Many princes supported Luther because they saw his movement as a means of weakening the Emperor. Charles V's success against Luther would only strengthen his authority and control. Some joined the movement not out of genuine religious conviction, but because they sought greater freedom from Habsburg authority. This explains why Catholic princes, like the Bavarian Wittelsbachs, made political alliances with Lutheran princes, even though they refused to tolerate the existence of Lutheranism within their territories.

Princes saw the material benefits of joining the Reformation cause. Although they might lose access to lucrative clerical offices, they could benefit from the secularisation of Church property and the receipt of Church taxes – Albrecht of Hohenzollern and Margrave Casimir of Brandenburg are notable examples. Some princes had no alternative and were forced to adopt Lutheranism due to popular pressure, such as the Archbishop of Mainz. Finally, some were attracted to Lutheranism out of religious conviction. This was especially the case with Frederick the Wise's successor, John of Saxony (1468–1532), and his son John Frederick I (1503–1554), as well as Philip of Hesse.

During the 1520s, little imperial pressure was exerted on the princes. Charles V was absent from the Empire between the Diets of Worms (1521) and Augsburg (1530) because he was committed to his other territories. He was dealing with the aftermath of the *Comuneros* revolt in Spain, and with the Habsburg–Valois wars in Navarre and Italy, and in the Netherlands. He managed to resist these attacks and succeeded in driving the French back. Yet it meant that Charles could not pressurise the Imperial Diets in the critical years of the Reformation.

The Reformation in the Swiss Confederacy

Overview

Like its German counterpart, the development of the Swiss Reformation owed much to political and social conditions. While the Swiss lands had secured independence from the Holy Roman Empire in 1499, they lacked a capital, a head of state or common laws. The newly established Swiss Confederacy was an association of cities and cantons, independent of any aristocratic overlord. In the words of Bruce Gordon, it was a 'jumble of alliances' and 'something of a political curiosity'.[12] It came to be dominated by the three major city-states of Zurich, Berne and Basle. The surrounding towns and countryside were often in conflict with these leading cities; Swiss peasants tended to resent the interference of the cities more than that of princes.

Ecclesiastically, the six dioceses of Constance (by far the largest), Basle, Chur, Lausanne, Sitten and Geneva did not correspond with the cantons within the Swiss Confederacy, making it more difficult for bishops to act decisively; it 'rendered effective ecclesiastical governance virtually impossible'.[13] Although most Swiss bishops came from leading families, they struggled to impose their authority in their dioceses. In similar fashion to the Holy Roman Empire, secular lords and magistrates were gaining increasing control of the Church's rights and privileges in the late medieval period. While there appears to have been a will to reform Church abuses, there was 'no effective means of implementing change'.[14] Any attempts at reforms by bishops were often blocked by various powers, including cathedral chapters, monastic communities and secular authorities, all of whom defended their own interests.

The state of the Swiss Church was affected by the willingness of successive popes to grant ecclesiastical privileges in exchange for Swiss mercenaries. However, the Church in the Swiss Confederacy was not in terminal decline. Far from it. There was a vibrant religious culture, characterised by popular saints' shrines and active participation in pilgrimages and processions. Even anti-clericalism was motivated by a yearning to see the Church reformed spiritually, rather than structurally or doctrinally.

Zwingli and the Reformation in Zurich

Zwingli's Reformation benefited both from the existence of humanist circles and from widespread anti-clericalism. There was a patriotic tone to Zwingli's reform, which also called for an end to the Swiss trade in mercenaries and represented his opposition to alliances with foreign powers, especially the French and the papacy. The grievances regarding mercenaries struck a resonant chord following the Swiss and imperial defeat against the French at the battle of Marignano in 1515, in which 6000 Swiss Confederates died. Opposition to the trade grew in spite of the extraordinary wealth that came from the employment of mercenaries – in 1497, over 3100 crowns were paid to the Zurich Council.

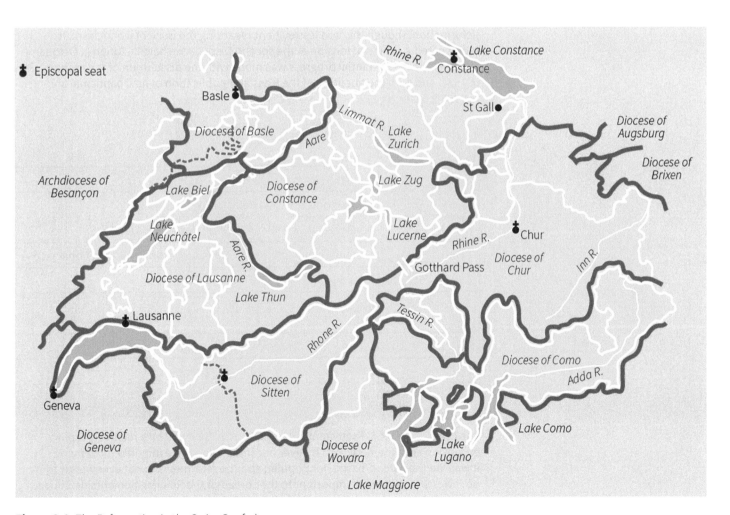

Figure 3.6: The Reformation in the Swiss Confederacy

ACTIVITY 3.9

Mercenaries in the 16th century

Using your wider reading, consider the following questions:

1. What was the function of mercenaries in this period?

2. How important were they in the context of the Holy Roman Empire, the Swiss Confederacy and the Italian city-states?

3. Read Chapters 12–14 of Machiavelli's *The Prince* and see what Machiavelli had to say about military affairs, but particularly the use of mercenaries.

The decisive element of the Zurich Reformation was the 'personality and preaching of Zwingli', though Gordon has also highlighted the importance of his colleagues, including Leo Jud, Kaspar Megander and Heinrich Uttinger.[15] Zwingli's charisma and inspired leadership was largely responsible for steering the Reformation in Zurich, though his pre-eminence hinted at the movement's fundamental weakness – namely, its 'utter dependence upon the character and thought of one man'.[16] He was supported by the Zurich Council, which was determined to maintain its control over the Church, especially against encroachments from outside powers, notably the Bishop of Constance. Zwingli was especially close to the Röist family, and Markus Röist (1454–1524), who was a highly regarded soldier and Bürgermeister in the years 1520–1523.

In the early 1520s, Zwingli attacked Catholic practices, such as abstinence from meat (March 1522), clerical celibacy (summer 1522) and monasticism (summer 1523). By October 1522, Zwingli had made his break with the Roman Catholic Church and its conception of priesthood, though the Reformation would still take a couple of years to emerge. From 1523 onwards, the City Council gave its full support to Zwingli's theology and called on its inhabitants to follow his teachings. This came at a time when he was especially vulnerable, accused of heresy by factions within and outside Zurich. Six hundred people attended a public disputation in Zurich in January 1523, to which Basle, Berne and Schaffhausen sent representatives, while the Catholic presence was negligible. The Zurich Council made its position clear, defending Zwingli and allowing him to preach. Röist's presence and support encouraged Zwingli to be more forthright in his views.

Zwingli's *Sixty-Seven Articles*, which formed the theological basis of the Disputation, were printed five months later. Zwingli maintained some coherence to Zurich's Reformation, though this was less evident regarding the issue of iconoclasm. It represented a source of tension at the second Disputation held in Zurich in October 1523. Yet more substantial progress was made with the dissolution of the monasteries in 1524, and with the abolition of the Mass and publication of new baptismal and marriage orders in 1525.

Timeline: Zwingli and the Zurich Reformation

1506	Zwingli's first parish at Glarus
1519	Elected priest at Great Minster in Zurich
9 March 1522	Sausage-eating incident in Froschauer's house
16 April 1522	Disputation in Zurich with delegation from Bishop of Constance
23 January 1523	First disputation in Zurich
26–28 October 1523	Second disputation in Zurich
8–15 June 1524	Council order to remove images from Zurich churches
1525	First evangelical communion service

The spread of the Reformation in the Swiss lands

The establishment of Protestantism in Zurich was followed by a relatively rapid expansion elsewhere, though it never became more than a minority movement; it was 'neither broad-based nor popular, and the reformers did not ever wish it to be'.[17] Nor was Zwingli as important to the spread of the Reformation outside Zurich. Unlike developments within the Holy Roman Empire, the Reformation in the Swiss lands lacked an obvious unifying cause, such as opposition to the papacy. Printing and preaching remained central to the adoption of Protestantism, which was also dependent on magisterial support. Zwingli's followers preached in various towns in the early 1520s, when Schaffhausen, St Gall and Appenzell all adopted the new teachings. In St Gall, Joachim von Watt, known as Vadianus, took the lead and his position was greatly enhanced by his election as Bürgermeister in December 1525. The threat of Anabaptism necessitated a more gradual Reformation, leading to the removal of the Mass in 1528 and the first evangelical service in 1529.

Although Luther's writings arrived in Berne as early as 1518, the evangelical cause did not receive widespread support initially. Yet in December 1522, the Bernese Council granted ministers permission to preach the Word of God without restrictions. The anti-clerical Carnival plays of Niklaus Manuel contributed much to the spread of evangelical ideas, though it took some years for the Reformation to establish firm roots. Even during the period 1524–1528, the Bernese did not fully commit to the Reformation, despite the enthusiastic support of the guilds. In due course, the Large Council came under the influence of the guilds and merchants, who remained the Reformation's most powerful advocates. The Council agreed to a religious disputation in January 1528, supervised by Vadianus, with over 250 theologians taking part, including Martin Bucer and Zwingli himself. That same year, the authority of the local bishop of Lausanne was rejected and monasteries were dissolved.

In Basle, support for the evangelical movement came relatively late, compared with Zurich. Despite this, Basle played an important role in the early years. Its population contained a high number of literate citizens and possessed a thriving printing industry, including printers such as Johannes Petri and Johannes Froben. From 1523, the Basle Council called on the clergy to preach from Scripture, though not to incorporate Luther's teachings. The Basle Reformation was inspired by John Hussgen, otherwise known as Oecolampadius, who was well known for the quality of his biblical commentaries and even assisted Erasmus with his edition of the Greek New Testament. He was also responsible for converting the artisans, securing the withdrawal of the bishop and encouraging the guilds to put pressure on the Council to adopt Protestantism in February 1529.

Zwinglianism and Lutheranism

These achievements in the Swiss Confederacy do not conceal the tensions between Zwinglianism and Lutheranism, especially regarding the Lord's Supper. These differences dated back to the emergence of Zwingli's Eucharistic theology in 1524 and 1525. Luther's *Sermon on the Sacrament of the Body and Blood of Christ*, published in 1526, triggered an exchange of critical works between Luther and Zwingli in the years 1526–1529. Although these divisions were exploited by Catholics, the two key reformers refused to concede over Eucharistic doctrines. In 1529, the Lutherans published the *Schwabach Articles*, which sought to distinguish Lutheran from Zwinglian ideas. Philip of Hesse arranged a meeting between Luther and Zwingli in October 1529, known as the Marburg Colloquy, but little progress was made. Luther initially refused to attend and only travelled to Marburg because he was pressurised by the Elector of Saxony. The two reformers agreed on the provision of communion in both kinds for the laity and rejected the sacrificial understanding of the Mass. However, they fell out over their different Eucharistic theologies and the split between the Swiss and German wings of the Reformation was sealed. On a personal level, Luther did not regard Zwingli as his equal and their relationship can only be described as fractious.

Opposition to the Reformation and the Kappel wars

Some states within the Swiss Confederacy did not allow access to the Reformation message. In particular, the Catholic cantons of Zug, Uri, Unterwalden, Lucerne and Schwyz, known as the Five Inner States, refused to show toleration and embarked on

ACTIVITY 3.10

Using your wider reading, draw up timelines for the emergence of Protestantism in Basle, Berne and Zurich, and identify three key factors that explain the rise of Protestantism in each town.

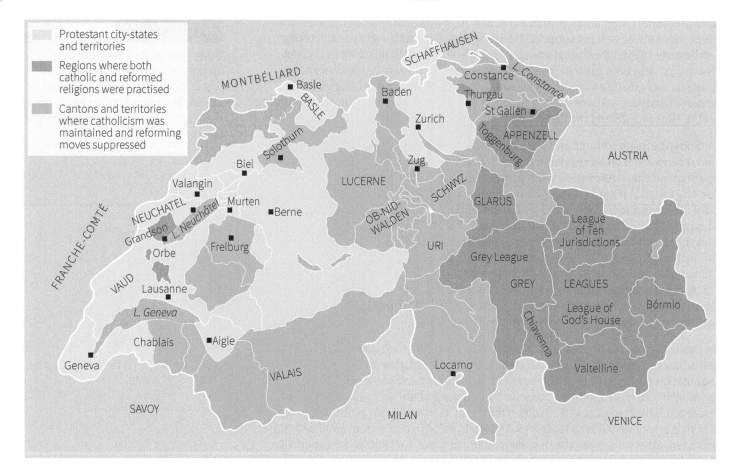

Figure 3.7: The Swiss Confederacy

an uncompromising spate of persecution. It was feared that Charles V might secure alliances with the Catholic territories and turn the Swiss lands into a Habsburg dependency. In April 1529, the Five Inner States concluded a Catholic Christian Union with Ferdinand of Austria, who promised 6000 foot soldiers and 400 cavalry in the event of war.

One of Zwingli's major differences with Luther was that the former condoned violence as a means to achieve religious ends. Towards the end of the 1520s, Zwingli sought to establish an aggressive alliance between evangelical states for the promotion of his cause. War seemed increasingly likely as evangelical cantons also established a military alliance, known as the Christian Civic Union. It consisted of Zurich and Berne, who signed an agreement in June 1528 and they were joined by St Gall in November. By 1529, the organisation included Biel, Mühlhausen, Basle, Schaffhausen and Strasbourg. Its *raison d'être* was to promise military support to any member who was attacked and to protect the Reformation. Thereafter, Zwingli was keen to incorporate other cities such as Lindau and Constance, but he failed to persuade Berne to join. While Zurich was eager to spread the Reformation by force and overcome their Catholic rivals in battle, Berne favoured diplomacy.

By 8 June 1529, Zurich had mobilised 4000 men for war. Zwingli expected the Catholic states to accept several key conditions, namely the free preaching of the Gospel, the abandonment of the Austrian alliance and the payment of war reparations. By the time the two sides met, the Catholic forces were significantly outnumbered. The Catholic commander, Hans Äbli of Glarus, decided to negotiate rather than fight, culminating in the First Peace of Kappel, signed on 26 June 1529. Although the Catholic states made some concessions, Zwingli had failed to convince the Protestant states, especially

Berne, to fight. The Bernese realised that there would be little support for war in the rural regions, something that Zwingli had misjudged. In April 1531, Berne reiterated its refusal to participate in military action.

Zwingli subsequently attempted to impose an economic blockade and, in response, Catholic forces mobilised in order to counter the effectiveness of the blockade; it may be that the Catholics were provoked by Zwingli's (albeit unsuccessful) attempts to secure an alliance with Francis I. In October 1531, the Catholics unexpectedly declared war on Zurich and found Zwingli and the city authorities unprepared. In the second Kappel war that followed, Zwingli's forces were outnumbered with 8000 Catholics to Zwingli's 2000 and the leader of the Swiss Reformation was tragically, though symbolically from Luther's perspective, killed on the battlefield in 1531.

The aftermath of the Kappel wars and the state of the Church by 1531

Throughout his life, Luther had hesitated to legitimise the use of force to promote the Gospel. Zwingli's death was followed by a peace treaty that anticipated the later 1555 Peace of Augsburg; each canton was allowed to dictate the religion of its inhabitants, except in the Common Lordships (such as Thurgau which were ruled jointly by the whole Confederation) where Catholic minorities were protected. Berne and Basle remained determined not to be involved in a religious war and sued for peace, while Zurich was more isolated than before. The terms of the First Peace of Kappel were cancelled and Catholics were granted the right to hear the Mass and receive the sacraments in areas where they were a minority. Evangelicals were not given the same rights.

The Second Kappel Peace guaranteed that there would be no further spread of Protestantism within the Confederation. While declaring that citizens in each state could adhere to their own religious beliefs, the Peace referred to Catholicism as the true faith. The Five Inner States also received war reparations from Zurich and Berne; these amounted to 8200 gulden, much more than the Catholic states had offered in the earlier peace. In Zurich, it took some time for Zwingli's followers to re-establish their authority, a process of consolidation that benefited enormously from the emergence of the more moderate Heinrich Bullinger as Zwingli's successor.

Practice essay question

> With reference to these sources and your understanding of the historical context, assess the value of these three sources to an historian studying the spread of the German and Swiss Reformations.

Extract A: Lazarus Spengler, city secretary of Nuremberg, memorandum on religion, 3 March 1525

In this Christian matter touching the Word of God there are two points of utmost grievance that concern Nuremberg alone, about which I as a Christian am also highly aggrieved. The first is the divisive preaching of the opposing proclaimers of the Word of God. I have seen publicly that a great number of Christians in this town are not turned away from their old errors but that the preachers who do not present the Word of God with a clear and right Christian understanding confirm them in their old human ways. Second, from such divisive preaching there must certainly follow disunity of magistrates, the dissipation of morale, morals and manners, the fracturing of civic unity and finally disturbance and recalcitrance towards the clergy or against the authorities who look on and permit them to preach.[18]

Extract B: Letter from the inhabitants of Blaufelden, a village north of Schwäbisch Hall, to the Margrave of Brandenburg-Ansbach, 1525

We have a parish priest and two other priests in our village, who are of no use to the community, but are harmful, scandalous and ruinous to the salvation of our souls, and who display no honourable Christian life or conduct. The parish priest is infirm, and cannot speak well enough to be understood, and he is so infected with bad breath or some odour that he is repulsive to pregnant women or the sick who wish to take the Sacrament. Moreover, he cannot preach the holy and divine Word to us, and if he could, we could not hear or understand him. We have here a preacher, the Rev. Hans Schilling, whose parents and ancestors grew up among us, and who preaches at our request. We can hear his sermons and he has instructed us diligently from Holy Scripture and taught us the holy Christian faith, love of neighbour, and that we should be subject and obedient to our authorities.[19]

Extract C: Zurich town council decree on Church attendance, 10 August 1531

The mandates on churchgoing issued last year has been poorly observed and people – young and old, men and women – wander idly about, hither and thither, during the sermon time, on the bridges, down the alleys, by the gates and alongside the moats. Therefore our lords order all persons who bear responsibility and oversight in the matter of churchgoing [to enforce the mandate] and hereby earnestly command that every person shall strictly observe the mandate to attend church on Sundays and holy days.[20]

Chapter summary

By the end of this chapter you should understand:

- the reasons for the spread of the radical and early Lutheran Reformation
- the significance of Luther, Melanchthon and Zwingli in the German and Swiss Reformations
- the motives of the imperial knights and peasants in their revolts, and the significance of these threats to the development of Lutheranism
- the transmission and reception of Luther's ideas in towns and in the countryside
- the development of the Reformation in the Swiss Confederacy.

Endnotes

1   R. Emmet McLaughlin, 'The Radical Reformation', in R. Po-Chia Hsia (ed.), *The Cambridge History of Christianity: Volume 6, Reform and Expansion, 1500–1660*. Cambridge University Press, 2007, p. 39.

2   Ulinka Rublack, *Reformation Europe.* Cambridge University Press, 2005, p. 61.

3   Cited in Thomas Brady, 'Emergence and Consolidation of Protestantism in the Holy Roman Empire to 1600', in Po-Chia Hsia, *Cambridge History*, pp. 22–23.

4   Robert Scribner, *The German Reformation.* London, Macmillan, 1988, p. 19.

5   Thomas Brady, 'The Reformation of the Common Man, 1521–1524', in C. Scott Dixon, *The German Reformation.* Oxford, Blackwell, 1999, p. 107.

6   See Peter Blickle, 'Communal Reformation: Zwingli, Luther, and the South of the Holy Roman Empire', in Po-Chia Hsia, *Cambridge History*, pp. 75–89.

7   Edited from a full text version posted at the University of Oregon: http://darkwing.uoregon. edu/~history/courses/archive/fall01/Docs-PeasantWar.html.

8   James Tracy, *Europe's Reformations.* Oxford, Rowman & Littlefield Publishers, 1999. p. 73.

9   Thomas Brady, 'Settlements: The Holy Roman Empire', in Thomas Brady, Heiko Oberman and James Tracy (eds), *Handbook of European History, 1400–1600: Late Middle Ages, Renaissance and Reformation,* Vol. II. Grand Rapids, MI, William B. Eerdmans, 1995, p. 351.

10   Tracy, *Europe's Reformations,* p. 77.

11   Martin Brecht, 'Luther's Reformation', in Thomas Brady, Heiko Oberman, and James Tracy (eds), *Handbook of European History, 1400–1600*, Vol. II. Grand Rapids, MI, William B. Eerdmans, 1995, p. 144.

12   Bruce Gordon, *The Swiss Reformation.* Manchester University Press, 2002, pp. 11, 25.

13   Gordon, *Swiss Reformation*, p. 27.

14   Gordon, *Swiss Reformation*, p. 26.

15   Gordon, *Swiss Reformation*, p. 45.

16   Gordon, *Swiss Reformation*, p. 49.

17   Gordon, *Swiss Reformation*, p. 86.

18   Pamela Johnston and Bob Scribner, *The Reformation in Germany and Switzerland.* Cambridge University Press, 1993, p. 41.

19   Johnston and Scribner, *The Reformation in Germany and Switzerland*, pp. 42–43.

20   Johnston and Scribner, *The Reformation in Germany and Switzerland*, pp. 60–61.

4 The expansion of the Reformation, 1531–1541

In this chapter we will focus on the Anabaptists and the geographical and social expansion of Lutheranism in the 1530s, as well as the religious and political divisions within the Empire.

Specification points:

- the geographical and social expansion of Lutheranism: Melanchthon; Luther; doctrine and leadership; position and problems of Charles V
- the development of the Radical Reformation; Anabaptism and the Münster rebellion
- religious division in Germany and the formation of the Schmalkaldic League
- the Diet of Regensburg and state of the Church by 1541.

The social expansion of Lutheranism

The Lutherans exploited Charles V's absence and the advantageous political conditions very effectively. With little deterrence from a remote emperor, Lutheran supporters did not hesitate to accelerate the process of reform. Political support for Lutheranism led to the removal of Catholic worship, the expulsion of the clergy and the closure of monasteries. Lutherans 'established through action a right of reformation they did not legally possess, and suppressed Catholic institutions and worship in their lands and cities'.[1] Yet at first, Luther and his followers gave little thought to the question of reorganisation so Lutheran reform was institutionalised gradually and rather haphazardly.

Lutheran princes and towns sought to strengthen Lutheranism in various ways. In the place of the old faith, Lutheran teachings and evangelical preaching were promoted. Lutheran clergy were recruited and trained, and they supervised the new orders of worship.[2] The Catholic Church's wealth was distributed and secular institutions, which handled marriage courts, poor relief and schools, replaced the older ecclesiastical ones. Luther encouraged rulers to act as 'emergency bishops' so that the Reformation could be enforced properly. This temporary measure soon became permanent. Bishops were replaced by organisations in which pastors and secular officials were expected to collaborate. In the cities, superintendents, who were accountable to the town council, were established to supervise the pastors. Lutheran princes sought to undermine the *Reichskammergericht*, which was the only institution to which Catholics could turn.

Reforming worship

Central to the social expansion of Lutheranism was the reform of worship. Luther's *Sola Scriptura* had highlighted the centrality of the biblical texts, which had to be made accessible to the laity. The Church had to grant access to the Word of God, something that Luther's vernacular orders of service made possible. There was some continuity with the pre-Reformation Church. Although marriage was no longer a sacrament, the Lutheran Church insisted on unions being blessed by the clergy before a communion table. For the baptismal rite, exorcisms – prayers calling on God to free the baptised from the Devil's powers – were reduced in number but not eliminated. However, the Eucharistic service was certainly different. Theologically, the sacrificial emphasis of the Mass was abandoned, while on a practical level, the clergy no longer had their backs to the people and faced the congregation. An important feature of the liturgy was to nurture key Lutheran ideals. According to James Tracy, 'the fundamental charge against the Catholic Church was a failure of indoctrination, from top to bottom … the new Protestant liturgy was part of a grand programme of Christian indoctrination'.[3]

Doctrine and politics

Naturally, Wittenberg continued to play an important role largely because of Luther himself, his principal colleagues and a thriving printing industry. Wittenberg provided printed catechisms, sermons and biblical commentaries, as well as polemical writings. Wittenberg's university trained new pastors, while Luther urged any towns without Latin schools to establish them for the preparation of their clergy and territorial officials. In the opening decade of the Reformation, Luther had called for obedience to the Emperor and supported his war against the Ottomans. Following the Diet of Augsburg in 1530, Luther composed his *Warning to His Dear German People* that was published in 1531, in which he called on Germans to resist any imperial orders to suppress Lutheranism. Initially, Luther opposed the idea of political resistance on theological grounds; he concluded that the Bible did not permit rebellion against divinely appointed rulers. But views on Protestant resistance evolved, arguing that Lutheran princes were not just individual believers, but rulers in their own right.

Leadership and church organisation

While the survival of Lutheranism owed much to the Schmalkaldic League's protection, the consolidation of the movement depended on a coherent church organisation. This required effective collaboration between the ecclesiastical and political authorities. In southern German and Swiss cities, the head of the Church sat together with the town mayor and leading members of civic councils on the ruling commissions of the Church.

Key term

Founded at the Imperial Diet of Worms in 1495, the *Reichskammergericht* (Imperial Chamber Court) tackled the Empire's legal proceedings. The decentralised nature of the Empire made it difficult to enforce laws and the Imperial Chamber Court was notoriously slow in dealing with cases.

ACTIVITY 4.1

Using this section and your broader reading, assess the significance of Johannes Bugenhagen, relative to the contributions of Melanchthon and Luther.

In territorial principalities, leading Lutheran churchmen were often counsellors to the prince.

Johannes Bugenhagen (1485–1558), a pastor in Wittenberg, assisted Luther in drafting church orders for the northern parts of the Empire. Thanks to Bugenhagen, Wittenberg became responsible for the provision of Church orders elsewhere in the Empire, including the cities of Brunswick, Hamburg and Lübeck, and the princely territories under Wittenberg's influence such as the Anhalt principalities, the Brunswick duchies, ducal Saxony and Brandenburg. Bugenhagen also served as Luther's confessor, worked on Luther's publications, translated Luther's Bible into Low German, and organised the Lutheran churches in the Duchy of Pomerania (1535) and further afield in the Danish kingdom (1537).

Luther's other associates, Johannes Brenz (1499–1570) and Andreas Osiander, composed a common church ordinance (1535) for the city of Nuremberg and the Margrave of Brandenburg-Ansbach, described as 'one of the most influential statements of Lutheranism in the Empire'.[4] Martin Bucer, who worked in the southern part of the Empire, drafted a church ordinance for the landgraviate of Hesse. All clergy and parishioners were expected to adhere to the church ordinances, and all other religions were prohibited. Essentially, Lutheranism 'had invested the sovereigns with the right to police their subjects' thoughts as they previously policed their actions'.[5]

Reforming the clergy

A key dimension of church organisation was the training of suitably competent and qualified clergy. Urban case studies reveal, perhaps unsurprisingly, that it took decades for Lutheranism to provide the right clerical personnel. For example, the Nuremberg town council formally introduced Lutheranism in 1531 and, in that year, investigated the clergy's views; the replies from 100 clerics (35 in the town and 65 in the countryside) reveal limited theological understanding. Yet all but the most intransigent was retained in office. As Bruce Gordon has noted, 'the most serious issue facing sixteenth-century reform movements in their transition from protest to institutionalisation was the provision of pastoral care for the laity by a trained, educated clergy'.[6] Matters could be complicated by the disputes over the right of communities to elect pastors. In some territories, princes or their officials appointed pastors, while in others, communities were encouraged to give their consent to or refuse appointments.

Lutheran discipline

Once in their posts, the parish clergy were responsible for disciplining their congregations through catechetical instruction, preaching and confession, which was intended to relieve the conscience. The model for Lutheran reform was electoral Saxony, where the 1533 ecclesiastical statutes sought to instil clerical discipline and enforce doctrine. The statutes declared that 'the authorities … are diligently to admonish their subjects, and exhort them to attend sermons and services, to hear his holy Word diligently.'[7] Initially, Luther had hoped that hearing the Gospel would be sufficient in reforming communities. In due course, Lutherans attached greater importance to a disciplinary process. Justus Jonas (1493–1555) contributed much to the development of Lutheran ideas about discipline. His work *Thoughts about Consistories* was particularly influential. Luther had distinguished between lesser excommunication, signifying exclusion from communion, and greater excommunication, which was the preserve of the secular authorities. In contrast to Luther, Jonas argued that church discipline should be handled by consistories and that those who were excommunicated should also face secular punishments.

As time progressed, church discipline 'became more and more influenced by the state … and under control of the so-called consistories, ecclesiastical governing bodies which were established by princely ordinances'.[8] German church ordinances dictated that clerical power should be limited to admonition and supervision; ministers should not be responsible for excommunication. Only princes could enforce physical or monetary punishments. Central to these practices was the superintendent who, as head of the local chapters of churches, worked closely with officials of the ruling prince to ensure that ordinances were upheld in the communities. Superintendents contributed to the work of the marriage courts, consistories and the visitations of parishes. By 1542, Saxony contained three courts, each composed of two lawyers and two theologians, which supervised the spiritual welfare of people, and enforced a uniformity of doctrine and worship. In practice, there were some regional variations; for example, in Hohenlohe in southwestern Germany, and in Magdeburg, the parish clergy had the right to impose lesser excommunications.

The key to church discipline was the Lutheran visitation system. In June 1527, Elector John the Constant ordered the first major Saxon visitation, which took place in the years 1528–1529, for which Melanchthon wrote the *Instruction of the Visitors to the Pastors in the Electorate of Saxony*. In addition to preaching, religious instruction and private confession, visitations played a vital role in the control of the clergy and laity. Luther accepted the need for state intervention to supervise the visitations. The instructions for visitors in electoral Saxony presented it as a biblical imperative, arguing that 'it is a godly and holy work for suitably instructed persons to visit the pastors and Christian communities'.[9]

The aims of visitations were: 'to provide information regarding church fabric, personnel and finances; and to control the religious orthodoxy and morality of the clergy and the laity'.[10] Record keeping for the visitations was meticulous, with scribes accompanying the visitors. In electoral Saxony, for example, it was discovered that peasants knew that the Pope was the Antichrist but had never heard of justification by faith alone.

Reinforcing Lutheranism's religious identity remained a key aspect of the movement's social expansion. Luther and his associates were determined that success should not come at the cost of sacrificing key principles. But this did not prevent Luther from seeking a rapprochement with like-minded supporters of the Gospel. It was in this context that the signing of the Wittenberg Concord took place in May 1536. It represented a timely agreement with Zwinglians, which Luther accepted because the Catholic Church was becoming more organised, seeking to convene a Council. Dialogue was made possible because hostility between Lutherans and Zwinglians had subsided since Zwingli's death. Melanchthon was impressed by Oecolampadius's treatise on the Eucharist, while Luther favourable to the opinions of Zwingli's successor, Heinrich Bullinger. The Concord was negotiated by the Strasbourg reformer Martin Bucer (1491–1551), and the meetings with Zwinglian representatives from the cities of Upper Germany were held in Luther's house in Wittenberg. Although the Concord failed to secure lasting unity, Luther agreed to collaborate with the Swiss against the Anabaptists. This allowed Lutheran influence to increase in the southern cities, especially in Augsburg. The two parties agreed on a form of words that covered their differences about the Real Presence. Bucer remained at the forefront of these negotiations and in the period 1534–1539, he travelled extensively within the Empire and the Swiss Confederacy, seeking to mediate between Zwinglians and Lutherans.

The Schmalkalden Articles of 1537 were of greater theological significance than the Wittenberg Concord. German princes had instructed theologians to produce a statement of faith and Luther responded with these Articles, which reasserted the key doctrinal points but also justified resistance, even to the Emperor, in the defence of the Gospel. The call for Protestant unity was reinforced by Pope Paul III's (r1534–1549) moves to reform Catholicism. Luther composed the Articles after the Catholic Church had announced the convening of a general council in Mantua for the same year. In 1539, Luther published his *On the Councils and the Church*, which assessed the relative importance of Church Councils and their authority. Luther believed that a Council

61

ACTIVITY 4.2

Research the Wittenberg Concord and the Schmalkalden Articles and write a brief comparison.

would be unacceptable to Lutherans and that no consensus would be reached, declaring the doctrine of justification to be 'the article on which the church stands or falls'.[11] Luther remained determined to consolidate Lutheran religious identity.

The development of the Radical Reformation and Anabaptism

Anabaptism in the Swiss and southwest German lands

Anabaptism spread to these areas, and some of the radicals involved were among the earliest advocates of reform. Its major figures included Andreas Karlstadt, Thomas Müntzer and Konrad Grebel, the last of whom emerged as the leader of the Swiss Anabaptists. Anabaptists accepted the majority of the central Protestant teachings. They supported the dismantling of the Catholic sacramental system and the rejection of priestly authority. They justified their beliefs on the Bible and on justification by faith, and underlined the importance of the laity. Yet Anabaptist views were distinctive for a number of reasons. They reappropriated certain Catholic elements, especially in their refusal to separate **justification** and **sanctification**. They were strongly influenced by late medieval mysticism, by monasticism and by Erasmus's writings, which emphasised interiority at the expense of the external manifestations of religion. They were also set apart by their marked emphasis on **millenarianism**.

Key term

Millenarianism was the belief that the end of the world was nigh and that humanity would soon be divided between the saved and the damned.

Anabaptists are famously characterised by their rejection of infant baptism. They interpreted baptism as a profession of faith by adults, and not a ritual by which infants could receive forgiveness for sin. Anabaptists believed that Luther had not gone far enough and was still too Catholic. They took Luther's views to what they thought was their logical extension. Some Anabaptists argued that even biblical texts placed too great an emphasis on the externals of religion. Without disregarding the Holy Scriptures, they believed that a purity of faith would lead to direct divine communication with the faithful via the Holy Spirit. Karlstadt had certainly influenced the early development of Anabaptism, especially through his rejection of infant baptism, his memorialist Eucharistic theology, and his biblicism.

Anabaptism was as prevalent in the Swiss Confederacy as it was in the Holy Roman Empire. The origins of Swiss Anabaptism can be attributed to radical Zwinglians in Zurich, who were led by Conrad Grebel (c1498–1526), Felix Mantz (died 1527) and George Blaurock (c1492–1529). These radicals were frustrated by Zwingli's hesitation and initial refusal to abolish the Mass, even more so because they knew that he despised it. In due course, they rejected adult baptism and, as the Zurich authorities did not tolerate their presence, they were forced to spread their doctrines in the countryside, where they also rejected the tithe.

Brüderliche vereynigung etzlicher kinder Gottes/ siben Artickel betreffend.

Item/Eyn sendtbrieff Michel sat-lers/ an eyn gemeyn Gottes/sampt kurtz-em/ doch warhafftigem anzeyg/wie er seine leer zů Rottenburg am Necker/ mitt seinem blůt bezeugethat.

M. D. XXvij.

Figure 4.1: Title page of the *Schleitheim Confession, The Seven Articles of the Brotherly Union of the True Children of God*, 1527

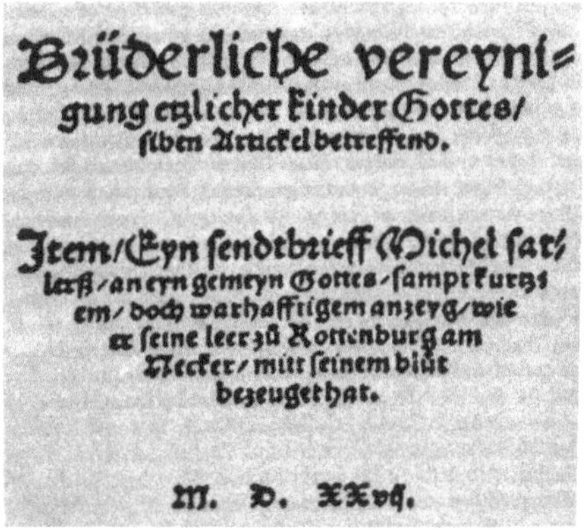

The Anabaptist movement had many different components. It spread as far as Waldshut in Austria, which became officially Anabaptist under Balthasar Hubmaier's (1480–1528) leadership. A second strand of southern Anabaptism was developed by Hans Denck (c1500–1527), which drew on a more mystical tradition. By 1527, attempts were made to unify the Anabaptists, and groups of south German and Swiss Anabaptists met in Schleitheim on the Swiss-German border and agreed on a set of articles that were composed by Michael Sattler.

Thomas Müntzer

One of the most prominent Anabaptists was Thomas Müntzer, author of the first published evangelical service in 1524. He asserted that there was no Real Presence in the Eucharist, and believed in spiritualism rather than biblicism. Müntzer's emphasis on the Spirit stemmed from the lack of visible improvement among Luther's followers. While he criticised infant baptism, he did not entirely abolish it. Müntzer pursued an

altogether different path from Luther, and even Karlstadt for that matter, when he condoned the use of force. Müntzer believed that the Spirit had urged him to become an armed prophet and lead the Lord's elect against the damned. Müntzer finally settled in the city of Mühlhausen in August 1524, where he formed the Eternal League of God in order to protect the Gospel. He fought in the Peasants' War in Thuringia, where his peasant army was crushed on 15 May 1525. Müntzer was captured, tortured and finally executed.

The Anabaptist Kingdom of Münster

By the end of the 1520s, the first generation of Anabaptists, including leaders such as Grebel, Mantz, Blaurock and Hubmaier, had died, at which point Anabaptism experienced a resurgence in the lower Rhine and the Low Countries. The principal source was Melchior Hoffman (1495–1543), who fled Denmark owing to his rejection of the Real Presence, and eventually moved to Strasbourg in 1530, by which time he had rejected infant baptism. Anabaptism in the northern provinces of the Low Countries was distinctive for its strong apocalyptic tradition. Following his travels to East Frisia and to Emden, Hoffman returned to Strasbourg, which he labelled the New Jerusalem, to await Christ's second coming, apparently scheduled for the year 1533. He was arrested the moment that he arrived in Strasbourg. In his absence from the Netherlands, Hoffman was succeeded by Jan Mathijs (d. 1534) and Jan Bockelszoon (1509–1536), and they later declared Münster in Westphalia the New Jerusalem.

Münster had already seen considerable tensions between Catholics and Lutherans. Initially, Lutherans were driven out, including the preacher Bernard Rottman, but he returned in due course and Lutherans gained a majority on the town council and secured control of the city's churches. In 1532, Catholic representatives left the city and planned their retaliation in collaboration with Count Franz von Waldeck, the newly elected Bishop of Münster. In the meantime, Rottman gradually adopted a more Zwinglian view of the Eucharist and also rejected infant baptism. In 1533, he encouraged the Anabaptists from Holland to come to Münster, and Mathijs and Bockelszoon responded to his call. Münster's citizens were influenced by Hoffman's writings, which had reached the town by 1534. An insurrection began on 9 February, and ill-advised concessions from the town authorities allowed the revolutionaries to secure thousands of converts, especially among women. The radicals' newly found legal status attracted more adherents from neighbouring towns and even from Holland.

Shortly afterwards, the Anabaptists gained a majority on the Council. Following a prayer meeting of armed Anabaptists six days after the insurrection, Münster's citizens were forced to convert or leave. An apocalyptic Council of Twelve elders was established, the goods of citizens who had fled were distributed and wives were also shared; the latter idea was based on the Old Testament, and intended to accommodate the growing numbers of unattached women. All images, manuscripts and musical instruments were destroyed, actions that were considered necessary preparation for Christ's second coming. Inspired by the Book of Revelation, all human regulations such as property, marriage and social distinctions were abolished. In practice, law and order virtually disappeared.

After Mathijs died, Bockelszoon introduced compulsory polygamy, dissolved the Council, made himself King of the New Jerusalem and claimed world rulership. On 30 August 1534, he defeated an attempt to besiege the city and in October he sent 28 followers to preach in neighbouring cities; almost all of them were seized and executed. It was not until April 1535 that the mutual jealousies of the princes and the dissensions between Catholics and Lutherans were put aside, permitting a joint expedition in support of the Bishop of Münster, largely funded by the Fuggers. The city offered remarkably stubborn resistance, though it was eventually taken on the night of 24 June 1535 owing to the treachery of several inhabitants. Male citizens were killed,

Figure 4.2: Portrait of Thomas Müntzer, 1609 engraving by Christoffel van Sichem

ACTIVITY 4.3

Using the material here and your own research, describe the main characteristics of Anabaptism. Include the variations between places, groups and people, and the way the beliefs of individuals changed and developed. How can you account for these variations?

ACTIVITY 4.4

Using this section and your wider reading, assess the immediate, short-term and long-term significance of the fall of the Anabaptist Kingdom of Münster.

and women and children were expelled. Events at Münster inevitably had a profound impact on all branches of the Anabaptist movement. As Emmet McLaughlin has asserted: 'Münster branded all Anabaptists as threats to society and human decency.'[12] For its part, the city of Münster was deprived of its privileges as an imperial city, and Catholicism was re-established.

The geographical expansion of Lutheranism

The geographical expansion of Lutheranism was important to its political survival. The urban Reformation had played a major part in the movement's consolidation. The legacy of the 1520s was vital, especially the daring protest at the 1529 Diet of Speyer. Between the years 1525 and 1545, Lutheranism gained 27 principalities, 30 counties and 19 lordships.

The formation of the Schmalkaldic League

The Emperor's response to the Lutheran Confession of Faith had represented an unambiguous affirmation of key Catholic teachings. He had also delegated the suppression of Lutheranism to the *Reichskammergericht*, which was dominated by Catholic judges. Anticipating military resistance from the Emperor, Elector John of Saxony and Philip of Hesse met in December 1530 at Schmalkalden, on the borders of Hesse and Saxony. In discussing how to deal with the *Reichskammergericht's* use of litigation against Lutheranism, it was agreed that Protestantism required a defensive alliance. The Schmalkaldic League, as the alliance came to be known, was initially supported by the Elector of Saxony, the Landgrave of Hesse, the Duke of Brunswick-Lüneburg, Prince Wolfgang of Anhalt, the two counts of Mansfeld and the cities of Magdeburg and Bremen. The League was established in 1531 immediately after the Diet of Augsburg, and restricted to the signatories of the Augsburg Confession. As indicated by Diarmaid MacCulloch, 'the League was only in existence to do God's work: it was not merely a diplomatic association of convenience'.[13] It was a military alliance with the purpose of defending and promoting the Reformation in the Holy Roman Empire. At two conferences held at Nordhausen and Frankfurt in November and December 1531 respectively, Lutherans worked on the League's military and financial details.

It was explicitly stated that the League's motives were defensive: 'this alliance has … no other reason than to defend and afford protection to ourselves, our subjects, in case we are attacked or interfered with because of the Christian and righteous cause for which our alliance has been formed'.[14] Yet this was the first time a section of the Holy Roman Empire had declared open resistance to the Emperor and to the Imperial Diets. Other territories joined the League when they converted to Lutheranism.

Yet not all Protestants did so. In February 1531, the Swiss cities refused to join the Schmalkaldic League, and Zwinglian theologians at Memmingen attacked the Catholic ceremonialism of the Lutheran liturgy. The political unity of Protestantism would forever be hampered by theological differences. Some Protestants were more willing to compromise their principles than others. Some south German cities like Strasbourg, which were Zwinglian in theology, did form part of the League, and accepted that Luther's doctrine of the Eucharist was the price to be paid for the League's protection. In contrast, the Swiss cities that continued to hold Zwingli's view of the Eucharist never joined. Strasbourg broke its alliance with the Swiss when it became a member of the Schmalkaldic League, and was subsequently joined by Augsburg. The death of Zwingli at the second Kappel war in 1531 undoubtedly worked to the advantage of Lutheranism, for the cities of northern Germany, previously sympathetic to Zwingli, increasingly favoured Wittenberg.

With the formation of the League, the outcome of future negotiations between Protestants and Catholics was uncertain, for Protestant princes had set themselves against the Emperor and his efforts to re-establish unity via the Imperial Diets. Lutherans were able to present such a powerful stance because of the extent of their geographical expansion. When Göttingen, Goslar, Eimbeck and Lübeck joined the League, and Hamburg, Rostock and Denmark became Protestant, the Schmalkaldic League was in almost complete control of the northern parts of the Empire. Northern princes, such as Dukes Barnim IX (1501–1573) and Philip I (1515–1560) who shared the Duchy of Pomerania, also joined the League. These north German Protestant powers were sufficiently confident that they planned to spread Protestantism further afield, sending agents to France, England, Denmark and Venice. The League's Constitution was approved at Schmalkalden on 23 December 1535, dividing responsibilities with the north controlled by the Saxon electors and the south under the Hessian landgrave. The Lutheran Confession of Faith represented the League's fundamental principles and helped to define their sense of unity. During the period 1531–1547, the League met a total of 26 times and the 1530s has been described as the League's 'halcyon days'.[15]

The Duchy of Württemberg

The rehabilitation of the Duke of Württemberg in 1534 was part of the League's objective of spreading the Reformation to southern Germany. It was regarded by some German Catholic princes and by the Emperor's foreign rivals as a necessary means of undermining Habsburg power. The Habsburgs had seized the Duchy of Württemberg's lands in 1519, after Duke Ulrich of Württemberg had murdered a knight in order to possess his wife and had been driven into exile by the Swabian League. Ulrich became increasingly determined to regain his territory. The expansion of Lutheranism and the emergence of the Schmalkaldic League provided him with a unique opportunity.

In January 1534, Francis I met Philip of Hesse at Bar-le-duc and promised extensive financial support. This came at a time when the Emperor and his brother were under considerable pressure both from within and outside the Empire. While Ferdinand and Charles continued to be preoccupied with the Ottomans and the French, within the Empire the Swabian League had become totally ineffectual. In November 1532, Philip of Hesse, and the electors of Trier and of the Palatinate had refused to renew their membership of the Swabian League. Some of the League's key former members, such as the cities of Ulm, Nuremberg and Augsburg, had subsequently established a separate alliance. In any case, the marked religious and political tensions within the Empire meant that the Swabian League was more likely to be hostile than supportive of the Emperor, and it was not long before it ceased to exist.

The staunchly Catholic Elector Joachim of Brandenburg had told Philip of Hesse that the Emperor's brother, Ferdinand, would receive no assistance from the electors, so Philip decided to use the Duchy of Württemberg as a demonstration of Protestant strength. The Schmalkaldic League, led by Philip of Hesse, financed by the French and supported by the Bavarians, marched on Württemberg in April 1534 with a well-equipped army of 20 000 foot soldiers and 4000 horsemen. Charles ignored Ferdinand's pleas for help, and the latter's lieutenant in Württemberg, Count Philip of the Palatinate, could only raise 9000 foot soldiers and 400 horsemen. The two sides met at Lauffen on 12 May, and by the end of June the whole of the duchy was overrun by the League. Peace was made with Ferdinand on 29 June, even though Francis I was pressing the Lutheran princes to expand further. The restoration of Ulrich was a big blow for the Habsburgs because not only had Lutheranism gained a vital stronghold in southwest Germany, but Württemberg was also situated between their Austrian and Swabian possessions.

Shortly after these events in Württemberg, the Schmalkaldic League contributed to the crushing of the Anabaptist Kingdom of Münster. In December 1535, the Schmalkaldic League reiterated its insistence on admitting only those who subscribed to the Confession of Augsburg, and the following became entitled to its protection: the Duchy of Pomerania, Anhalt and the cities of Augsburg, Frankfurt, Hanover and Kempten.

Members of the League renewed their rejection of the *Reichskammergericht*. Since his restoration as Duke of Württemberg, Ulrich had overseen a Zwinglian reform programme. In the mid-1530s, his duchy was divided into two different regions, supervised by the Lutheran pastor Erhard Schnepfen and the Zwinglian Ambrosius Blaurer respectively. When Johannes Brenz was invited as a theological adviser, he successfully introduced a more moderate strand of Lutheranism, and established one of Lutheranism's most influential territorial churches. Ulrich finally joined the League in 1536 and Württemberg became a key territory in the southwest for Lutheranism, thereby helping the movement to eclipse Zwinglianism as a confessional force among the princes.

Timeline: Members of the Schmalkaldic League in the 1530s

1530–1531	Elector of Saxony, Landgrave of Hesse, Duke of Braunschweig-Lüneburg, Count of Anhalt, Count of Mansfeld, and the towns of Strasbourg, Ulm, Constance, Reutlingen, Memmingen, Lindau, Biberach, Isny, Lübeck, Magdeburg, Bremen
1532	Count of Brandenburg-Ansbach, and the towns of Esslingen, Heilbronn, Schwäbisch-Hall, Kempten, Weissenburg, Windesheim, Braunschweig, Goslar, Einbeck, Göttingen, Nordhausen, Hamburg
1535	Duke of Pomerania, Duke of Württemberg, Count of Anhalt-Dessau, and the towns of Augsburg, Frankfurt, Hanover.[16]

The development of the Schmalkaldic League

The personal and religious differences between John Frederick and Philip of Hesse caused problems for the League. Philip was contemptuous of John Frederick whom he thought was uninspiring, while John Frederick had doubts about Philip's orthodoxy. Philip was inclined to Zwinglian views and certainly resented being dictated to both by Wittenberg's theologians and by their elector. In spite of the tensions between the League's most influential members, the League's power continued to grow in the 1530s. This was partly due to the succession of Protestant sons to influential Catholic princes. Joachim II (1505–1571) replaced Joachim I, who died in 1535, as Elector of Brandenburg. He refused to join the Catholic League of Nuremberg in 1538 (see section 'The Catholic League of Nuremberg'), and converted to Lutheranism in 1539. Joachim II's brother, Margrave John of Brandenburg, who ruled in Cottbus and Peitz, had also joined the Schmalkaldic League in 1537. Heidelberg, the Elector Palatine's capital, was described as the most Lutheran city in Germany; the Elector himself wavered between Lutheranism and Catholicism.

In ducal Saxony, Henry II (d. 1541) replaced Duke George in 1539 and Lutheranism was introduced immediately, with assistance from neighbouring electoral Saxony. He adopted similar visitations and church orders. Interestingly, Duke George had made his brother's succession conditional on his rejection of Lutheranism and joining the Catholic League of Nuremberg. If Henry rejected the terms, the duchy would pass either to the Emperor or his brother Ferdinand. Yet the inhabitants of ducal Saxony had long resented Duke George's repressive measures and his conditions proved unenforceable. In 1540, the estates within ducal Saxony sanctioned a Lutheran Reformation that Duke Henry had already initiated without their consent.

In April 1539, the Truce of Frankfurt was signed between the Habsburgs and the German princes, presenting terms that were similar to the Peace of Nuremberg. The truce yielded temporary concessions until a general council of the Church met. Charles V accepted the mediation of the half-hearted Catholic Elector Palatine Ludwig

V and equally doubtful Protestant Joachim II of Brandenburg, who had refused to join the Schmalkaldic League or accept the spiritual guidance of Wittenberg. The Protestant terms were certainly demanding: the establishment of a permanent peace which no Council and no assembly of estates should have the power to break; the Nuremberg League was to have no new members; the Schmalkaldic League could have as many new members as possible; all processes of the *Reichskammergericht* were to be suspended for 18 months. Charles conceded to a suspension of the *Reichskammergericht's* activities for six months and quietly gave consent to the point concerning the Nuremberg League, though the organisation was not dissolved, and the latest recruits to Lutheranism enjoyed immunity. Beyond that nothing was settled, and much depended on the extent of the Emperor's troubles elsewhere.

By the late 1530s, the Protestant princes were the dominant force in the north. East of the Rhine and north of the river Main, only the northwestern prince-bishops and one lay prince, the Duke of Brunswick-Wolfenbüttel, remained Catholic. By this stage, the Lutherans possessed two electoral votes, Saxony and Brandenburg, and the heir to the Palatinate appeared to be Protestant. If Cologne fell, Lutherans would gain a majority in an imperial election. Despite these notable advantages, the League was eager to secure a more permanent alliance with the King of France, a view that was voiced by John Frederick, the Elector of Saxony, who was himself influenced by his Chancellor Gregor Brück (1485–1557).

The League certainly attracted ever-increasing international attention; both Francis I and Henry VIII courted the German Protestants as potential allies. In December 1535, French and English ambassadors even sought admission to the League, though both were rejected owing to their profession of Catholicism (despite Henry VIII's break with Rome).

Relations between the League and the Holy Roman Empire

During the 1530s, the Schmalkaldic League had a profound impact on imperial governance. The Imperial Diet did not meet during the years 1533–1540, though Ferdinand could have called a Diet in Charles's absence, albeit not without his permission. The Schmalkaldic League's leaders negotiated with the Emperor through envoys. The League worked tirelessly against the stiff opposition presented by the *Reichskammergericht*. There was widespread resistance to the Court's numerous writs for the restoration of Church properties. One of the judges, Count Wilhelm Werner von Zimmern (1485–1575), highlighted the court's vulnerability amid the increasing Lutheran threat: 'because the Protestant Estates had prevailed and spread so much, the members of the Chamber Court lived in a state of heightened insecurity and at times were in danger when they dared to venture out'.[17]

Out of necessity, Lutherans challenged the *Reichskammergericht* because the secularisation of Church property had provided the financial basis of Lutheran churches. On 30 January 1534, Lutherans formally rejected the *Reichskammergericht* as a partisan body in an agreement called the Peace of Cadan. The signatories insisted that Ferdinand should prevent any proceedings against the Schmalkaldic League. Ferdinand was forced to comply and, in exchange, the Elector of Saxony withdrew his opposition to Ferdinand's election as King of the Romans. The Peace of Cadan's protection did not extend to those towns and territories that had not joined the League; numerous Protestant states were liable to practical ruin as a result of the *Reichskammergericht's* verdicts. This caused immense friction because Catholic princes had more than religious motives for executing the judgments of *Reichskammergericht*; 'as executors of the Court's decrees they could legally seize the lands of recalcitrant cities or lords, and under the guise of religion extend their territorial power'.[18]

Figure 4.3: Portrait of Philip of Hesse, woodcut by Hans Brosamer, c1530

ACTIVITY 4.5

Using this section and your wider reading, draw up a timeline indicating Philip of Hesse's association with Lutheranism. How significant was Philip of Hesse to the consolidation of Luther's movement?

Philip of Hesse's bigamy

There are additional reasons why Lutheranism experienced mixed fortunes in the late 1530s and early 1540s. Not only was it discovered that Philip of Hesse, one of the movement's leading princes, was a bigamist, but Luther and Melanchthon supported his bigamy on the condition that it remained a secret. While Philip had married Duke George of Saxony's daughter in 1523, he subsequently married a young Saxon noblewoman, Margarethe von der Saale. Philip could not bear his wife, and with divorce out of the question, he justified bigamy on Old Testament precedents. The moral effect of this revelation, once it leaked out, was dramatic. Luther, Melanchthon and Bucer were all aware of, and had approved, Philip's second marriage but insisted that knowledge about its existence should be concealed. A ceremony had taken place on 4 March 1540 and news soon leaked out. John Frederick and Ulrich of Württemberg refused to guarantee Philip immunity for his crime, the legal penalty for which was death – according to paragraph 121 of the Holy Roman Empire's criminal code, promulgated in 1532.

By later seeking to make his peace with the Habsburgs, Philip of Hesse caused a rift in the Schmalkaldic League, which had potentially disastrous consequences. Charles V turned it to his advantage. In the autumn of 1540, Philip began negotiations with Charles's leading councillor Granvelle and on 13 June 1541 he concluded an agreement with the Emperor. Philip abandoned all relations with England, France and the Duchy of Cleves. He also promised to disrupt any communication between those territories and the Schmalkaldic League, as well as siding with Charles on all political questions and to recognise Ferdinand as Charles's successor in the Empire.

Despite the League's apparent weaknesses, by 1541 Duke Maurice was in charge at Dresden and so the two Saxon territories were now committed to the Lutheran cause, at least for the time being. When Charles returned to the Empire in the early 1540s, the Schmalkaldic League had become a powerful body, with a military council and a reasonably coherent financial system. And Charles continued to be hampered by his countless external problems.

Charles V: his position and his problems

Charles's failed attempts to suppress Lutheranism were largely due to his repeated absences. He delegated authority to his brother Ferdinand, who could not wield the same power as him. Ferdinand's election as King of the Romans in Cologne on 5 January 1531, a title sometimes held by an Emperor's successor, made little difference. Charles consistently misjudged the nature and gravity of the Lutheran threat. He assumed 'that political or economic ambitions – particularism and the confiscation of Church lands – were more prominent in the actions of the dissident princes than issues of faith.'[19] This helps us to understand Charles's actions in the aftermath of the Diet of Augsburg; the adoption of the Recess on 19 November insisted on the Edict of Worms, the restoration of church property and the reconstitution of the *Reichskammergericht*.

The Emperor was eager to resist the secularisation of church property, while not targeting the Lutheran princes directly. Charles was deliberately cautious in the 1530s, resorting to the law, rather than using force. It was out of necessity given that only Elector Joachim of Brandenburg and Duke George of Saxony would have willingly gone to war for Charles V at that time. A.F. Pollard shrewdly pointed out that 'each Catholic prince desired the suppression of heresy, but no one would set his face against the enemy for fear of being stabbed in the back by a friend'.[20] Even the most powerful Catholic princes, the Wittelsbach rulers of Bavaria, frequently conspired with Philip of Hesse against the Habsburgs.

The Ottoman diversion

Just when Charles wanted to enforce a harsher line on Lutheranism, he suspended the actions of the *Reichskammergericht* on 8 July 1531. He was too concerned and fearful of the Ottoman advance and urgently required the assistance of the Lutheran princes. On 23 July 1532, a truce was signed at Nuremberg in which Protestants were incorporated into a general peace of the Empire. As a result of various private discussions, all lawsuits before the Imperial Court were suspended until the next Diet or until a general religious Council was called. The agreement was kept secret from the Catholics so as not to cause consternation, but this at least ensured Protestant military support against the Ottomans. This breach of the Edict of Worms was necessitated on the grounds that Charles V relied on princely support to drive back Suleiman, while Ferdinand also wished to strengthen his position in Eastern Europe. This compromise gave the green light for the consolidation and further legitimisation of Protestantism within the Empire.

For the Habsburgs, the Ottoman threat had become their top priority. Although the 1529 siege of Vienna had failed, nothing could stop the Sultan from returning. Ferdinand attempted to dissuade the Ottomans from attacking by offering to pay a tribute, and to cede the Hungarian lands to Jan Zápolya on the condition that they were returned on Zápolya's death. On 26 April 1532, the Ottomans launched a new campaign with 250 000 (only half of whom were combatants) against 80 000 well-equipped imperial troops. Charles instructed Ferdinand to secure peace with the Ottomans, but Suleiman was not in the mood for negotiation. In the campaign that followed, the Ottomans were largely unsuccessful; a tiny imperial garrison at Güns held up the massive Ottoman army between 7 and 28 August. Although the Ottomans were only 60 kilometres from the city, they made no further attempts to march on Vienna, and started their retreat in September.

Charles did not exploit these circumstances to seize Hungarian territory for Ferdinand. In any case, German soldiers refused to go beyond the frontiers of the Empire, so preoccupied were they with their own self-defence. For his part, Ferdinand abandoned his claims to Turkish Hungary and in 1533 he recognised Zápolya as the ruler of the client kingdom of Hungary. At this stage, it would seem that Suleiman wanted to avoid a direct occupation of Hungary. Ottoman priorities lay in the East with their recent expansion into Syria and Egypt and in the Mediterranean, though this was not necessarily clear to Charles at the time.

The Mediterranean

In the Mediterranean, Charles intervened in response to the corsair raids on Spain. He gained the invaluable support of the Genoese admiral Andrea Doria. With Barbarossa's support, the Ottomans seized Peñón of Algiers, while the imperial fleet temporarily secured Patras and Coron. In 1535, Doria's ships successfully recaptured Tunis; Barbarossa was expelled, and Muley Hassan, a Moorish ally of the Spanish, was reinstated. At this point, Barbarossa was appointed commander of the Ottoman navy and the establishment of a new Holy League in 1538 did little to consolidate the imperial position in the Mediterranean, as indicated by the battle of Preveza in the same year. In Elton's words, 'Preveza undid Charles's Tunisian triumph, revived Barbarossa's reputation, and secured the eastern Mediterranean for the Turkish navy'.[21] Three years later, Charles attempted to conquer Algiers, but his campaign ended in disaster.

In the same year as the battle of Preveza, 1538, Ferdinand secured a treaty with the childless Zápolya, which guaranteed the latter's control of the Hungarian throne on the condition that Ferdinand should be his successor. Once the Sultan heard about this, he was enraged, for Suleiman regarded Hungary as his and Zápolya as his viceroy, so he threatened war in 1539. However, before his death on 23 July 1540, Zápolya had

ACTIVITY 4.6

In a group, share out the names of people and places named in this section on the Mediterranean and carry out private research. Then pool what you have found out to gain a fuller picture of the challenges Charles V faced on his southern and eastern frontiers.

ACTIVITY 4.7

For this activity, use a mind-map format on a large blank sheet. Using material in sections 'Relations with France' and 'The Catholic League of Nuremberg' (and any further research of your own), sketch out the difficulties Charles faced in his dealings with France, Italy, the Netherlands, and the leading Lutherans and Catholics in the Holy Roman Empire.

had a son, called John Sigismund. His widow and her minister George Martinuzzi, the Bishop of Grosswardein, repudiated the 1538 treaty and crowned John Sigismund. The Ottoman reaction was to end the nominal independence that the Hungarians had enjoyed under Zápolya. In August 1541, the Ottomans captured Buda, turning Hungary into a Turkish province. The Diet of Speyer, summoned in January 1542, offered substantial money for the war, but imperial troops were ill equipped and poorly commanded by Joachim of Brandenburg. Although the army did get as far as Pest and started to besiege it, they were ultimately unsuccessful. Thereafter, Suleiman extended his control over the Hungarian cities of Pécs (known as Fünfkirchen), Székesfehérvár (Stuhlweissenburg) and Esztergom (Gran).

Relations with France

While the Ottomans were his chief concern, Charles was equally preoccupied with the French in the 1530s. The Habsburgs had sought to isolate France diplomatically. This necessitated a less confrontational religious policy within the Empire. As Pollard has argued, 'temporal security was a more urgent need than the maintenance of the Catholic Church,' so that in 1534, 'the suspension of all the ecclesiastical cases in the *Reichskammergericht* was the price which Ferdinand paid for the Lutheran rejection of an alliance with Henry VIII and Francis I'.[22]

In the early 1530s, Charles had restored Francesco Sforza to the Duchy of Milan. When the latter died without heirs in 1535, Francis I revived his claims to Milan, fearing that Charles would take the opportunity to seize Milan. Francis I attacked Piedmont and Savoy, Charles's ally in 1536, and communicated with the Ottomans, Henry VIII and the Lutheran princes. By March 1536, French troops occupied Savoy and Piedmont. In response, Charles invaded Provence and Picardy, but achieved little at considerable expense. Francis also attacked the southern borders of the Netherlands, and the French occupied Hesdin and pushed into Artois. Although Henry VIII and the Lutheran princes remained neutral, Francis I more than held his own in the years 1536–1538. A stalemate culminated in an agreement signed at Aigues Mortes between May and June 1538, in which Pope Paul III was the principal mediator. The ten years' truce between Charles and Francis subsequently negotiated by Paul III at Nice in 1538 marked a considerable recovery from the earlier humiliation experienced by Francis I at Pavia in 1525.

The Catholic League of Nuremberg

In October 1536, Charles V unwisely sent Matthias Held, the Imperial Vice-Chancellor, to negotiate with the Schmalkaldic League. Held was a bitter opponent of Lutheranism and an ardent supporter of the *Reichskammergericht*. Instead of attempting to persuade the Lutherans, he tried to intimidate them and organised Catholic resistance, against Charles V's instructions.

In 1538, Charles ignored the Peace of Cadan and Ferdinand's later concessions, and required Protestants to submit to a proposed Council and to the *Reichskammergericht's* demands. Charles proceeded to build up a Catholic alliance, and on 10 June 1538, the Catholic League of Nuremberg, the brainchild of Matthias Held, was formed. Under the nominal patronage of Charles V, Ferdinand, the archbishops of Mainz and Salzburg, the dukes of Bavaria and George of Saxony, Eric and Henry of Brunswick joined the League. Although presented as a defensive alliance, the insistence on enforcing the *Reichskammergericht's* decrees did threaten war. The League never played a serious part in the policies of the Emperor, who only reluctantly accepted its existence. While most Catholic princes were willing to denounce Lutheranism, they were generally reluctant to help the Emperor suppress it by force.

Further north, Charles encountered problems in 1539 with a revolt in Ghent, which later spread to Alost, Oudenaarde and Courtrai. Although it was easily crushed by

February 1540, the revolt represented yet another distraction from his German affairs. Elsewhere, it appeared as though Guelders might fall into the hands of a ruler who wanted to join the Schmalkaldic League. William, heir to the united Duchy of Jülich-Cleves-Berg, also had claims to the neighbouring Duchy of Guelders, whose duke had died without issue in 1538. The estates of Guelders accepted William's claims and in February 1539 William succeeded his father in Cleves. William's sister was already married to the Elector of Saxony, and at the end of 1539, another sister, Anne, married Henry VIII. This was a serious threat to Charles because William of Cleves had succeeded in creating a powerful state in the northwest of Germany next to the Lower Rhine, the vital route that linked the Emperor's Italian and south German possessions with the Netherlands.

While Duke William was an Erasmian, and the duchy adopted a more compromising stance between Rome and Wittenberg, it was clear that the Duke would continue to pursue the anti-Habsburg traditions of Guelders. He established contacts with the Schmalkaldic League and welcomed the advances from England. However, Charles wasted little time and defeated the Duke in 1543 and William lost control of Guelders.

Religious division in Germany

By the late 1530s and early 1540s, moderate theologians on both sides of the religious divide were seeking to reconcile their conflicting doctrinal positions. In 1540, Charles V summoned an Imperial Diet in order to kick-start discussions between the two religious parties. The emergence of influential theologians dedicated to the cause of religious unity – who included not only Martin Bucer but also Johann Gropper (1503–1559), a Catholic theologian who was Chancellor of Cologne – increased the hope of success. The first attempt at reconciliation took place at the Diet of Haguenau, which met in June 1540. The Protestant estates upheld the Augsburg Confession, which was rejected by Catholic princes; the Diet made no significant progress.

In the same year, Charles accepted the Augsburg Confession as a basis for discussion at the Imperial Diet of Worms, which took place between November 1540 and January 1541. The eleven Catholics – including Ludwig of the Palatinate, Joachim of Brandenburg and William of Cleves – and 11 Protestants who participated in the discussions made some progress. With more concrete discussions starting in January 1541, Johannes Eck and Melanchthon remarkably collaborated on a statement about original sin, which they drafted in four days. Bucer and Gropper focused on the question of justification, and prepared what came to be known as the 'Regensburg Book'.

The Diet of Regensburg

These meetings were followed by the Imperial Diet of Regensburg, which Charles attended. Beforehand, Charles had secretly commissioned Gropper and Bucer to draft articles on key points of doctrine. Parallel to the Imperial Diet of Regensburg (March–July 1541), there was a religious colloquy, with three theologians on each side of the religious divide. While Gasparo Contarini led the moderate Catholics, Philip Melanchthon was the pre-eminent Protestant theologian in attendance. Pope Paul III had sent Contarini to be his representative, and the choice of Contarini appeared to bode well and there was optimism on both sides.

The articles reflected a certain consensus regarding justification by faith and culminated in a joint definition that brought the sides closer together. The Emperor was very hopeful, and even Eck and Calvin could see nothing wrong with the formula. However, the agreement on justification was the only achievement of note and was quickly repudiated by the Pope and Luther. The latter summarised his views to Melanchthon in unambiguous terms: 'agreement on doctrine is plainly impossible, unless the pope will abolish his popedom'.[23]

ACTIVITY 4.8

In his analysis of the Diet of Regensburg, Diarmaid MacCulloch has argued that 'the theologians proceeded over the next two months to ruin the deal before the politicians had any opportunity to do so'.[25] Could the Diet of Regensburg have succeeded or, at the very least, ended differently?

Debates on more conflicting theological issues emerged such as the Church's authority, and ultimately negotiations seriously faltered over the Lord's Supper. Contarini would not concede on transubstantiation, and Protestants were not prepared to say that confession to a priest was necessary. However determined Charles was to achieve a theological understanding, it became clear that all the major protagonists, Bucer, John Frederick, Contarini and Aleander, the papal ambassador, were unconvinced.

Although there were further attempts at religious compromise in the early 1540s, they were unsuccessful. The failure of religious compromise was clearly indicative of the hardened theological divisions between Catholicism and Protestantism. The Diet of Regensburg marked a turning point in Charles V's policy. He had considered force in 1530 but rejected it, and had followed a policy based on the hope of compromise. As Tracy noted, 'no one realised it at the time, but with the failure of Regensburg colloquy, the moment for theological compromise had come and gone'.[24] As the chance for reconciliation faded, so too did the reputations of those who had promoted the idea of compromise. Charles V realised that, sooner or later, he would have to restore imperial unity by force.

The state of the churches by 1541

The survival of Lutheranism in the years 1531–1541 certainly benefited from the Catholic Church's inability to convene a Church Council. Ever since 1521, the idea of a general council to restore religious unity had repeatedly been urged. in the Empire, the proposed national Church Council lacked the support of either the Emperor or the Pope. As the German princes awaited a solution, they were told that evangelical preachers could be tolerated as long as a Reformation was not introduced. The imperial estates demanded a Church Council at each of the Imperial Diets, and the reference to a pending Church Council proved an effective strategy, for the notion that religious divisions would be settled at some stage in the future was sufficient to make compromise in the present a possibility. In any case, Protestants considered a Church Council to be a human institution, capable of error and, worse still, subject to the influence of Rome; Scripture alone was the arbiter of God's will.

In 1532, the Imperial Diet suspended any religious discussions before the imperial High Court and declared that if no ecumenical council were summoned in the interim, the following Diet, planned for 1534, would craft a religious compromise on its own authority. Charles sought reconciliation with the Pope and the convening of a general council in February 1533, but that was a dismal failure. Pope Clement VII secured an alliance with France, cemented by the marriage between Clement's niece Catherine de' Medici and Francis I's heir, Henri de Valois. Pope Clement VII refused to convene a Council partly due to conciliarist fears. He was also resistant to an Imperial Diet challenging the role of a Council in discussing and determining doctrine, so the Pope urged Charles and Ferdinand not to convene the 1534 Diet.

When Clement VII died in September 1534, he was replaced by Alexander Farnese (1468–1549), Pope Paul III, who accepted that a general council should be called. But he was equally determined that a Council should not threaten papal supremacy. Paul III was keen for the Emperor and Francis I to make peace, but believed that progress was being undermined by the latter. In the late 1530s and early 1540s, the main obstacle to a Council was now not in Rome but in Paris. The French church, particularly its bishops, was distrustful of papal motives and feared a loss of independence. All the different political and ecclesiastical powers also needed to identify a location for the Council. Mantua, though Italian, was independent and sufficiently near to the Alpine passes from a papal perspective, but this was not well received by the imperial powers. John Frederick rejected the Pope's attempts to convene a Council at Mantua in May 1537, and in its place suggested an alternative council to be held at Augsburg under the Schmalkaldic League's protection. In any case, Lutherans were reluctant to be involved because the terms of the summons referred to targeting heresy, not merely to eradicate abuses.

German Catholics, led by the Bavarian dukes, were hesitant to support a papal Council and demanded instead a Council of the German Nation. They wished to avoid a scenario in which promoting their religion would force them to support their emperor. While Charles was, in any case, distracted again by external affairs, Paul III attempted to call a Council for 1538, but the outbreak of war between France and the Emperor forced him to dismiss various cardinals and bishops. Eventually, Paul called his bishops to Mantua in 1539, and subsequently summoned them to Trent in 1542. It would take a further three years for the Council of Trent to be convened.

Practice essay question

> With reference to these sources and your understanding of the historical context, assess the value of these three sources to an historian studying the obstacles encountered by the Lutheran movement.

Extract A: *The Seven Articles of Schleitheim*, Canton Schaffhausen in the Swiss Confederacy, 24 February 1527

I. Baptism shall be given to all those who have learned repentance and amendment of life, and who believe truly that their sins are taken away by Christ, and to all those who demand it for themselves. This excludes all infant baptism, the highest and chief abomination of the Pope. In this you have the foundation and testimony of the apostles. Matt. 28, Mark 16, Acts 2, 8, 16, 19.

VI. The sword is ordained of God outside the perfection of Christ. It punishes and puts to death the wicked, and guards and protects the good. In the Law the sword was ordained for the punishment of the wicked and for their death, and the same (sword) is (now) ordained to be used by the worldly magistrates.[26]

Extract B: Examination of the clergy in the city of Ulm, 7 June 1531

Johannes Mann, chaplain at Reutti: formerly had a wife and has been a priest for twelve years; previously he learned much at the schools and at the papal and episcopal courts during the time when he was a priest and followed the papist beliefs, but has been partly enlightened for about two years and has partly given them up.

Hans Widemann, parson at Sontbergen (endowed by the town council): considers the Articles to be Christian, though has not the skill to defend them; previously held the Mass to be good, but is willing to be told better.[27]

Extract C: Brandenburg Church Statutes of 1540: On Fasting

As a territorial prince, we have the power, after taking good advice, to issue political statutes that serve the common good, provided that the conscience is not bound before God; also so that the young and ignorant folk become accustomed to moderation. Now since Christ ordained no specific times for fasting nor made no distinction in food, it is therefore unjust to make specific laws which bind the

ACTIVITY 4.9

Using this section and your wider reading, consider whether political rulers contributed more than theologians to the deteriorating relations between the Catholic and Lutheran Churches?

conscience contrary to God's Word and Christian freedom. Now since the young and the common folk are too ignorant and inclined to excess, if one did not compel them to do so, they would not learn moderation and would fall into excessive gorging and guzzling; so it is fitting that the secular authority consider passing statutes which each father of a household should make his servants observe. Now since it is not suitable to enact new special times for fasting, it is more convenient to retain those which have been customary, namely Friday and Saturday each week and the forty days of Lent. And since meat is out of season during Lent and our principality of Brandenburg is well supplied with fish, it is not unreasonable to ordain that throughout this period the communities should abstain from meat.[28]

Chapter summary

By the end of this chapter you should understand:

- the nature and development of Anabaptism, as well as the failed experiment of the Anabaptist Kingdom of Münster
- the reasons for the social and geographical expansion of Lutheranism, with particular emphasis on the consolidation of the movement in the 1530s
- the political background for these developments, including the formation and growth of the Schmalkaldic League, alongside the continuing problems faced by Charles V
- the attempts to heal the religious divide, particularly at the Diet of Regensburg, and the reasons for their failure.

Endnotes

1 Thomas Brady, *German Histories in the Age of Reformations, 1400–1650.* Cambridge University Press, 2009, p. 222.

2 Thomas A. Brady, 'Emergence and Consolidation of Protestantism in the Holy Roman Empire to 1600', in R. Po-Chia Hsia (ed.), *The Cambridge History of Christianity: Volume 6, Reform and Expansion, 1500–1660.* Cambridge University Press, 2007, p. 21.

3 James Tracy, *Europe's Reformations, 1450–1650.* Oxford, Rowman & Littlefield Publishers, 1999, p. 248.

4 C. Scott Dixon, 'The Princely Reformation in Germany', in Andrew Pettegree (ed.), *The Reformation World.* London and New York, Routledge, 2000, p. 157.

5 Scott Dixon, 'Princely Reformation', p. 161.

6 Bruce Gordon, 'The New Parish', in Po-chia Hsia, *Companion to Reformation World*, p. 411.

7 Pamela Johnston and Bob Scribner (eds), *The Reformation in Germany and Switzerland.* Cambridge University Press, 1993, p. 127.

8 Ute Lotz-Heumann, 'Imposing Church and Social Discipline', in Po-chia Hsia, *Companion to Reformation World*, p. 251.

9 Johnston and Scribner, *Reformation in Germany and Switzerland*, p. 120.

10 Lotz-Heumann, 'Church and Social Discipline', p. 253.

11 Martin Brecht, 'Luther's Reformation', in Thomas Brady, Heiko Oberman and James Tracy (eds), *Handbook of European History, 1400–1600*, Vol. II. Grand Rapids, MI, William B. Eerdmans, 1995, p. 145.

12 R. Emmet McLaughlin, 'The Radical Reformation', in Po-chia Hsia, *Companion to Reformation World*, p. 52.

13 Diarmaid MacCulloch, *Reformation: Europe's House Divided, 1490–1700.* London, Allen Lane, 2003, p. 174.

14 Brady, *German Histories*, p. 221.

15 Brady, *German Histories*, pp. 220–221.

16 Mark Greengrass, *The European Reformation, c1500–1618.* London and New York, Longman, 1998, pp. 87–88.

17 Brady, *German Histories*, p. 223.

18 A.F. Pollard, 'The Conflicts of Creeds and Parties in Germany', in A. Ward, G. Prothero, and S. Leathes (eds), *The Cambridge Modern History, Volume II: The Reformation.* Cambridge University Press, 1934, p. 232.

19 Elton, *Reformation Europe*, p. 97.

20 Pollard, 'Conflicts of Creeds', p. 215.

21 Elton, *Reformation Europe*, p. 113.

22 Pollard, 'Conflicts of Creeds', p. 233.

23 cited in Elton, *Reformation Europe*, p. 101.

24 James Tracy, Europe's Reformations p. 90.

25 MacCulloch, *Reformation*, p. 230.

26 The Schleitheim Confession. Crockett, KY, Rod and Staff Publishers, Inc., 1985.

27 Johnston and Scribner, *Reformation in Germany and Switzerland*, p. 123.

28 Johnston and Scribner, *The Reformation in Germany and Switzerland*, p. 127.

5 The second wave of Protestant Reform, 1541–1564

In this chapter we will study the career and rise to prominence of John Calvin. We will focus on the spread of Calvinism throughout Europe, as well as discuss the Schmalkaldic wars and the reasons for the survival of Lutheranism.

Specification points:

- Calvin: influences on early life and the evolution of doctrine; publications; early reform work and ministry in Strasbourg
- the practice of Calvinism in Geneva: support and opposition; the impact of his relationship with Servetus; Calvin and Luther; attitudes, similarities and differences; Calvin's authority and concordat with Zurich and Geneva churches
- the spread of Calvinism: France, Scotland, Netherlands, Germany, Poland and eastern Europe
- religious war in Germany; the death of Luther; the Peace of Augsburg and the abdication of Charles V; principles and problems of the Peace of Augsburg.

John Calvin

Influences on his early life

Calvin was born in Noyon, Picardy on 10 July 1509; little is known about his early life. Despite his mother's piety, he later criticised her Catholic faith. Calvin's father was an administrator for a local bishop, enabling him to secure a benefice, the chaplaincy at

Noyon cathedral, for his son. In 1523, he studied at the University of Paris, and in 1527 was appointed an absentee curate of Marteville, a village near Noyon – he resigned that post in May 1534. On his father's instructions, in 1527, he studied law, first at Orléans then at Bourges. He abandoned his legal training in 1531 when his father died and returned to Paris, entering the newly founded Collège Royal. He studied classical languages, and was influenced by Erasmus and French evangelicals, including Jacques Lefèvre d'Étaples, and Nicholas Cop, rector of the University of Paris. He fled Paris with Cop in December 1533 after a controversial sermon by the latter, at which point he underwent a conversion experience.

He finally left France after the Affair of the Placards (18 October 1534), during which placards denouncing the Mass were put up in Paris, Blois, Rouen, Tours and Orléans. Calvin found refuge in Basle, where he studied theology and the Bible, as well as the works of Martin Luther and St Augustine. He visited the court of Renée, Duchess of Ferrara, where he met numerous Protestant refugees, Geneva, which had recently turned Protestant, under the influence of Guillaume Farel (1489–1565), and spent several years in Strasbourg (1538–1541).

Timeline: John Calvin's early years and career

1509	Birth of Calvin
1521	Appointed to the chaplaincy at Noyon Cathedral
1523	Attended University of Paris
1527	Studied law at Orléans, then Bourges
1531	Returned to Paris, studying at the Collège Royal
1533	Left Paris with Nicholas Cop
1534	Fled France after the Affair of the Placards, initially residing in Basle

Evolution of doctrine and publications

Following his flight from France, Calvin embarked on his major project, the *Institutes of the Christian Religion*, first published in Latin in 1536. Calvin was one of the Reformation's most systematic thinkers and the *Institutes* gave him an international reputation. Described as a 'classic of Protestant theology',[1] the *Institutes* is hailed 'as the most orderly and eloquent presentation of Reformed Protestant theology and ethics ever written'.[2]

Intended to complement the Bible, the work presents very clear summaries as well as new emphases. In a sense, it resembles a **catechism**, expounding key biblical teachings, such as the overwhelming **omnipotence** and **omnipresence** of God, the thorough corruption of human nature by original sin and the belief in election and predestination.

There were various revisions of the *Institutes* during Calvin's life, with the final edition produced in 1559. Although he discouraged detailed analysis of predestination, he presented his defence of the doctrine in the 1559 edition: 'No one who wishes to be thought religious dares simply deny predestination, by which God adopts some to hope of life, and sentences others to eternal death … for all are not created in an equal condition.'[3]

In addition to the *Institutes*, Calvin wrote biblical commentaries on the Old and New Testaments.[4] He drew up a catechism for the young (published in 1542), and gave the

ACTIVITY 5.1

Using the section 'Evolution of doctrine and publications' and your wider reading, draw up a detailed mind map to explain the key themes of the *Institutes*. Why was it such an influential work?

Figure 5.1: Calvin

Genevan Church liturgical form. In 1542, he composed a hymnal composed of Psalms from the Bible, which developed into the famous Genevan Psalter of 1562, set to 125 simple melodies in poetic metre. He composed various theological and polemical treatises, including his works to the Nicodemites in France. During his Genevan ministry, he delivered countless sermons: Calvin alone delivered approximately 4000 sermons between 1538 and 1564. Calvin also wrote numerous letters to the faithful and to potential supporters abroad.

Calvin was reluctant to engage on some issues, such as the concept of resistance. In his 1559 edition of the *Institutes*, he devoted only a brief paragraph to the subject; under certain circumstances, magistrates could use their power to defy an idolatrous ruler. Left deliberately vague, Calvin's views on the matter lacked substance and he was increasingly overtaken by events in France and the Netherlands. His theological standing was recognised by contemporaries; Melanchthon was 'quite willing to acknowledge that Calvin was without peer when it came to theology'.[5]

Early reform work and ministry in Strasbourg

Calvin benefited enormously from his Strasbourg years. As a pastor, he ministered to the city's French refugee community. Calvin also taught at Johann Sturm's academy as a professor of biblical exegesis. Calvin was greatly influenced by Strasbourg's leading reformer, Martin Bucer. This was evident in Calvin's views on the Eucharist: both rejected the **Real Presence**, believing in a spiritual communion with Christ. Calvin observed Bucer's establishment of an evangelical church, focusing on religious conformity and the drafting of a liturgy. Calvin read Bucer's works with interest, notably his *De Regno Christi*.

During the years 1540-1541, Calvin attended religious colloquies at Haguenau, Worms and Regensburg. He continued to publish works, including the second Latin edition (1539) and first French translation (1541) of the *Institutes*. He also published his *Commentaries on the Epistle to the Romans* and wrote an *Epistle to Sadoleto*: a response to the Bishop of Carpentras (a diocese in neighbouring France), who had called on Geneva to return to Catholicism. Meanwhile, growing tensions in Geneva encouraged the city authorities to recall Calvin.

The practice of Calvinism in Geneva

Support for Calvinism in Geneva

Calvin returned to Geneva in 1541 and he resided there permanently until his death in 1564. The city authorities wanted Calvin to preach and resume his teaching. He became a member of the Company of Pastors and was appointed their unofficial leader; he chaired its weekly meetings, which planned services and provided an opportunity for mutual correction. The year of his return marked the publication of his *Ecclesiastical Ordinances*, which defined the Genevan Church's framework and constitution. Geneva was restructured into three parishes with ten pastors, and the *Ordinances* asserted that the clergy should function as co-administrators of the city.

The Church was composed of four different orders: pastors, teachers, elders and deacons. Pastors were expected to preach, administer the sacraments and enforce discipline; teachers provided religious instruction, defined doctrine and trained those who were preparing for the ministry; elders were laymen who supervised and admonished the faithful; deacons looked after the sick, the poor, orphans and abandoned children.

Calvin did not claim originality, arguing for a return to the early Church. The *Ordinances* were inspired by the Strasbourg and Zurich models; the Genevan elders performed a similar function to the Strasbourg churchwardens. In Geneva, the elders were integral to how the Church controlled society. Twelve elders sat on a committee, known as the Consistory, and represented the city's governing councils.

On his arrival, Calvin encountered incompetent ministers, and by 1546 he had established a more reliable ministry. He refined his understanding of the relationship between the secular and ecclesiastical authorities, realising that civil government was essential for the Church to function properly. He asserted that God ordained the civil authorities, though they were not meant to administer the Church. The power of excommunication became the foremost issue. The Genevan magistrates wanted Calvin to preach and be a legal adviser, but not to act as a secular ruler. Yet Calvin's pre-eminence as a theologian gave him considerable status in Geneva. His authority was not unquestioned during the 1540s and 1550s, though he gradually consolidated his position.

The city council increasingly collaborated with the Consistory, a court that focused on disciplinary and moral matters. Its members, pastors and lay elders, were elected annually. The Consistory was vital to the Calvinist concept of discipline and was a formidable and intrusive institution, summoning approximately 7% of the adult population every year, including nobles and patricians. Surviving Catholic practices, such as Latin prayers, the Rosary, and abstaining from meat were targeted. It dealt primarily with religious offenders, particularly negligence in Church attendance. The Consistory also addressed social issues such as marital problems, disputes within families and among neighbours.

The Consistory possessed limited powers of enforcement, and excommunication was the punishment in only the most serious cases. One of its functions was to secure admission of guilt and a declaration of penitence. It was neither a court of law nor empowered to impose civil penalties such as a fine, imprisonment, banishment or death. Yet discipline was enforced even for minor misdemeanours; in 1547, a parishioner was imprisoned for leaving noisily during a sermon. The Genevan regime tended to be less punitive with first-time offenders, though small fines and imprisonment on bread and water were common punishments. Most cases were unrelated to doctrine. Out of the 584 cases recorded in 1550, 238 represented quarrels within families or neighbourhoods, 160 consisted of sexual misdemeanours, gambling or dancing. During Calvin's time in Geneva (1541–1564), a total of 58 people were executed and 76 were banished.

Opposition to Calvin and the impact of his relationship with Servetus

Calvin's return was not welcomed by everybody. There was constant opposition from 1541, often led by the leading Genevan families, especially the Perrins. In 1546, for example, there was resistance from Ami Perrin and François Favre, who had been reprimanded by the Consistory with no respect for their status. These opponents opposed the rigours of the new ecclesiastical regime. There was also conflict between the Consistory and the Senate over excommunication; both ministers and senators were convinced that each held power over excommunication.

One of the most serious clashes involved baptismal names. Calvin was eager to avoid saints' names due to their associations with Catholicism. The controversies arose when babies were re-baptised with Old Testament names without parental consent. Calvin's principal enemies were known as the Libertines or Perrinists, who favoured greater freedom from clerical supervision. Although never more than a political minority, they frequently disobeyed laws.

This conflict intensified with the arrival of French refugees, leading to the fear (on the part of the Libertines) that foreigners were taking over the city. When the anti-Perrinists gained a small majority in the Senate in 1555, numerous French refugees were made bourgeois, allowing them to vote. In response, the Perrinists participated in a drunken riot on 16 May, described as an attempted coup. Many were arrested and tried for treason, some were executed and the rest were expelled. Ami Perrin and his family were forced to leave Geneva and their property was seized; the money was subsequently used to establish the Genevan Academy. Within six months of the riot, a third of Geneva's ruling elite had disappeared and the political landscape had changed immeasurably, to Calvin's obvious benefit.

Theological opposition

There was also some theological opposition to Calvin. In 1542, Calvin quarrelled with Sebastian Castellio, who denied that the Song of Songs was a religiously inspired book. He was later dismissed as rector of the Latin school due to his criticisms of Calvin's teachings on predestination, the Trinity and Christ's descent into Hell. The Genevan Council reprimanded Castellio, who was banished and subsequently moved to Basle, as Calvin was determined to expel any radicals from Geneva. In 1551, Jean Bolsec attacked Calvin's teachings on predestination, accusing him of regarding God as the author of sin. Although Bolsec had powerful protectors, he too was banished from the city. Calvin became determined to exclude any radicals in the building of his godly community. The Bolsec controversy led Calvin to publish in 1552 his most sustained treatment of predestination.

Michael Servetus

Calvin's response to one opponent gave Geneva a reputation for intolerance. A Spanish spiritualist, Michael Servetus, decided to visit Geneva in 1553. That same year, Calvin had condemned Servetus's anti-Trinitarian writings. Despite this, Servetus foolishly entered the city, whereupon he was seized. Calvin took charge of the proceedings, requesting verdicts from Zurich, Berne, Basle and Schaffhausen. Calvin sought to share the blame for the following death sentence, which received unanimous support from those cities and from Bullinger and Melanchthon. In response, Castellio published a book in 1554, condemning the execution and advocating a theory of toleration based on the Bible. Perrin's support for Servetus had contributed to the former's exile.

Another theological opponent was Joachim Westphal. Like Castellio, Westphal did not reside in Geneva. As a Lutheran minister in Hamburg, he wrote against the *Consensus Tigurinus* in 1552 (see section 'Calvin's authority and concordat between Zurich and Geneva churches'). Westphal condemned Zwingli and Calvin as heretics for denying the Real Presence. Calvin responded because Westphal's attacks threatened to undermine Lutheran–Reformed relations in Frankfurt and Wesel. In 1555, Calvin published his work defending the Consensus in Geneva and Zurich, triggering a pamphlet war. While Westphal attacked Calvin's work, this in turn led Calvin to publish a second defence in 1566. Westphal refused to be silenced and published his *Answer to some of the outrageous lies of John Calvin* (1558). This controversy reinforced Calvin's authority in Geneva.

By 1555, Calvin had become the pre-eminent force in Geneva. By packing the electorate with his supporters, notably French refugees, Calvin's authority was never seriously challenged again. The newly elected Council agreed not to interfere in the Church's decisions and refugees were granted full voting rights. Many of the refugees – some of whom were nobles – became pastors, and they inspired a thriving printing industry. Printers included Robert Estienne, previously the French King's printer, who devised the system of numbered verses in addition to normal chapter numbering, and his son Henri, as well as Jean Crespin, Antoine Vincent and Laurent de Normandie.[6] Calvin was in complete control by 1555, with a third of the former ruling elite in exile, and the remaining families fully supportive. At this time, the Consistory became even stricter; in 1553, 16 were excommunicated, whereas over 100 were excommunicated in 1560.

Calvin and Luther: attitudes, similarities and differences

There were theological similarities between Luther and Calvin. Calvin owed much to Luther. Both believed that man is justified by faith alone, that good works contributed nothing, and that faith was God's gift to man. Both rejected the fundamental tenets of Roman Catholicism. They denied the Catholic emphasis on priestly mediation and intercessory prayers to saints and to Mary. Both rejected purgatory and the Catholic penitential system.

However, there were differences between the two reformers, some more obvious than others. With his humanist training, Calvin emphasised the importance of serving a public moral good. In contrast, for Luther everybody was a sinner. While both insisted on *sola fide*, they drew different conclusions from it. Calvin and his followers believed that 'they were carrying out the purest of all Reformations, nothing less than a reform of the Reformation'.[7] While both believed in predestination, the notion of double predestination (that God had predestined some men to be saved and others to be condemned) became a characteristic core of Calvinism. Admittedly, Calvin himself did not emphasise it as much as some of his followers. Related to this were Calvin's frequent references to God's providence, which 'belonged to the central nervous system of his theology'.[8]

Most importantly, Luther and Calvin had different Eucharistic theologies. The latter rejected the former's belief in a Real Presence. While Luther perceived images and statues to be *adiaphora*, Calvin supported **iconoclasm** if magistrates supervised it. That some Lutheran and Catholic communities shared churches was abhorrent to Calvin. The main differences between the two reformers can be found in Church organisation rather than theology: 'Calvinism was less connected to a specifically new Protestant doctrine than to a renewed religious practice … stricter notions of membership and exclusion.'[9] The responsibility to impose discipline became a distinctive mark of the Calvinist Church.

Calvin's authority and concordat between Zurich and Geneva churches

Calvin was eager to establish a reliable group of pastors. As the overseer of the Company of Pastors, he managed to recruit gifted, educated and financially secure ministers. Calvin's ascendancy was key to the Company and to the different congregations. He had no rival 'in intellectual energy, in seriousness of purpose, or in unremitting zeal'.[10] Unlike earlier bishops, he had no formal powers of Church and state, but his religious authority was unquestioned, at least for the final decade of his life.

His pre-eminence owed much to his extensive preaching. In the early part of his career, he delivered sermons three times a week on weekdays and three times on Sundays until 1549. Every week, he held catechism classes, engaged in theological debates and led Bible studies. Calvin was the 'visible face – and audible voice – of authority in the city' and was sufficient to attract the attention of his Swiss counterparts, especially Zwingli's successor Heinrich Bullinger.[11]

Calvin was acutely aware of the ongoing tensions about the Eucharist and had personally observed the tensions between Zwinglian and Lutheran ministers in Berne. Having been presented with Bullinger's treatise on the Lord's Supper, Calvin wrote to Bullinger. In May 1549, Calvin accompanied Farel to Zurich and the subsequent discussions culminated in the 26 articles of the *Consensus Tigurinus*. The document rejected **transubstantiation** and **consubstantiation**; Calvin believed in Christ's spiritual presence in the Eucharist.

Key term

Adiaphora (literally, 'things indifferent') are not essential to faith, but form part of Christian practices and worship. The definition of *adiaphora* depends on the interpretation of theologians. The Lutheran definition of *adiaphora* was contained in the Confession of Augsburg, but became a source of disagreement between Lutherans after the 1548 Augsburg Interim imposed by Charles V.

ACTIVITY 5.2

Using a large blank sheet, create a mind map to chart Calvin's influence, featuring the personalities and theology of the Reformation; the growth of the Reformation; church life and civic life; and any other aspects that you think significant. Provide examples for the items you list.

The *Consensus Tigurinus* was published in 1551 after the Swiss churches had adopted the agreement; Calvin completed a French translation, while Bullinger worked on the German edition. The agreement was the fruit of several years of correspondence, Calvin's visit to Zurich and considerable diplomacy from Zurich and Genevan theologians. It is remarkable that Calvin and Bullinger signed their names to a joint statement on baptism and on the Eucharist. It was of sufficient international significance to influence the confessions of faith in Poland (1557), France (1559), Scotland (1560), and the Rhine Palatinate (1563).

The spread of Calvinism abroad

The spread of Calvinism abroad was facilitated by Calvin's success in Geneva. Calvin managed to 'present his Protestantism as vital to solving local political problems and securing social order'.[12] His achievements increased Geneva's international profile. Calvin and his followers clearly intended to spread their ideas beyond Geneva. A sermon delivered on 29 June 1562 was indicative of Calvin's ambitions; 'Let [God] work this miracle of grace not just here and for us, but for all people and nations of this earth.'[13]

Within Calvin's lifetime, missionaries were even sent to Brazil (in 1556). Similarly, Calvin's letters shows that he was not provincial in his aspirations. In addition to corresponding with key reformers like Bullinger and Bucer, Calvin sent letters and copies of his works to supporters in different countries ranging from Scotland to more distant Poland. In many respects, Geneva was operating as an international missionary centre. From a printing perspective, Laurent de Normandie's inventory numbered 35 000 books, including 10 000 books and pamphlets by Calvin, and Geneva had as many as 34 printing presses by the early 1560s. In 1559, the Genevan Academy opened as a seminary for trainee pastors, with Theodore Beza (1519–1605) as its first rector. Geneva gained the reputation as a 'Protestant Rome', and was visited by numerous Protestants and religious refugees.

The rise of international Calvinism also benefited from the growing divisions within Lutheranism, following Luther's death in 1546. The moderate Philippists followed Melanchthon who sought Protestant unity, whereas Gnesio-Lutherans led by Flacius Illyricus (1520–1575) upheld the purity of Luther's teaching. Calvinism did not suffer similar divisions thanks to the smooth succession from Calvin to Beza, who had arrived in Geneva in 1559 and lived until 1605. Calvin had called on the Company of Pastors to support Beza and not to introduce change. Beza did his part by writing Calvin's biography and editing a popular **hagiography** of Protestantism.

France

If we accept that Calvin 'understood clearly enough that different circumstances demanded a variety of approaches to church building', this was even truer of his followers abroad.[14] By the time Calvin was fully established, Geneva was filled with French refugees. With exiled printers and the Company of Pastors, Geneva was well placed to be a missionary church. In fact, in the Edict of Châteaubriand (1551), the French authorities identified Geneva as the key centre for printing Calvinist books. Robert Kingdon has contributed much to our understanding of how the Genevan Church assisted the Calvinist mission to France, which reached its climax in the early 1560s.[15] Yet developments took place in France that were independent of Geneva. Despite being the bastion of French Catholicism, 'it was Paris, not Geneva, which ignited the explosion'.[16]

In 1555, a Calvinist church was first established in Paris which included two noble pastors, François de Morel and Antoine de la Roche-Chandieu. Two years later, the disruption of a Calvinist prayer meeting by Catholics, known as the Rue St Jacques affair culminated in 130 arrests, including 30 nobles. The willingness of Calvinists, and indeed some nobles, to defy the Catholic authorities is further illustrated by the attendance of thousands at a public sermon in the Pré-aux-Clercs in 1558. The following year, Calvinists organised their first national synod, which was presided over by Pastor François de Morel. Seventy-two Calvinist churches were represented, and Calvin sent over a draft confession of faith (35 articles in total), which was largely accepted, albeit with slight modifications. Arriving late, Calvin's Genevan representative was rather overtaken by events. The confession of faith, already at variance with the Genevan Confession, was later modified in 1571 to form the Confession of La Rochelle. Significantly, the synod established the key structures of the Calvinist Church, ranging from the regional **colloques** to the provincial and national synods. The consistories inevitably formed the foundation of the entire Calvinist system and gave each community its separate identity and strength.

The rise of Calvinism took place in spite of the Catholic regime's determined attempts to suppress it, as evidenced by the Edict of Écouen and the execution of Anne du Bourg, a member of the Paris Parlement, both in 1559. The late 1550s and early 1560s saw an 'explosion of Calvinist conversions'.[17] Louis, Prince of Condé, estimated a figure of 2150 churches for the year 1562, though the more recent estimate of 1750 seems more accurate.[18]

ACTIVITY 5.3

Chart the rise of Calvinism in France using a timeline. Pick out the main *persons* involved in one colour and the *events* in another colour, and do your own research to add detailed information boxes on each.

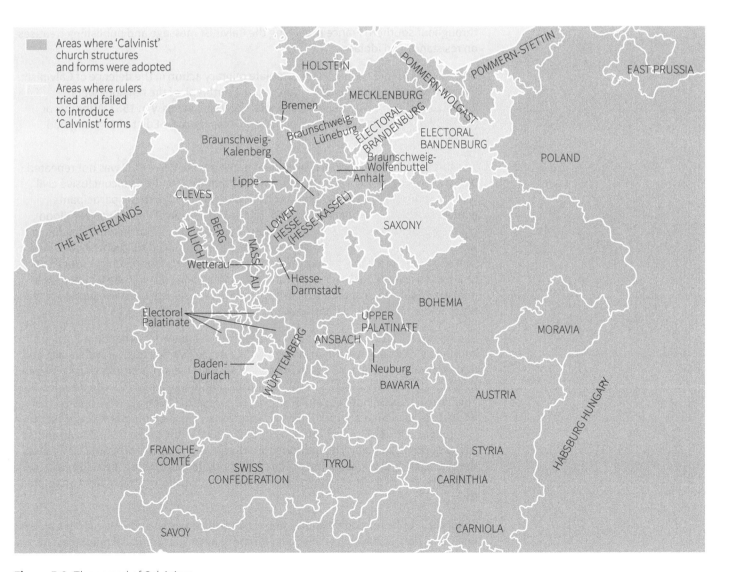

Figure 5.2: The spread of Calvinism

French Calvinism spread for numerous reasons. In addition to Genevan support, Calvinist preachers contributed greatly and their itinerancy was vital in allowing more remote communities to hear the message. Pierre Viret travelled throughout the Midi (the south), especially Nîmes, Montpellier and Lyon, while Jean le Masson preached in communities from the Pyrenees to Carcassonne and then to Montauban between 1555 and 1570. Noble support gave Calvinism confidence and greater security. Jeanne d'Albret, the Queen of Navarre, converted in 1560, while Louis, the Prince de Condé and a prince of the blood, became the official protector of the **Huguenot** Church. Huguenot numbers increased to 10% of the population. French Calvinism represented a cross-section of society, though 50% were nobles. The one exception was in the Cévennes where commercial links with Nîmes had stimulated a rural industry. Calvinism thrived in urban communities with numerous converts from merchants, craftsmen, doctors, and the local elites, especially lawyers and notaries.

With increasing support, Calvinists became more militant. There were riots in Rouen and La Rochelle as early as 1560, and iconoclasm spread in that decade, often incited by preaching. Calvinism took hold in many southern towns, such as Castres, Nîmes and Montauban, as early as 1561. Calvin favoured restraint and hesitated to support armed resistance, but he was overtaken by events. Condé and Beza supported the plan to seize the young king Francis II, known as the Conspiracy of Amboise (1560), while Calvin distanced himself from the project. A more powerful voice in France came from Pierre Viret (1511–1571). Initially based in Lausanne, from 1559 Viret travelled throughout southern France preaching the Calvinist message and publishing treatises on resistance and idolatry.

Beza was also more willing to contemplate military action in the defence of Calvinism. Growing religious tensions contributed to the outbreak of the religious wars, which were triggered by the massacre of Protestants at Vassy in 1562. Attempts at reconciliation, illustrated by the Colloquy of Poissy and the Edict of January, had failed.

The surge in Huguenot popularity evident in the period 1559–1562 was not repeated but the years 1570–1572 provided renewed optimism. After three inconclusive civil wars, Beza presided over the Synod of La Rochelle in 1571, and the participants agreed on a confession of faith resembling the Confession of Flemish and Walloon churches drafted at Emden that year. The Huguenots were granted some freedom of worship, as well as four garrison towns (*places de sûreté*), and Huguenot nobles had signed a treaty of mutual support with William of Orange. Admiral Coligny was now Charles IX's favoured adviser and he planned to reconcile the warring factions via a joint expedition against the Spanish Netherlands. With Dutch Calvinist support, the prospects were good and Charles was interested.

Catholics were less enthusiastic and suspicious of a broader international Calvinist conspiracy. Tensions were high in August 1572 as the kingdom's leading Calvinist and Catholic nobles attended the festivities that followed the symbolic marriage between the Protestant Henri de Navarre and the King's Catholic sister Marguerite de Valois. The Catholic Guises opted to strike and on 22 August 1572 Coligny was the victim of a failed assassination attempt. This was followed by a pre-emptive strike against the Huguenots, with 2000 slaughtered in Paris, and 3000 in the provinces. While in earlier decades Calvinism had spread throughout Normandy, Picardy and the Île-de-France, the events of 1572 led to a drastic reduction of Huguenots in those areas. Some Calvinists recanted, others went underground or into exile, and the majority migrated south.

Given the number of noble deaths – Henri de Navarre was spared – Huguenot survival is striking. Calvinist authors called for resistance against a tyrannical monarchy. Beza's *On the Right of Magistrates* and Philippe du Plessis-Mornay's (1549–1623) *Vindiciae contra Tyrannos* declared that resistance was legitimate as long as the magistrates coordinated it. Cities controlled by Protestants entered a state of official warfare with the King. In 1574, a Huguenot constitution was published, which openly rejected the monarchy, though southern France did not develop a separate state or become a Huguenot republic, as Janine Garrison has suggested.[19] Such was their strength that only four years after the massacres, the Huguenots were given even greater religious concessions at the Peace of Monsieur, negotiated by the King's brother the duc d'Alençon. This led to the formation of a Catholic League, whose objective was the expulsion of heresy.

While France enjoyed relative peace between 1577 and 1584, the death of Alençon in 1584 triggered a major religious and constitutional crisis because the heir to the throne was now the Protestant first prince of the blood, Henri de Navarre. This led to the re-formation of the Catholic League, which secured Treaty of Joinville with Spain (1584). Paris was seized by Catholic radicals, known as the *Seize* because they divided the capital into 16 districts for administrative purposes. The Day of the Barricades (1588) persuaded Henri III to flee Paris for his own security. He then felt sufficiently insecure and humiliated by the war hero Henri de Guise to order his assassination and that of his brother the Cardinal de Lorraine. In response, the Catholic League gained numerous new adherents, particularly in the northern towns and Henri III was forced to make an alliance with Henri de Navarre. Within a year, Henri himself was assassinated and the Catholic League now fought Henri de Navarre for the throne.

In July 1593, Henri IV abjured Calvinism at the cathedral of St Denis, and he took control of Paris in March 1594. While the Huguenots felt uncertain about their future, their anxiety was lessened by the implementation of the Edict of Nantes (1598). Although this dictated that the Catholic Mass should be restored everywhere, the edict granted considerable concessions to the Huguenots, as well as 100 garrison towns. This was followed by a period of relative peace and coexistence, until Louis XIII provoked a second phase of religious wars with his restoration of Catholicism in Béarn. The later wars lasted for seven years, and included the demise of Montauban, La Rochelle, and Nîmes. The fall of La Rochelle in 1629 culminated in the Peace of Alès and the loss of Huguenot political privileges. Religious toleration came to an end later with the revocation of the Edict of Nantes in 1685 by Louis XIV, who outlawed Protestantism, resulting in the emigration of 200 000 Huguenots.

England

Calvin's ideas became prevalent in Elizabethan England and persisted into the reigns of the early Stuarts. Owing to the large Protestant exile communities in England, especially in London, one could hear Protestant sermons in English, Latin, French, Flemish, Italian and even Spanish. A Reformed theology of grace emphasising predestination was consistent with most branches of English Protestantism. The links between English and continental Protestantism were strengthened during Mary Tudor's reign, as many English Protestants went into exile in Protestant towns such as Frankfurt, Strasbourg, Zurich, Geneva and Emden.[20]

One of Calvin's followers in England was William Whittingham, who is considered the 'first Englishman who can be called a Calvinist' – he was later appointed dean of Durham.[21] Calvin ordained Whittingham and his Calvinist credentials were reinforced by his contribution to the Geneva Bible of 1560. In spite of its **episcopal structure**, England was one of the largest markets for Calvin's writings in the later 1500s. English readers had an 'almost insatiable appetite for Calvin's works'; 50 editions of Calvin's works were published in Elizabeth I's reign.[22] While Genevan Calvinists recognised the strategic importance of Protestant England, English Protestants showed solidarity with international Protestants, especially in London, by becoming actively involved in the affairs of the 'stranger' churches (the exile communities).

ACTIVITY 5.4

Using this section and your wider reading, account for Huguenot survival in the period 1563–1598. You may wish to consider the following themes: noble and urban support for Calvinism; the resilience of the Calvinist movement; divisions within Catholicism; monarchical weaknesses; geographical factors; foreign intervention in the civil wars.

Key Term

An **episcopal structure** represents the administration of the Church by bishops. While this was the norm in the Roman Catholic Church, the spread of Calvinism beyond Geneva led to different types of church structures, though the majority abandoned the use of bishops.

While English Calvinists have been described as a partisan cause outside the mainstream of English society, the reception of Calvinism in Elizabethan and Jacobean England was more broadly based. Even elements of the Elizabethan Settlement contained interpretations of salvation, faith, grace and predestination that were 'consistent with the Reformed consensus on these matters and directly indebted to specific Reformed sources at some points'.[23]

English Calvinism was not necessarily the same as Puritanism: few Elizabethans referred more frequently to Calvin to support his arguments than Archbishop John Whitgift, an outspoken Puritan opponent. Whitgift and his Puritan adversary Thomas Cartwright both quoted Calvin frequently, though English theologians were equally likely to reference Heinrich Bullinger. In any case, with Calvin's death in 1564, Calvinism no longer necessarily signified Calvin or Geneva, but instead a rather loose alliance of Calvinist churches, universities and academies in Europe. While Calvinist theologians certainly existed in England, such as William Whitaker, William Fulke, Laurence Chaderton, William Perkins and John Reynolds, there were many other authors, theologians and ministers who appropriated Calvinist ideas without considering themselves to be Calvinist.

Scotland

The links between Geneva and Scotland were embodied in John Knox, who had visited Geneva, describing it as the 'most perfect school of Christ'.[24] Elizabeth I's accession in November 1558 opened up new possibilities, an opportunity seized by Knox himself. In May 1559, Knox delivered a sermon in which he advocated an anti-French, anti-papal and pro-English alliance. Several months later, in July 1559, a Protestant 'Congregation', representing a cross-section of society from nobles to townspeople, seized various towns in central Scotland and entered the capital Edinburgh, where Knox was installed as the first Protestant minister. The regent was deposed in October 1559 and Scotland's rebellion was strengthened by the arrival of English troops in March 1560. A Reformation Parliament was convened and met in August 1560, and the rejection of papal authority, the abolition of the Mass and the adoption of a Calvinist confession of faith were enshrined in law. While Mary Stuart returned from France in 1561 following the death of her husband François II, she later fled to England in 1568. This was a rather peculiar revolution, since not a single major office in either the executive or judicial functions of government changed hands; for example, the Earl of Huntly, the greatest Catholic magnate in Scotland, remained as Chancellor.

John Knox was the driving force behind the religious changes. Where Calvin had earlier counselled caution, Knox declared that it was entirely justifiable to resist idolatrous rulers. Between 1559 and 1560, the Catholic Church was dismantled and iconoclastic disturbances became widespread, though there was fierce resistance to Calvinism from some nobles and especially northern Scotland's rural inhabitants so Catholicism was not completely eradicated.

Knox was the only Scottish Calvinist with direct experience of Geneva, and realised the importance of enforcing Calvinism at parish level. The *First Book of Discipline*, presented in January 1561, was composed by the 'six Johns' (Douglas, Winram, Row, Knox, Willock and Spottiswoode). Calvinism gained aristocratic support, the most influential being Lord James Stewart, the Earl of Moray. In addition to appointing George Buchanan as principal of St Leonard's in 1566 at the University of St Andrews, Moray was one of very few Scottish nobles who acted as if he believed in international Calvinism. St Andrews became a vital centre for Scottish Calvinism, so when Andrew Melville returned to Scotland in 1574 after visits to Paris and Geneva he was, by 1580, appointed principal of the university's theological faculty, St Mary's College; Melville's 'most significant contribution lay in the reorganisation of St Mary's as the major seminary in Scotland'.[25]

The Calvinist Church was largely successful in establishing an effective ministry, even though this took at least 40 years to achieve. From the 1630s onwards, the Scottish Kirk (as the Church was known) was organised by Presbyters (elders) rather than bishops, following the Genevan model. A clear Church structure was established, ranging from the Kirk Session, to presbyteries, synods and then the General Assembly. While 17th-century Scotland had become a Calvinist nation, 'there is little doubt that the nobility rather than the clergy were the key instruments in the course of the Scottish Revolution'.[26] This is especially demonstrated by the National Covenant of 1638, known as the 'noblemen's covenant', in which nobles promised to protect the Church.

The Netherlands

During the 1550s, Calvinism appeared in the French-speaking provinces closest to France and spread to the northern provinces of Brabant and Flanders. As in France, the first Reformed Church in Antwerp was founded in 1555, yet the key missionary centre for Dutch Calvinism was not Geneva. Before 1566, only 12 out of 84 preachers active in the southern Netherlands had links with Geneva. Instead the town of Emden provided refuge and counsel, and a key printing industry in northwestern Europe after 1553; the first Dutch translation of Calvin's *Institutes* was published in Emden in 1560.

There were further differences between the Netherlands and Geneva. The Reformed Church order in the Low Countries was not based on the *Ecclesiastical Ordinances*, which were not published until the 1560s in the Netherlands. The Dutch Church Order was written by John à Lasco, and subsequently revised by Jan Utenhove and Martin Micronius. Discipline was also a feature of the Dutch Reformed churches.

The rise of Calvinism in the Netherlands took place within the context of considerable religious and political conflict. In the early years of his reign, Philip II provoked tensions by creating new bishoprics in 1561, even though this made strategic sense and was driven by the objective of supervising clerical reform and the campaign against heresy. But these initiatives were unpopular: noble families feared a loss of control; abbots resisted the anticipated loss of monastic properties that would be used to endow the new bishoprics; and many magistrates refused to allow the bishops within the city walls. The nobility were apprehensive about the appointment of Antoine Perrenot de Granvelle as Archbishop of Mechelen, even more so when his elevation to the Cardinalate meant that he took precedence over the leading Dutch nobles, notably William of Nassau, Prince of Orange (1533–1584).

Philip's failure to visit the Netherlands exacerbated an already tense situation, especially given that his natural supporters, the Dutch aristocracy, felt alienated. At the same time, they were expected to defend Catholicism and suppress Calvinism. Living in the Netherlands had taught the nobles that compromise was a political necessity. In 1565, aristocratic sentiment was such that 400 nobles signed a petition for the relaxation of the heresy laws. While Philip deliberated, thousands of Calvinists flocked to the countryside to hear sermons; this hedge preaching, as it was known, clearly illustrated how powerful the movement was becoming. On 10 August 1566, sermons gave way to widespread iconoclasm, especially in the Flanders textile district; over 400 Catholic churches were sacked in two weeks in Flanders alone. In that year, there were already Calvinist churches in the chief Walloon towns and Ghent, Bruges and Hondschoote in Flanders.

The Duke of Alba

In response, Philip sent the Duke of Alba to the Netherlands, accompanied by 10 000 troops. He established a Council of Troubles to eliminate Calvinism by force. Although partly successful, Alba was unable to suppress the movement, even though many Calvinist leaders fled to the Holy Roman Empire, Emden and England. The survival of Dutch Calvinism owed much to their Church structures, which included consistories

ACTIVITY 5.5

As you work through this section, draw up a timeline in three columns to analyse the rise of Dutch Calvinism. In the central column, chart the main events in the Netherlands. Use the left-hand column to note Calvinist influences from and events in Switzerland and France, and the right-hand column to record influences from and events in Spain.

on a parish level, the *classis* that served the same function as the French *colloque*, together with provincial and national synods.

William of Orange coordinated Dutch Calvinism from the late 1560s onwards and was ably assisted by the scholar-statesman Philippe van Marnix Sainte Aldegonde, who had spent some time in Geneva. Philippe became a key propagandist for the cause, and his brother Jean was a military commander who died in the early stages of Revolt. The coordination of different Dutch Calvinist communities, included those in exile in Heidelberg and Frankenthal, was facilitated by the organisation of a general synod in Emden in 1571; by that stage, there were only 16 Calvinist 'Churches under the cross' left in all the Netherlands suggesting that Alba's repression was not altogether unsuccessful.

With Orange's withdrawal to the Holy Roman Empire in 1568, the resistance of the Calvinist privateers, known as the Sea Beggars, helped Dutch Calvinism to survive. They disrupted Spanish trade, especially in the Channel, and were a major obstacle to Alba's restoration of royal authority. The Spanish regime lacked money, so Alba tried to collect a tenth-penny tax in 1572 which was badly received in the Netherlands. The Sea Beggars, who seized the port of Brill in the same year, exploited this effectively. Many exiles returned, including William of Orange, who now officially converted to Calvinism. In defence of traditional liberties, Orange favoured religious toleration.

During the years 1572–1576, the Dutch Revolt was confined to Holland and Zeeland, and rebel access to the sea was vital. The Spanish were set back by their financial troubles. The declaration of bankruptcy in 1575 in Castile meant that there were insufficient funds to pay Spanish troops in the Netherlands. Out of frustration, in July 1576, Spanish soldiers sacked Antwerp, resulting in the death of 8000 civilians and burning of 1000 houses. The Spanish 'Fury' united loyalist (Spain's natural allies) and rebel deputies, who signed the Pacification of Ghent in November 1576, in which the signatories agreed to expel all Spaniards from the country.

Spain's position later improved, thanks to the appointment as governor of Alessandro Farnese, Duke of Parma (1545–1592), who took control of Spanish forces in 1578. Farnese exploited the divisions between radical Calvinists and more moderate Catholic nobles in the French-speaking provinces. Although some Catholics favoured religious toleration, they were horrified by the violent suppression of Catholicism in Ghent and other cities. In January 1579, the Calvinists in the northern provinces strengthened their position by establishing the Union of Utrecht, which protected Calvinism and prohibited Catholicism. In May 1579, a counter-alliance was formed by Farnese, known as the Union of Arras.

Farnese made significant military progress, seizing an increasing number of towns including Antwerp in 1585. Yet Calvinism survived because Philip insisted that Farnese should lead several military expeditions to France against the Protestant Henri de Navarre in the early 1590s. By 1585, the Dutch States General had also concluded a treaty with England, which brought much-needed military and financial assistance to the cause. Dutch Calvinists were also expertly led by Johan van Oldenbarnevelt, chief legal adviser to the States of Holland (1586–1618) and Maurice of Nassau (1567–1625), William of Orange's son, an able strategist and innovator in military tactics.

By 1600, Calvinists were the dominant force in the northern provinces of the Netherlands, and their position was sufficiently entrenched that war with Spain continued until 1648, despite the signing of the Twelve Years' Truce in 1609. Yet Calvinists were never an absolute majority in the United Provinces. The Genevan model could not be replicated, as an uneasy coexistence with Catholics and Anabaptists was the norm in the Netherlands. As Carlos Eire has argued, 'ironically, then, an officially Calvinist state became the most tolerant place in all of Europe, proving that Calvinism was not necessarily intolerant and inflexible, but rather quite adaptable'.[27]

In the 17th century, the Synod of Dort (1618) marked the triumph of Calvinist theology within Dutch Protestantism, though divisions remained. Jacob Arminius (1560–1609) had adopted a more flexible stance on predestination. In 1610, his followers (Arminians) summarised their beliefs in a treatise entitled *The Remonstrance*, a document that was strongly rejected by the Counter-Remonstrants who reaffirmed double predestination.

Central Europe

Calvinism enjoyed some success in those regions that were politically fragmented or lacked strong centralising monarchies, and where it gained protection from local rulers. These territories represented widely dispersed 'Calvinist islands'.[28] This was evident both in the Holy Roman Empire as well as in Eastern Europe.

Germany

Calvinism made initial progress in the territories neighbouring France and the Netherlands, gaining followers in Anhalt, Hesse and in the Upper Palatinate. The rise of Calvinism can partly be explained by Lutheranism's weaknesses. Despite gaining recognition within the Empire in the Peace of Augsburg (1555), Lutheran theologians became increasingly disillusioned by the state of their own Church. Lutheran visitations revealed non-attendance at church and relative ignorance of basic Lutheran teachings. The Lutheran **Formula of Concord** (1577) forced Protestants to choose sides and ensured that there would be little chance of future cooperation between Lutherans and Calvinists; the theological differences made reconciliation unlikely. In fact, some of the Philippists, the followers of Melanchthon, became crypto-Calvinists and later Calvinists in towns such as Wittenberg, Hamburg, Bremen, Heidelberg and Breslau.

The shift from Lutheranism to Calvinism was evident among the princes. Strikingly nobles converted from Lutheranism to Calvinism when they had already appropriated former church lands and had direct control over their church, as well as enjoying the protection of the 1555 Peace of Augsburg. Henry Cohn has clearly outlined their importance; 'the hallmark of Calvinism in the Empire was the leading part played from the outset by princely rulers'.[29] The control of religion allowed rulers to strengthen their authority over the state, even though the economic benefits were less than expected. Calvinism was partly instrumental in the creation of a more absolutist style of government. There were also few Calvinist urban Reformations owing to the Peace of Augsburg (1555), which meant that cities became politically weaker than the princes, and there was greater pressure to observe imperial laws. Individuals with Calvinist sympathies were more likely to move to the courts and universities of princes willing to overlook the Peace of Augsburg.

The Palatinate was the most important part of the Empire to convert. The Wittelsbach rulers who adopted Calvinism provided a real haven for the Reformed cause. They supervised the rise of Heidelberg University, which ultimately outshone even Geneva, and directed the formulation of the Heidelberg Catechism and Church Order (both published in 1563), which helped to shape the development of international Calvinism. Elector Frederick III (r1559–1576) introduced Calvinism when it had no legal standing in the Empire due to the Peace of Augsburg.

In addition to the university, Heidelberg had a printing industry (publishing the first German edition of Calvin's works) and the Wittelsbachs founded the famous Bibliotheca Palatina. The Palatinate became a model for other German Calvinist churches, in which Kaspar Olevianus played a significant role. He convinced the authorities to adopt consistorial excommunication. In his preface to the Heidelberg

ACTIVITY 5.6

Using this section and your own further reading, assess the extent to which the development of Calvinism in the Netherlands was helped and/or hindered by the fact that it was a Spanish territory.

 Key term

Lutherans subscribed to the **Formula of Concord** in 1577, though this confession of faith was published in 1580, on the fiftieth anniversary of the Augsburg Confession. The composition of the Formula of Concord was largely motivated by an attempt to bring to an end decades of internal divisions within Lutheranism. The 13 articles encouraged greater unity within Lutheranism, facilitating a more effective response to Calvinist and radical threats throughout Europe.

Catechism, Frederick emphasised the importance of religious uniformity, and even participated in an iconoclastic tour of the provinces in 1565. He also provided military assistance to his co-religionists in France and in the Netherlands, and his troops were commanded by his younger sons John Casimir and Christopher. While Frederick's eldest son Louis VI (r1576–1583) restored Lutheranism, John Casimir later acted as regent of the Palatinate for his nephew and reinstated Calvinism. Yet the military defeat of Elector Frederick V at the battle of White Mountain in 1620 ensured that he lost his Bohemian crown and Heidelberg itself fell to a Spanish army two years later.

While in Brandenburg the Lutheran ruler Johann Sigismund converted to Calvinism, electoral Saxony came under Calvinist influence during 1571–1574 and 1586–1591. By 1605, a number of smaller principalities adopted Calvinism, such as Nassau-Dillenburg in the Wetterau, Lippe (except for the Lutheran city of Lemgo), Zweibrücken, Baden-Durlach and Hesse-Kassel. Estimates suggest that one out of the 16 million inhabitants in the German lands were Reformed Calvinists by 1618. By 1620, two out of the four lay electors of the Empire, Brandenburg and Palatinate, were Calvinist, as were five dukes in Silesia and one in Anhalt, the landgrave of Hesse-Kassel, 17 imperial counts, the imperial cities of Bremen and Colmar and the territorial town of Emden. These Calvinist territories contributed to the foundation of the three Reformed universities of Heidelberg, Marburg and Frankfurt an der Oder, and the Reformed academies of Herborn and Bremen.

Eastern Europe

The Calvinist faith spread rapidly in Eastern Europe in the late 1500s, but only in Hungary did it survive in the longer term. As in the Holy Roman Empire, the political

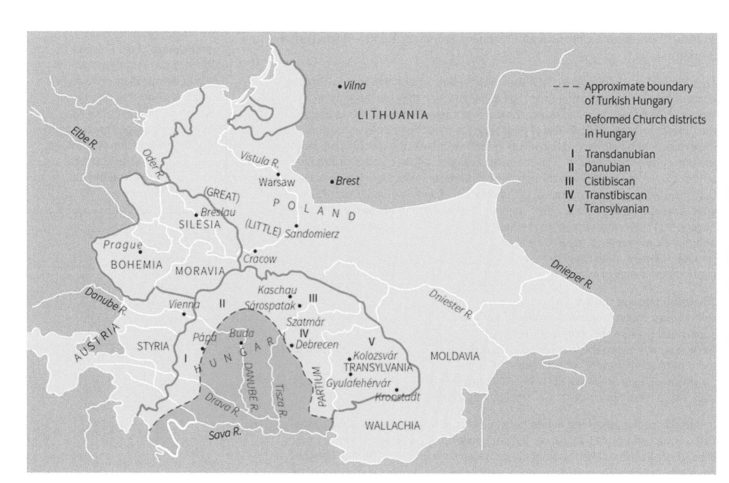

Figure 5.3: The spread of Calvinism in Eastern Europe

conditions were favourable: 'The power of the nobility and relative weakness of the crowns also offered noble converts or privileged communities unusual latitude to found new congregations or experiment with new forms of worship.'[30]

Poland-Lithuania

In the kingdom of Poland and the Grand Duchy of Lithuania, Calvinism found fertile soil owing to the existence of a weak monarchy and powerful nobility. The Grand Duchy of Lithuania was a religiously diverse state that included Orthodox Christians, Jews, Lutherans, and Anabaptists. Religious toleration was observed and made law in 1573. At its peak, 45% of nobles were Calvinist, and between 20% and 25% of the population.

While there were 400 Calvinist churches in Lithuania, there was approximately half that number in Poland. John à Lasco (1499–1560), who had established a Calvinist Church in Emden and an exile church in London, helped to spread Calvinism in Poland. Internal divisions over the Trinity and a vigorous Counter-Reformation (driven by Cardinal Stanislas Hosius and the Jesuits) checked Protestant expansion. Yet the Warsaw Confederation of 1573 allowed Polish nobles to retain Protestant churches on their lands. Furthermore, 36 out of the 69 members of the upper house of the Polish Diet were Protestants (28 of them being Reformed).

Hungary

Habsburg-ruled Hungary, including Moravia and Transylvania, was very receptive to Calvinism, in spite of Habsburg hostility. A Czech nobleman, Karel de Zerotin, arrived in Geneva in 1582, returned to central Europe and became governor of Moravia. He established Calvinist churches, which were later challenged by the Habsburg restoration of Catholicism in the Thirty Years War. Calvinism grew in response to fears of the Counter-Reformation under Cardinal Martinuzzi, insecurity regarding the Ottomans, and anti-Habsburg sentiments. Protestantism became a 'vehicle for the aristocracy to assert their autonomy against the Habsburgs'.[31]

Hungarian Calvinism originated from Basle and Zurich, rather than Geneva (though Moravia seems to be an exception); Beza knew no one in Hungary when he appealed for funds on behalf of Geneva in 1592. The Second Helvetic Confession was introduced at Debrecen in 1567, completing a process largely accomplished by the synods of Tarcal and Torda, held in the years 1562–1563. Hungarian Calvinism survived despite the movement's internal tensions and its conflict with Lutheranism. In the end, Hungarian Calvinism adopted an episcopal structure, and Reformed Protestants made up between 40% and 45% of the Hungarian population. By 1564, most of the Hungarian nobility was Reformed, though among the highest echelons of the aristocracy, three out of 36 magnates who sat in the upper house of the Hungarian Diet were Protestant. By 1570, most noblemen and magistrates in market towns were Reformed.

In eastern Hungary, Calvinists led successful resistance against the Jesuits in Transylvania, though the western and northwestern regions had no Protestant organisations until 1576. Habsburg pressure for a Counter-Reformation provoked a rising in 1604 under István Bocskai, the first Reformed prince of Transylvania. By 1608, Protestants had gained full constitutional recognition, which was supported by Bethlen Gábor, who ruled in the years 1613–1629. The Calvinist clergy gained the guarantee of full tax exemption in 1614, and the grant of hereditary nobility by 1629.[32] In later years, the monarchy, with Jesuit help, successfully converted Calvinist nobles, partly by promising them quality education in Jesuit schools. A royal edict of 1668 made it a capital crime for Catholics to abandon the faith. The Habsburgs acquired Transylvania in the early 1690s and Calvinism went back on the defensive.

Religious war in Germany and the death of Luther

Charles V's preoccupations in the early 1540s

Religious war in Germany could not take place until Charles V was at peace elsewhere. In the early 1540s, Charles was preoccupied with the Habsburg–Valois Wars. Francis I had launched a three-pronged offensive against Catalonia, Milan, and Antwerp and Louvain. In 1542, Francis I's forces overran Luxemburg and a Franco-Turkish fleet captured Nice. Although the French had little military success and Charles remained the dominant power on the Italian peninsula, Charles was preoccupied with this war and unable to focus on the Holy Roman Empire. The Peace of Crépy, signed in 1544, brought a temporary end to the Habsburg–Valois struggles the treaty stipulated that France should not make any alliances with German Protestant princes.

Further afield, Charles and his brother Ferdinand faced the threat of Ottoman expansion in the Mediterranean and in Eastern Europe. Suleiman the Magnificent's alliance with Barbarossa strengthened his fleet and made the Ottomans a threat to Charles in the western Mediterranean, especially when Suleiman was granted access to French ports. An attempt by Charles to seize Algiers in 1541 was a total failure and came to nothing, allowing the Barbary pirates the freedom to devastate the coastal economy.

Charles V largely failed to contain the Muslim threat in the Mediterranean because he could not seize and retain the North African ports. Throughout the 1530s and early 1540s, Suleiman also consolidated his position in Eastern Europe, especially in Hungary. Although Vienna itself was not directly threatened after 1532, Ottoman presence in Europe also prevented Charles from dealing with German problems. The truce of 1547, signed between the Habsburgs and the Ottomans, secured central Hungary for the Turks, established Transylvania as an independent state under Turkish rule, in exchange for Ferdinand's control of western Hungary and an annual tribute paid by the Habsburgs.

War as a last resort and Protestant survival

With the failure of religious compromise in the 1540s, the Emperor was left with only one viable option, the use of force. In 1542, Charles was confronted with the Schmalkaldic League's occupation of Brunswick, a duchy previously controlled by the Catholic Duke Henry V. The League considered extending its membership to the Duke

Voices from the past

Abraham Scultetus, court preacher at Heidelberg

I cannot fail to recall the optimistic mood which I and many others felt when we considered the condition of the Reformed churches in 1591. In France there ruled the valiant King Henri IV, in England the mighty Queen Elizabeth, in Scotland the learned King James, in the Palatinate the bold hero John Casimir, in Saxony the courageous and powerful Elector Christian I, in Hesse the clever and prudent Landgrave William, who were all inclined to the Reformed religion. In the Netherlands everything went as Prince Maurice of Orange wished, when he took Breda, Zutphen, Hulst and Nijmegen. But what entered our heads? We imagined that a golden

age had dawned. But this was folly, for within twelve months, the elector of Saxony, the count Palatine, and the landgrave of Hesse all died, King Henri of France deserted the true faith, and all our golden hopes went up in smoke.[33]

Using this extract and your broader reading, answer the following questions:

1. What evidence was there for princely support of Calvinism in Europe?
2. What impact did this have on society and ordinary people?
3. What was the interplay between princely allegiance to Calvinism and the doctrine of predestination?

of Cleves, who occupied part of the Low Countries with French assistance. Charles responded by assembling an army in 1543 and quickly overcame the duchy, forcing the Duke to renounce his claims. Thereafter, events abroad changed to the extent that Charles V found himself in a stronger position, enabling him to put pressure on the German princes.

Charles benefited from a changing political climate. In October 1545, the Turks agreed to a truce because they were threatened by war in Persia and by a dynastic dispute. In 1544, the Peace of Crépy with France removed one of the most important threats to Charles V. At the same time, England and France were now engaged in a bitter war. In early 1547, both Henry VIII and Francis I died, further strengthening Charles V's hand. So Charles decided to confront the Schmalkaldic League on the battlefield. While Charles V persuaded the Swiss to remain neutral, Pope Paul III offered 12 000 soldiers and a loan of 200 000 crowns for Charles to fight the German Protestants.

Within the Empire, the Catholic duke of Bavaria was won over to the Emperor's side, guaranteeing the passage of imperial troops through Bavaria. Of greater significance was the reconciliation of Duke Maurice of Saxony to the Emperor's side. He was promised the electoral title if he supported Charles with troops and cash. When Charles returned to the Empire in 1545, he implied that he would resume religious negotiations. He granted concessions to the original 14 Protestant cities of 1529, provoking divisions within Protestantism. In truth, he was concealing his military preparations. The Schmalkaldic League, disaffected by Philip of Hesse's bigamous marriage, was relatively unprepared. These changing fortunes were exacerbated by Luther's death in February 1546. Despite its progress, suddenly Lutheranism appeared vulnerable and its survival was under threat.

The First Schmalkaldic War

In the First Schmalkaldic War, Charles V's forces defeated the Schmalkaldic League at the Battle of Mühlberg in April 1547. Wittenberg surrendered, John Frederick was taken prisoner, Philip of Hesse's fortresses were dismantled and Maurice of Saxony became the new elector of Saxony. Following the Mühlberg victory, Charles V imposed the Augsburg Interim in 1548. Although Protestants were offered minor concessions, including clerical marriage, and communion in both kinds, it was a hard-line Catholic religious settlement. The seven sacraments and the Latin Mass were restored and transubstantiation was retained. The Protestants were profoundly affected by the combined impact of Luther's death and their military defeat.

Figure 5.4: Charles V, by Titian

However, Charles V's military successes were short-lived. There was growing opposition to the Habsburgs and the princes began to desert the Emperor's cause. Maurice of Saxony, fearing for his own position, owing to his betrayal of John Frederick, distanced himself from Charles V. Maurice was as successful in choosing the right moment to abandon Charles as he had been to desert the Schmalkaldic League. The implications of Maurice's decision were far-reaching, enabling 'German Protestantism to snatch victory from the jaws of their defeat'.[34]

Charles V's failure to consolidate his military victory at Mühlberg was testimony to the Protestantism's insurmountable strength by the mid-1540s. There had been considerable resistance to the Interim. In Magdeburg, Matthias Flacius (1520–1575) led Lutheran clerical opposition and his position was greatly strengthened by Duke Maurice's decision to abandon the Emperor. Although the negotiations at Augsburg in 1547 offered Charles an opportunity to consolidate his power, they revealed that anti-Habsburg antagonism was too deep-seated. Bavaria went back to its natural opposition to the Habsburgs, especially since Charles V had not properly rewarded its contribution.

Charles V proposed to establish a new League to preserve peace, but this was viewed as a cynical enterprise to strengthen the Habsburgs. There was increasing hostility to the imperial garrisons in the Empire. Though few in numbers, they created an impression of the Empire being occupied. The hatred was directed at Spaniards, and increasingly focused on Charles himself, who refused to listen to the Diet's complaints. At this time, Charles also faced dynastic problems. He tried to put forward his son, Philip, as Ferdinand's successor. This caused tensions with the princes and with Ferdinand himself, whose son Maximilian was the next heir, further weakening Charles V's position.

The resurgence of Charles V's external problems and the Second Schmalkaldic War

There were also tensions between Charles and the papacy. While Charles wanted to convene a Church council, Paul III refused to manage the Council according to Charles's objectives. While Paul III favoured the restatement of Catholic doctrine, Charles, with his eye on wavering Lutherans, required discreet silence on doctrinal matters to maintain political unity. Charles V's concessions to the 14 Lutheran cities had also offended the Pope. Charles V's prestige abroad was rapidly waning. By 1550, the war between England and France had come to an end and it was anticipated that this peace would be followed by war with the Emperor. Simultaneously, the Ottomans advanced again in Hungary.

In 1552, the Treaty of Chambord was signed between German princes and Henri II, the new French King. Henri II intervened in German affairs as the champion of national liberties against the Emperor. Charles V's attempts to besiege Metz failed in 1553, indicating the extent of his powerlessness. The Habsburgs were forced to sign the humiliating Treaty of Passau, drafted by Elector Maurice of Saxony and Ferdinand. Maurice demanded security against Habsburg aggression, the restoration of princely privileges and a guarantee for the Lutheran religion, irrespective of the Council of Trent's proceedings. After Passau, Charles V empowered his brother Ferdinand to settle the religious question with an Imperial Diet.

The Peace of Augsburg (1555) and the abdication of Charles V

Despite the existence of a Catholic majority, Protestants were a sufficiently strong political force to pressurise the Imperial Diet. They forced Ferdinand to recognise the Lutheran Confession of Augsburg and the following terms were also signed: security was granted to all Lutheran princes; episcopal jurisdiction in their lands was to cease; Lutherans were no longer subject to heresy laws, nor subject to Church jurisdiction; they were allowed to retain all ecclesiastical property secularised before the Treaty of Passau (1552). For the future, each territorial secular prince was allowed to choose between the Catholic and Lutheran faiths, and his decision was to bind all his subjects (hence, the phrase *cuius regio eius religio*, translated as 'his the territory, his the religion'). The Lutheran confession was thereby placed on the same legal footing as Catholicism, though equality was not extended to Calvinism, Zwinglianism or Anabaptism.

The Peace of Augsburg did not symbolise religious tolerance; it was a legal and political compromise between two sides exhausted by war. Although this granted Lutheranism official religious and legal recognition within the Empire, it was testimony to how political the movement had become. German territorial princes had gained mastery over the Church as well as the state. By mid-century, the leadership of the Reformation movement was firmly in the hands of the princes. However, even the princes were restricted to Roman Catholicism or Lutheranism. In the preceding 25 years, every conceivable means of restoring religious unity had been exhaustively tried out. The peace transformed the Empire from a religious entity into a political alliance, diminishing with it Habsburg and the Catholic Church's authority. It was intended as a provisional solution, yet remained imperial law for over two centuries. Soon after the Peace of Augsburg, Charles relinquished his power in the Netherlands (1555) and in Spain (1556), abdicating in favour of his son Philip. Charles then retired to the monastery of Yuste in Estremadura, Spain.

Practice essay question

With reference to these sources and your understanding of the historical context, assess the value of these three sources to an historian studying the strengths and weaknesses of Calvinism.

Extract A: Theodore Beza, *Life and Death of John Calvin*

And it was not without cause that every man had his refuge to him: for God had adorned him so wise and good counsel, that never man repented him of the following of it, but I have known many fall into great and extreme inconveniences which would not believe him. This has been found so by many experiences and proofs, namely in the seditions which happened in the years 1548, 1554 and 1555 to break and disorder the discipline of the Church.[35]

Extract B: Third National Synod, Orléans, April 1562

The Princes and other great Lords following the Court, in case they would have churches instituted in their houses, shall be desired to take for their pastors such as are ministers in churches truly reformed, bringing with them sufficient testimonials of their lawful calling to the ministry; and who shall before their admission subscribe the Confession of Faith of the churches in this kingdom and our church discipline. And that the preaching of the Gospel may be more successful, the said protestant Lords shall be requested, every one of them, to erect a consistory composed of the ministers and other persons most eminent for piety in their said family, by which consistory all scandals and vices shall be suppressed, and the rules of discipline observed.[36]

Extract C: Reformed Churches combine to defend their confession in Germany. From the Genevan Register of the Company of Pastors.

On the last day of May [1575] M. de Bèze said that in view of the fact that at the end of July the Estates of the Holy Roman Empire were to meet at Frankfurt to elect the King of the Romans, we had to fear that some sort of decree would be issued there against those of our confession, given that it was clear that the Saxons at least were in favour of something of the kind. Monsieur Ursinus has written from Heidelberg that the Company of Pastors there thinks it desirable that magistrates of our confession should be present at those Estates to urge that despite the difference between us and the Lutherans on the matter of the Lord's supper, nevertheless we all profess the true Communion of the body of Jesus Christ together with the other principal points of the faith, and that the diversity on the Supper should not divide us, nor prevent those of our confession from being included in the comprehensive peace settlement.[37]

Chapter summary

By the end of this chapter you should understand:

- the reasons for the significance of John Calvin and his impact on the religious and political affairs in Geneva
- the spread of Calvinism throughout Europe and the reasons for its success, as well as the extent of its expansion
- the reasons for Charles's initial victory and subsequent defeat against the Schmalkaldic League, culminating in the Peace of Augsburg.

Endnotes

1 I. John Hesselink, 'Calvin's Theology', in Donald K. McKim (ed.), *The Cambridge Companion to Calvin.* Cambridge University Press, 2004, p. 74.

2 Carlos Eire, 'Calvinism and the Reform of the Reformation', in Peter Marshall (ed.), *The Oxford Illustrated History of the Reformation.* Oxford University Press, 2015, p. 83.

3 Cited in Eire, 'Calvinism and Reform', p. 85.

4 Wulfert de Greef, 'Calvin's Writings', in McKim, *Cambridge Companion*, pp. 44–45.

5 Hesselink, 'Calvin's Theology', p. 74.

6 Mark Greengrass, 'The Theology and Liturgy of Reformed Christianity', in R. Po-Chia Hsia (ed.), *The Cambridge History of Christianity: Volume 6, Reform and Expansion, 1500–1660.* Cambridge University Press, 2007, p. 113.

7 Eire, 'Calvinism and Reform', p. 76.

8 Greengrass, 'Theology and Liturgy', p. 116.

9 Ulinka Rublack, *Reformation Europe.* Cambridge University Press, 2005, p. 104.

10 Gillian Lewis, 'Calvinism in Geneva in the Time of Calvin and of Beza 1541–1608', in Menna Prestwich (ed.), *International Calvinism, 1541–1715.* Oxford, Clarendon Press, 1986, p. 46.

11 William G. Naphy, 'Calvin and Geneva', in Andrew Pettegree (ed.), *The Reformation World.* London and New York, Routledge, 2000, p. 319.

12 Rublack, *Reformation*, p. 113.

13 Cited in Rublack, *Reformation*, p. 113.

14 Andrew Pettegree, 'The Spread of Calvin's Thought', in McKim, *Cambridge Companion*, p. 207.

15 Robert Kingdon, *Geneva and the Coming of the Wars of Religion.* Geneva, Librairie Droz, 2007.

16 Menna Prestwich, 'Calvinism in France, 1555–1629', in *International Calvinism, 1541–1715.* Oxford, Clarendon Press, 1986, p. 85.

17 Prestwich, 'Calvinism in France', p. 71.

18 Prestwich, 'Calvinism in France', p. 85.

19 See Janine Garrison's *Les Protestants du Midi.* Toulouse, 1980, or her *History of Sixteenth-Century France, 1483–1598: Renaissance, Reformation and Rebellion.* London, Palgrave, 1995, and the discrediting of Garrison's interpretation by Philip Conner, *Huguenot Heartland: Montauban and Southern French Calvinism During the Wars of Religion.* Farnham, Ashgate, 2002.

20 Andrew Pettegree, *Marian Protestantism: Six Studies.* Farnham, Ashgate, 1996.

21 Patrick Collinson, 'England and International Calvinism, 1558–1640', in Prestwich, *International Calvinism*, p. 199.

22 Pettegree, 'Calvin's Thought', p. 210.

23 Collinson, 'England and International Calvinism', p. 213.

24 Eire, 'Calvinism and Reform', p. 93.

25 Michael Lynch, 'Calvinism in Scotland, 1559–1638', in Prestwich, *International Calvinism*, p. 235.

26 Lynch, 'Calvinism in Scotland', p. 253.

27 Eire, 'Calvinism and Reform', p. 99.

28 Eire, 'Calvinism and Reform', p. 104.

29 Henry J. Cohn, 'The Territorial Princes in Germany's Second Reformation, 1559–1622', in Prestwich, *International Calvinism*, p. 138.

30 Philip Benedict, 'The Second Wave of Protestant Expansion', in Po-Chia Hsia, *Cambridge History of Christianity*, p. 127.

31 Rublack, *Reformation*, p. 140.

32 R.J.W. Evans, 'Calvinism in East Central Europe: Hungary and her Neighbours', in Prestwich, *International Calvinism*, p. 182.

33 Cohn, 'Germany's Second Reformation', p. 135.

34 Thomas A. Brady, 'Emergence and Consolidation of Protestantism in the Holy Roman Empire to 1600', Po-chia Hsia, *Cambridge History of Christianity*, p. 24.

35 Alastair Duke, Gillian Lewis and Andrew Pettegree (eds), *Calvinism in Europe, 1540–1610.* Cambridge University Press, 1992, pp. 22–23.

36 Duke, Lewis and Pettegree, *Calvinism in Europe*, p. 93.

37 Duke, Lewis and Pettegree, *Calvinism in Europe*, pp. 60–61.

6 The Catholic Reformation, 1531–1564

In this chapter we will study the papal revival led by Pope Paul III and his reform-minded cardinals, especially the Council of Trent. We will analyse further evidence for a Catholic resurgence, such as the new religious orders, notably the Jesuits, and the foundation of the Roman Inquisition.

Specification points:

- papal revival: Paul III; report into the state of the Church; the Roman Inquisition; Paul IV and Pius IV
- spiritual regeneration: new religious orders; Loyola and the Jesuits; beliefs and discipline and influence
- the Council of Trent: the three sessions; doctrine and the extent of reform
- the impact of reform by 1564; the response of monarchy, clergy and laity; geographical variation; the spiritual and political role of the Church.

Papal revival

The principal means of reforming the Church was via a general council, which could only be convened by the Pope. The fundamental problem with the late medieval Church stemmed from the refusal of successive popes to summon Councils. Popes resisted reform because they knew that thoroughgoing reform would undermine their own power and wealth. Calling a Council would reflect an admission that abuses were rife. In any case, popes feared councils due to the conciliarist threat, tensions that had plagued the late medieval papacy. Popes had other priorities, and were equally devoted to temporal affairs.

Background: the papacy, 1513–1534

The popes that preceded Paul III were not fully committed to Church reform. During the papal election of 1513, the future Leo X had promised to complete the work of the Fifth Lateran Council, but once he was elected, he did very little. Leo was a stereotypical Renaissance Prince. The second son of Lorenzo the Magnificent, he was tutored by Marsilio Ficino and Pico della Mirandola, and was a leading patron of the arts. He commissioned Raphael to redecorate the papal apartments. For most of his pontificate, he ruled Florence from 1512 to 1521, as well as Rome. Despite some reforming gestures, it was Leo X's attempts to raise money for the rebuilding of St Peter's that provoked the indulgences controversy in 1517. Leo X's reaction to Luther's early revolt was surprisingly lacklustre. As Duffy argued, he 'failed utterly to grasp the seriousness of the crisis and the need for drastic action to hold the Church together and to meet the legitimate demands of the reformers'.[1]

His successor, Adrian VI (r1522–1523) had been tutor to Archduke Charles, the future Emperor Charles V, and acted as Regent of Spain following the death of Ferdinand of Aragon. Adrian was strongly influenced by the Devotio Moderna, had a reputation for piety and integrity, and, as Pope, celebrated Mass on a daily basis. (See Chapter 1 for section on Priests and the 'mixed life')

Following his election, he sought to moderate the *Curia's* extravagance and reduce the number of personnel working in the Vatican. He even sent an envoy, Francesco Chieregati, to the 1522 Imperial Diet of Nuremberg; the latter was despatched with a document that acknowledged papal corruption and promised reform of the *Curia*. The uniqueness of this document 'lies primarily in the public admission of guilt which Adrian makes and in his excoriation of Rome as the fountainhead of the evil and corruption that had come'.[2] Yet like Leo X before him, he showed no interest in debating with Luther, whom he dismissed as a condemned heretic. He undertook some reform, yet this came to an abrupt halt with his death in 1523.

Clement VII (r1523–1534), though a Renaissance aristocrat and illegitimate son of Giuliano de' Medici, was hard working and free of sexual scandal. He was also the patron of Raphael and Michelangelo, and commissioned the painting of the Sistine Chapel. Although a beneficiary of nepotism – his uncle Leo X had appointed him as Cardinal in 1513 – Clement founded new religious orders, including the Theatines and the Capuchins, which indicates his dedication to reform. Yet Clement's difficult relationship with Charles V prevented any effective collaboration in the suppression of Lutheranism: 'with Pope and Emperor at odds, any attempt to deal with the religious revolution was sterile from the beginning'.[3] Clement was intimidated by the imperial presence in Italy, and as a result, he vacillated between the two major European powers and constantly dithered. His powerlessness was clearly reflected in 1527 with the sack of Rome by imperial mercenaries, many of whom were Lutherans.

Ultimately, it was the half-hearted nature of the early 16th-century papacy's commitment to reform that explains why so few major changes were enacted; 'over the longer run, early modern popes and their courts instituted more effective reform, but they exhibited personal inconsistencies that help explain why change came so slowly'.[4]

Paul III (r1534–1549)

Although similar inconsistencies were evident in Paul III's career, he made a more systematic attempt at reforming the Church. Paul III 'governed the Church with one foot, as it were, in the Renaissance and the other in the movement for reform and

---

ACTIVITY 6.1

Bearing in mind your reading about the thinkers of the Reformation so far in this course, write a paragraph about the papacy in the early years of the 16th century. Explain briefly how the state of the papacy may have encouraged the development of reform among theologians and the faithful.

renewal'.[5] He did see the papacy as a source of prestige. His own promotion in the Church were thanks to his sister Giulia, who was Alexander VI's mistress. As a Cardinal, Paul III had a mistress, a relationship that produced four illegitimate children. As a diplomat, he recognised the importance of being on friendly terms with France and the Holy Roman Empire. He was a shrewd political operator and decades of experience in papal diplomacy meant that Francis I and Charles V welcomed his election.

Paul III was concerned that no more countries should break with Rome like Henry VIII, whom he excommunicated. Paul supported Charles V in his war against the Schmalkaldic League. Although his first appointments as cardinals were his teenage grandsons, Paul III did appoint several influential, reform-minded cardinals in the 1530s, the most important of which was Gasparo Contarini (1483–1542). The other newly appointed cardinals included Reginald Pole, Henry VIII's cousin, Gian Matteo Giberti, Bishop of Verona, Jacopo Sadoleto, Bishop of Carpentras, and Giampietro Carafa, Archbishop of Brindisi.

Report into the state of the Church

Contarini, Charles V's ambassador, was a diplomat and author of the *Compendium*, a work outlining a strong commitment to Church reform. Similarly, in 1516, Contarini published a work on the duties of bishops, entitled *De officio episcopi*.[6] Once appointed Cardinal, Contarini was asked by Paul III to preside over a reform Commission, which included all the recently appointed cardinals, as well as Gregorio Cortese, Abbot of San Giorgio Maggiore in Venice, Federigo Fregoso, Bishop of Gubbio, Jerome Aleander, papal nuncio, Carafa, Archbishop of Brindisi and Tommaso Badia, Dominican Master of the Sacred Palace; members of the *Curia* were not invited to participate.

The Commission investigated Church abuses for three months. The findings were published as the *Consilium de emendenda ecclesia* (*Advice concerning the Reform of the Church*) and presented to the Pope in March 1537. The *Consilium* highlighted the following abuses within the Church: simony (buying and selling of church offices), pluralism (holding of more than one church office), absenteeism (non-resident office-holders), and the corruption within the religious orders. The Commission was radical, urging Paul III to reform the *Curia* itself. The Church's problems, including the rise of Protestantism, was blamed on the papacy and his senior clerics. The report was confidential, but copies circulated widely and even reached Luther, who published his own edition, with a critical preface and marginal commentary, in 1538.

Figure 6.1: Portrait of Pope Paul III, by Titian

Voices from the past

The *Consilium de emendenda ecclesia* (Advice concerning the Reform of the Church), 1537

Read the following extract and answer the questions that follow:

The first abuse is the ordination of clerics and especially of priests, in which no care is taken, no diligence employed, so that indiscriminately the most unskilled, men of the vilest stock and of evil morals, are admitted to Holy Orders and to the priesthood. From this has come innumerable scandals and a contempt for the ecclesiastical order, and reverence for divine worship has not only been diminished but has almost by now been destroyed. Therefore, we think that it would be an

excellent thing if your Holiness first in this city of Rome appointed two or three prelates, learned and upright men, to preside over the ordination of clerics. He should also instruct all bishops, even under pain of censure, to give careful attention to this in their own dioceses.[7]

1. What does the *Consilium* suggest about the state of the Catholic Church?
2. How significant is this in the light of the source's provenance?
3. Why did the Catholic Church not act sooner to address and rectify these problems?

The Roman Inquisition

Paul III founded the Roman Inquisition in 1542 in order to target Protestantism. The failure of doctrinal discussions at the Diet of Regensburg in 1541 was an important watershed. By the early 1540s, the Catholic moderates, particularly the *spirituali*, had been discredited. The establishment of the Roman Inquisition represented the abandonment of compromise. The regulations of the Holy Office declared that heretics should not be shown any toleration. In 1542, the flight from Italy and conversion to Protestantism of Bernardino Ochino, Vicar-General of the Capuchin Order, sent shockwaves around the Catholic world. Protestantism had infiltrated one of Catholicism's most recently founded institutions. The death of Cardinal Contarini in the same year, the leading Catholic moderate, all but destroyed the Catholic party that advocated reconciliation with Protestantism. The increasing prominence of Cardinal Carafa, an arch-conservative, illustrated which faction was taking control of the *Curia*. Carafa was to play a central role in the Roman Inquisition when he became Pope Paul IV (r1555–1559).

The Roman Inquisition supervised a network of courts throughout western Christendom. Its inquisitors did not require the local bishop's permission to operate; the papacy affirmed that inquisitorial courts were superior to both ecclesiastical and secular courts. While there were 43 tribunals in the Italian city-states, excluding Sicily, Lucca and Naples, the Roman Inquisition had some jurisdiction north of the Alps, notably in Avignon, Franche-Comté, Carcassonne, Toulouse and Cologne.

Yet Rome's jurisdiction was not all encompassing. Spain and Portugal already had their own Inquisitions, established in 1478 and 1536 respectively. Some Catholic territories resisted what they perceived to be Rome's interference in their affairs. The strand of French Gallicanism, upheld by the Paris Parlement and the Sorbonne, meant that it did not operate everywhere in France.[8] Closer to Rome, Venice, which was heavily dependent on trade, organised its own Inquisition. It was less severe because it was reluctant to persecute individuals who were vital to their economy. In any case, by the late 1560s, Protestantism was less of a concern since it had never really gained a proper foothold in the Italian city-states. By the late 1560s, the Venetian tribunal increasingly recognised the Roman tribunal, a change that was directed by papal diplomacy.

In the early years (1542–1544), the Inquisition targeted individuals, and even conducted trials against several prominent bishops, particularly those who had close connections with the *spirituali*, such as Pier Paolo Vergerio. After 1544, heresy became more difficult to detect, which necessitated a closer supervision of the book trade. Paul IV in 1557 formally established an Index of Forbidden Books, which became the means of issuing the papal censure of books.

Paul IV (r1555–1559)

From an early stage, Giampietro Carafa was reform-minded, joining the Oratory of Divine Love in Rome and later co-founding the Theatines, an order dedicated to strict poverty and eradicating Church corruption. He was by far the most reactionary of Paul III's cardinals, opposing compromise with Lutheranism. He was suspicious of the *spirituali* and their attempts to seek reconciliation with Lutherans. Nor did he conceal his dissatisfaction with the Peace of Augsburg, which had granted Lutheranism recognition within the Empire. In July 1542 Carafa was appointed as one of the six Inquisitors General. Eager to impose his own personal stamp on the Church, he deliberately avoided reconvening the Council of Trent after it had been suspended in 1552, believing that he could push forward a comprehensive reform programme without it.

Speak like a historian

Eamon Duffy's comparison of the pontificates of Paul III and Paul IV

Read the extract below, and with wider reading, answer the questions that follow:

Paul III and Paul IV embodied two different visions of reform. In Paul III reform was still recognisably part of the surge of positive energies which we call the Renaissance. It could accommodate the theological exploration of the Spirituali as well as the austere orthodoxies of Carafa, and it harnessed daring religious experimentation, such as Loyola's Jesuits and their new intensely personal spirituality. Under Paul IV reform took on a darker and more fearful character. Creativity was distrusted as dangerous innovation, theological energies were diverted into the suppression of error rather than the exploration of truth. Catholicism was identified with reaction. The contrast was of course not absolute: Paul III encouraged the use of force against heresy, and Paul IV valued the work of the new religious orders..[9]

1. Do you agree with Duffy's interpretations of the pontificates of Paul III and Paul IV?
2. Which of these two popes did more to advance the cause of reform?

In the mid-1550s, he devoted most of his attention to the Roman Inquisition, thereby confirming his virulent opposition to Protestantism. He targeted the remnants of the *spirituali*, including Cardinal Giovanni Morone, who was imprisoned in Rome and released only in the next pontificate. Paul IV later attempted to recall Pole to Rome on charges of heresy, even though he was instrumental, as Archbishop of Canterbury, in effecting England's reconciliation to Rome during Mary Tudor's reign (1553–1558). Even the Primate of Spain, Archbishop Carranza, who had helped Mary Tudor to restore Catholicism in England, was imprisoned on charges of heresy. In 1559, the Index of Forbidden Books was reissued with an amended and expanded list of heretical books.

Timeline of Popes in the era of Catholic renewal

1513–1521	Leo X
1522–1523	Adrian VI
1523–1534	Clement VII
1534–1549	Paul III
1550–1555	Julius III
1555	Marcellus II
1555–1559	Paul IV
1559–1565	Pius IV

Pius IV (r1559–1565)

In contrast with his recent predecessors, Pius IV was undoubtedly a pope in the Renaissance tradition. Not only did he have three illegitimate children, but his career was also greatly enhanced when his brother married into Pope Paul's III family. In turn, as Pope, he was equally nepotistic and his favours led to the promotion of his nephew Carlo Borromeo. Yet, in this instance, Pius IV's favouritism led to the emergence of one of the 16th century's greatest reformers. Borromeo became the model bishop of the Tridentine era: pious and devout; resident and active in his diocese. Of considerable importance to Pius's pontificate were his amicable relations with both the Austrian and

Spanish Habsburgs, in particular Emperor Ferdinand and Philip II; Paul IV's hostility to the Habsburgs had not helped the cause of reform. Pius was also reasonably devout and a good administrator. Crucially, he reconvened the Council of Trent in January 1562 and confirmed all the Tridentine decrees, and during his pontificate yet another Index of Forbidden Books was published in 1564. By that date the structures of reform were in place and Catholic renewal could begin to flourish.

Spiritual regeneration

New religious orders

Many new orders were founded in the 16th century, including a variety of different groups, both in terms of size, type of membership and activities. None of these orders was founded with the specific intention of combating Protestantism. Their principal commitment was to religious reform on parish level.

Oratories of Divine Love

The Oratories of Divine Love were mainly lay confraternities (see section 'The laity and the growth of confraternities') or brotherhoods, though they also included some priests. The first Oratory was founded by a Franciscan friar, Bernardino da Feltre, in Vicenza in 1494, though a more formidable one was established in Genoa in 1497. The Genoese oratory was founded by Ettore Vernazza and inspired by the superior of the hospital of Pammatone, Caterina Fieschi Adorno, better known as St Catherine of Genoa. Vernazza was Catherine's disciple and the oratory's focus on charity and the care of the sick derived from her example.

The best-known oratory was founded in Rome between 1514 and 1517. Although modelled on the oratory in Genoa, the Roman oratory's membership was more exclusive, with approximately 50, mainly aristocratic members, including Gaetano da Thiene, and Giampietro Carafa. There was further expansion into northern Italy after 1517, with Bartolomeo Stella establishing an oratory in Brescia and Gaetano da Thiene travelling to Verona and Venice. The members of these oratories were obviously reform-minded, with a strong emphasis on prayer, worship and charitable work. The oratories did not represent a religious order because members did not take vows.

Theatines

The Theatines were founded in 1524, when four members of the Roman Oratory of Divine Love took vows of poverty, chastity and obedience at St Peter's Basilica in Rome: Gaetano da Thiene, better known as Cardinal Cajetan (1480–1547); Giampietro Carafa (1476–1559), cardinal and later Paul IV, and author of the Theatine rule and the order's first superior; Bonifacio de' Colli; and Paolo Consiglieri. Its membership was very small, with 14 and 21 members in 1527 and 1533 respectively, and only priests were allowed to join. The intention of the founders was to establish a society of priests (monks and friars were not invited), which would engage in pastoral work but live in a community under a superior and according to monastic vows.

The Theatines were a highly ambitious and extremely talented group, indeed a school for future bishops. Their activities included prayer and works of charity, as well as promoting episcopal reform. Cajetan set an example by giving up a lucrative office in the Vatican in order to combat the decadence of the parish clergy. The Theatines were different from earlier orders because 'they recited the traditional priestly office in common and their vow of poverty forbade them to hold benefices or to beg'.[10] They were also the first order to found papal missions abroad and acquired an international reputation.

ACTIVITY 6.2

Make notes, from the information here and from your own research, on the two popes described above. Then answer the following questions:

1. How do these popes compare to those during the years 1513–1534?

2. How effective do you think each of the three was in shoring up Catholicism against the forces of the Reformation?

ACTIVITY 6.3

Create a table to compare the salient features of the new religious orders. Think about their way of life; their guiding principles; those who joined; the effect they wished to have on the Church and on society; and any other aspects you think significant.

Capuchins

The Capuchins were founded by Matteo da Bascio (1495–1552) in July 1528, in the diocese of Camerino, and emerged from the Observant Franciscans. Da Bascio and his followers, including Ludovico and Raffaele da Fossombrone and Paolo da Chioggia, sought to observe the rule of St Francis more strictly. While da Bascio was elected Superior in 1529, Ludovico da Fossombrone took over shortly afterwards and laid the foundations for the order's remarkable growth (from 700 in 1535 to 6000 in 1587).

Less exclusive than the Roman Oratory of Divine Love, the order still benefited from aristocratic support, especially the patronage of Caterina Cibo, Duchess of Camerino, and Vittoria Colonna, who defended the Capuchins against the Observant Franciscans. It was under Ludovico da Fossombrone's leadership that the Capuchin *Constitutions* were first drafted in 1529. Subsequently revised in 1536, the *Constitutions* outlined the main aims of the order: a commitment to total poverty, ministering to the underprivileged, including orphans, plague victims and the sick. They highlighted the centrality of the Mass and worship.

Despite their successes, the Capuchins attracted controversy. First, they were opposed by the Observant Franciscans who labelled them as fanatics. Some of the Capuchins came to be associated with the *spirituali*, who were later criticised for holding Protestant sympathies. These suspicions were confirmed when Bernardino Ochino, Vicar-General of the order, converted to Protestantism and fled to Calvin's Geneva. This major crisis almost led to the order's demise, but the Capuchins survived and managed to recover after an investigation exonerated the Order.

Ursulines

The Ursulines were established by Angela Merici in 1535 as an exclusively female, lay order. Merici had previously become involved with the Oratory of Divine Love in Brescia, and assisted in a hospital of incurables. In the 1520s, she gathered together a group of virgins and widows, who dedicated themselves to working with orphans and the sick. Merici rejected the notion of an enclosed order, displaying her clear commitment to an active religious life dedicated to charitable works. In 1536, the Bishop of Brescia gave the Ursulines his approval and the Pope officially recognised them in 1544.

This intention to live a free and active life was gradually undermined by the changing perspectives of the Catholic Church. Largely due to the Council of Trent, the Ursulines experienced considerable change in the second half of the 16th century. From 1546, they were forced to wear a habit, and in 1566, they were forced to live in communities. Carlo Borromeo invited the Ursulines to assist him with Milan's programme of religious instruction; in 1576, he required that each bishop in his ecclesiastical province establish the Ursulines in his diocese. By 1595, the Ursulines had, under duress, become a traditional enclosed order of nuns. The Council of Trent's restrictions on female religious activity were largely responsible for these changes.

Ignatius of Loyola and the Jesuits

In 1534, the foundations for the Jesuits were laid in a small chapel dedicated to St Denis at Montmartre in Paris, where Ignatius of Loyola and his first companions made a vow to travel to the Holy Land in order to convert Muslims. These companions – Pierre Favre, Francis Xavier, Diego Laynez, Alfonso Salmeron, Nicolas Bobadilla and Simon Rodriquez – came from a variety of European countries. On arriving in Italy, the order soon gained official approval as the Society of Jesus from Pope Paul III in 1540. This took place with the timely intervention and support of Gasparo Contarini.[11] The Jesuits took four vows, the last of which prescribed that Jesuits should take a vow to the Pope to travel anywhere in the world to spread the Gospel. The Jesuits were not obliged to recite prayers in community, so that they could remain itinerant. Ignatius discarded regular prayer times in order to allow greater flexibility to pursue a more active ministry. Ignatius 'wanted not only a new balance of contemplation and activity, but he sought to integrate the two creatively in Jesuits as *contemplatives in action*'.[12]

The order was carefully structured according to *Constitutions*, which were completed during the 1550s in Ignatius's lifetime, and confirmed by Pope Julius III. The order was divided into provinces in order to manage its expansion; by 1553, there were six different provinces, a figure that doubled within three years. The order was highly structured in term of personnel, with Provincials in charge of each province who were ordered to communicate regularly with the Jesuit headquarters in Rome. Ignatius of Loyola was appointed the Order's first General and ably led the Jesuits until his death in 1556. The dynamism and discipline of the Jesuits allowed them to grow extremely quickly: from 1000 members in 1553 to 3500 by 1565.

Ignatius of Loyola

One key source of inspiration for the Jesuits was the life of Ignatius of Loyola, their founder. Born in 1491 of noble descent, Ignatius entered military service in 1517 and had a striking conversion experience, following a serious injury sustained from a cannon ball at the siege of Pamplona in 1521. After a retreat at the Benedictine monastery of Montserrat, he moved to Manresa where he began composing a religious text known as the *Spiritual Exercises*. He travelled to the Holy Land on pilgrimage and on his return decided to embark on his education in Spain at the universities of Alcalá and Salamanca, and later at the University of Paris, where he studied from 1528 to 1535. He subsequently moved to Italy where the Society of Jesus was founded.

Beliefs, discipline and influence

The *Spiritual Exercises*

The *Spiritual Exercises* were central to Ignatius's beliefs, discipline and influence. The text represented the central part of Jesuit spirituality, and was a manual for spiritual living. The *Exercises* 'originated in religious experience, first the author's and then others'.[13] A spiritual director, normally taking charge of a four-week retreat, guided believers through the *Exercises*. Not all retreatants would make it through the entirety of the retreat and the stages were very flexible to accommodate their different capabilities. The focal point was the life of Christ, on which believers meditated and based their personal renewal.

The spirituality of the Jesuits placed them at the crossroads between the late medieval and early modern periods. Ignatius and the early Jesuits drew considerable inspiration from key late medieval works of spirituality, such as the *Imitation of Christ*, Jacobus de Voragine's *Golden Legend* and Ludolph of Saxony's *Life of Christ*, while simultaneously developing their own form of practical spirituality as manifest in the *Exercises*. Hence, the method of following Christ was not merely found in **spiritual contemplation** but also in **apostolic action**.

Education

The Jesuits had limited plans for education initially, and it was never the intention to create a teaching order at the expense of other concerns or of their mobility. Initially, the first Jesuit colleges were little more than hostels for young Jesuits attending universities. Yet they were increasingly set up for the training of Jesuits and the first college to admit non-Jesuits (known as externs) was in Messina, established in 1547. Another college was opened in Palermo in 1549, and two years later, the Roman College was established. Thereafter, Ignatius encouraged the Jesuits to found colleges throughout Europe and beyond; by the time of his death in 1556, there were approximately 33 colleges.

ACTIVITY 6.4

Research the lives of the founders of all the new orders described. Explain how their different histories gave rise to the different characteristics of the orders they founded.

Figure 6.2: Ignatius of Loyola

In later years, many schools and universities were opened and taken over by Jesuits for the purpose of educating the laity. Many Jesuits also staffed the newly founded seminaries, which became so central to **Tridentine** reform. The rapid expansion did have its problems as some colleges lacked the necessary finances and personnel. This explains the Jesuits' decision to stem the growth of colleges in 1565.

Timeline: The growth of the Jesuits

1540	Jesuits founded by Pope Paul III
1548	First Jesuit college established in Messina (Sicily)
1551	College founded in Rome
1553	6 Jesuit provinces in full operation (India, Portugal, Castile, Aragon, Brazil, Italy)
1555	55 Jesuits in Goa supervised by Francis Xavier
1556	35+ colleges (19 in Italy), 12 provinces (Italy, Sicily, Upper Germany, Lower Germany, France, Aragon, Castile, Andalusia, Portugal, Brazil, India, Ethiopia), 1000 members
1565	3500 members

Missions

Jesuits believed that their personal conversion was incomplete if it was separated from their missionary life. They became excellent preachers and communicators with local inhabitants, teachers in schools, universities but also in basic Christian instruction, and performers with their use of drama and music. The Jesuits contributed 'disproportionately to the flood of dictionaries and grammars of non-European languages'.[14] They were innovative in the use of processions, confraternities, social welfare, art and architecture. They also made considerable use of noble patronage; King John III of Portugal had a Jesuit confessor, Simão Rodrigues who resided at Court, and his benefaction led to the founding of a College in Coimbra in 1542. The most famous missionary was Francis Xavier (1506–1552), who spent much of his time in India, especially Goa and Japan. The Jesuits experienced considerable growth in Japan until the rise of persecutions in the late 1590s, and also brought European culture to China, where they 'created a synthesis of Christian faith and Confucian ethics'.[15] The Jesuits were also active in Spanish and Portuguese America, as well as on the African continent.

Fig. 6.3: Francis Xavier, Jesuit missionary

The Jesuits experienced varying degrees of success in Europe. They were less effective in England and France. They were not invited to England during Mary Tudor's reign, so their arrival was delayed until the rule of the Protestant Elizabeth I. They were immediately perceived as a political and religious threat. Many Jesuits were forced to work underground and sought to remain incognito, though some were arrested and executed for their faith, such as Edmund Campion. In France, the strong undercurrent of Gallicanism meant that the Jesuits were not as welcome as one would suppose. They were generally opposed by the Paris Parlement and by the Sorbonne, and tensions mounted to such a degree that they were expelled from France between the years 1594–1603.

The Jesuits first arrived in Germany in the early 1540s, shortly after their foundation. Most prominent of all were Peter Favre and especially Peter Canisius (1521–1597). The Jesuits were very successful in Germany, mainly due to their effective courting of the nobility, especially the Wittelsbach dukes of Bavaria. Duke Albert V of Bavaria oversaw Jesuit activities and took advantage of their dynamism to consolidate Catholicism in Bavaria. This was undertaken via preaching and publishing books, especially Canisius's *Catechism*. With noble support, the Jesuits took over many of the leading universities, most notably Munich, Dillingen and Ingolstadt. Bavaria became an important missionary centre for the spread of Catholicism in Germany.

The Council of Trent

Why was the convening of the Council of Trent delayed?

Given that Luther made his theological breakthrough in 1520, it is curious that a general council was not convened sooner. So why did it take so long? The perennial fear of conciliarism was reinforced by the belief that convening a council was tantamount to acknowledging the Church's failings. The *Curia* resisted Paul III's measures to end absenteeism and pluralism at the highest level of the hierarchy. Although the popes were responsible for convening councils, they were not solely to blame for the delays. As the ruler of the greater part of western Christendom, Charles V was vital to the organisation of a successful Council. While firmly committed to Catholicism, he was also driven by dynasticism, especially against the Valois dynasty.

Charles also had a different understanding of what councils should achieve. He wanted a general council to deal exclusively with the reform of abuses, allowing him to seek a doctrinal consensus with Lutherans. Paul III, on the other hand, demanded that the Council address doctrinal, as well as disciplinary, matters. Equally significant for Charles was the coordination of Christian forces in order to confront the Ottomans. He depended on Protestant and Catholic princes for money and troops. And Francis I, despite professing Catholicism, pursued his own dynastic interests, even to the point of securing alliances with German Protestant princes in order to weaken Charles V.

The timing of the Council depended on the existence of peace between Francis I and Charles V. The Council was formally summoned by Paul III on 22 May 1542 and meant to meet in November 1542, but an Ottoman alliance with France led Suleiman to take Buda and Francis I to declare war against the Emperor. Eventually, the Peace of Crépy in 1544 between the Habsburg and Valois dynasties provided a window of opportunity. The location of the Council was also controversial. Charles V wanted the council to be based in the German lands because they had been the most exposed to Lutheranism. He had threatened to convene a German council, independent of Rome. Given the papacy's fear of Councils, Paul III insisted on having a council within the Italian city-states. For that reason, a compromise location was found in Trent, situated south of the Alps but still part of the Holy Roman Empire.

Doctrine

The principal agenda of the Council was to define key doctrines, especially in response to Protestantism, and to reform Church abuses. As Duffy remarks, 'its mere existence was a triumph of papal diplomacy, and so was the fact that, despite Charles V's efforts to prevent it, the Council from the start dealt with both doctrine and practical reform.'[16] The treatment of doctrine at Trent indicates that the Catholic Church pursued an anti-Protestant agenda, a convincing justification for the literal use of the term Counter-Reformation. There was a deliberate policy not to discuss theological differences among Catholics; the main thrust of the Council's bishops and theologians was 'towards delineating clearly the Catholic stance vis-à-vis the Protestants'.[17] Each decree was divided into two sections: the first included a presentation of Catholic teachings; the second represented canons rejecting Protestant beliefs. Each canon was followed by the phrase 'anathema sit', meaning 'let it be condemned'. Doctrines shared by Protestants and Catholics were avoided.

This reactionary approach was reflected in the dominance of conservative theologians, especially the Dominicans and the Jesuits. That the first period of the Council covered

ACTIVITY 6.5

For this activity, use the material in this section and your own research. On a blank sheet, draw a diagram to show the geographical spread of the Jesuits during their first few decades. Add boxes giving details of their activities, the growth in numbers, and assessing the cultures they would have encountered. You may like to bear in mind that the Jesuits are still, in the 21st century, a major feature of the Catholic Church.

ACTIVITY 6.6

Briefly assess the advantages and disadvantages that the Council of Trent's meetings happened over such an extended period.

the greatest amount of doctrine illustrates where the papacy's priorities lay. Although the reform of abuses was discussed in this initial phase, it was clearly overshadowed by theological concerns. The Tridentine emphasis on theology illustrates how the Counter-Reformation based its attack on a rejection of the fundamental Protestant beliefs, as well as on a total reassertion of papal power. In Duffy's words, 'the Council's teaching on the contested points – justification, the seven sacraments, transubstantiation, purgatory – was uncompromising, but clear and cogent'.[18]

Church authority

Trent reaffirmed the Catholic view that Church tradition, defined by the doctrinal statements formulated in Church Councils and the writings of the early Christian Church, was of equal validity to the Bible, thereby rejecting *Sola Scriptura*. The Vulgate, the official Latin version of the Bible, was confirmed as the sole authoritative version of the Bible, indicating the Church's opposition to vernacular translations of the Scriptures. The Roman Catholic Church was put forward as the sole interpreter of the Bible. Trent also reasserted the view that original sin did not completely destroy human nature, so that human beings were given a clean slate through baptism. It confirmed the necessity of good works, living a good life and earning merit in this life, while emphasising the centrality of confession and doing penance to remove sins. This reinforced the understanding of priesthood, as well as the Catholic sacramental system. The Church also defended the belief that any sins that were not confessed in this life could be purified in purgatory; all of these teachings directly contradicted Protestant doctrines.

The sacraments

Trent reaffirmed the belief in seven sacraments, reinforcing the need for priestly mediation. In response to Protestant criticisms about clerical corruption, Trent declared that the administration of the sacraments was undertaken *ex opere operato*, irrespective of the qualities and merits of priests.

Unsurprisingly, Trent firmly defended the belief in transubstantiation and stressed the sacrificial element of the Mass, particularly the central role played by the priest without which the sacrifice would be impossible. The status of priests was reinforced, with an insistence on celibacy, and communion in both kinds (bread and wine) being reserved for priests only. The Tridentine decrees clearly rejected the vernacular liturgy; all worship had to be in Latin.

Discipline, abuses and the extent of reform

In addition to this doctrinal focus, Tridentine decrees also focused on discipline. This is not to say that there was no significant reform undertaken in the period prior to the convocation of the Council.

The key role of bishops

The centrepiece of Tridentine reform was the emphasis on the episcopacy. The Council of Trent emphasised the 'role of the bishop as pastor, as opposed to that of an ecclesiastical officer-holder with rights of jurisdiction'.[19] They were meant to provide strong leadership at all levels. First, importance was attached to their personal example. They were expected to show integrity, acting as shepherds within their communities. They were to reside within their diocese. They were called upon to preach and administer the sacraments, not delegating any responsibilities. They were to check that parishes were being run smoothly via conducting visitations every two years. They were to establish one seminary per diocese and to set up religious schools. They were also meant to chair diocesan and provincial synods in order to any problems within the Church.

The emphasis on episcopal reform was not uncontroversial, for the non-residence of bishops had been sanctioned by the *Curia*. As Po-chia Hsia has argued: 'Any reform in this important issue touched on the prerogative of Rome; after all, the edifice of patronage at the papal curia rested on the foundations of plurality of benefice and non-residence.'[20] There were further potential problems for the papacy in the discussions regarding whether episcopal residency was divinely ordained, implying that the Council's authority (as a body of bishops) might possess greater authority than the Pope.

Once the final session of the Tridentine Council was concluded, it did not take long for some dioceses to implement its decrees. In Milan, Carlo Borromeo (1538–1584) responded immediately to the Council of Trent's demands and became a model bishop. By 1565, he had been appointed Archbishop of Milan, and was shortly afterwards elevated to the Cardinalate. Borromeo held 11 diocesan synods and six provincial councils during his time as Archbishop. He established three seminaries and supervised regular visitations to the parishes within his archdiocese.

The role of parish priests

Priests were expected to be vital instruments of Tridentine reform in the parishes. Like the bishops, priests were to lead by example and show integrity. They were urged not to keep a mistress and to avoid excessive drinking. They were asked to administer the sacraments, preach, provide religious instruction, and maintain parish records (especially of baptisms, marriages and funerals), which were checked during episcopal visitations.

The impact of reform by 1564

The extent of the Catholic recovery by 1564 was significant. The Council of Trent was starting to make its presence felt throughout Europe. Although it took several decades for Tridentine reforms to be enforced, the Council's directives and the greater sense of purpose that emanated from a reinvigorated papacy prepared the way for a more thorough Catholic recovery. Even within the German lands, a Catholic resurgence was taking place.

Political factors and geographical variations

The Church's recovery was greatly influenced by political factors. In England, the fate of Catholicism was entirely dictated by political developments. Once Elizabeth established Protestantism, it was no longer a question of recovery but rather of survival. Similarly, in the German lands, Lutheranism was recognised as a legitimate religious denomination by the Peace of Augsburg in 1555. According to the principle of *cuius regio eius religio*, Catholicism was excluded from a number of territories within the Empire. Political judgements led popes to make compromises with rulers that, despite benefiting the papacy and the Church, could undermine local bishops. The policy of accommodating secular rulers, evident in the 1550s and early 1560s, was also pursued in later decades. The Counter-Reformation benefited much from the aristocratic leadership represented by Philip II of Spain (r1556–1598), which had an important impact by 1564.

The spiritual and political role of the Church

Despite this Catholic recovery, the papacy did not reform itself, despite its willingness to address the issue of reform at Trent. Despite reconvening the Council in 1562, Pius IV was a pope in the Renaissance tradition, making the most of the office to promote members of his own family. In 1564 the *Curia* was still a relatively corrupt institution, which continued to hamper its effectiveness in bringing about a full Catholic recovery. Members of the *Curia* were asked to condemn practices on which their prestige and

---

ACTIVITY 6.7

Using the information in this chapter and your own research, assess whether the Council of Trent was an appropriate and timely response to the growth of the Reformation movement.

ACTIVITY 6.8

Thinking about the religious life of the laity, compare the appeal of confraternities to the response of the lay faithful to the Reformation.

incomes relied. The abuses at the highest levels of the Church did not disappear in subsequent decades.

While popes were reluctant to leave the central administration of the Church to the provinces, cardinals were hesitant to return to their own dioceses for fear of losing their influence at the papal court. This fundamental problem was destined to provide a continuing obstacle to the course of Catholic reform. Yet there were some improvements at the highest levels of the Church. Pluralism, simony and absenteeism were far less common, and some leading clerics acquired an impressive reputation for integrity and even sanctity, such as the Jesuit and Cardinal Robert Bellarmine and the Oratorian Cesare Baronius.

The clergy

The Tridentine decrees sought to improve the state of the clergy and this was given high priority by the popes during the Council. Integral to the reform of the clergy was the explicit distinction that was made between the clergy and the laity: Catholic theology reasserted the unique mediatory powers of the priesthood. For that reason, the duty of preaching sermons was restricted to the clergy – hence the Tridentine emphasis on seminaries. However, while some dioceses were carefully monitored, others received few regular visitations, leaving priests to their own devices. In those parishes, the rural clergy tended to function not as agents of a Tridentine Church, but rather as intermediaries between the rural population and the Church authorities. By 1564, some dioceses remained in a state of disrepair because the Council's decrees had not had sufficient time to be fully enforced. In France, the chaos provoked by the wars of religion left many dioceses without the presence of a bishop.

The laity and the growth of confraternities

Confraternities

During the Counter-Reformation, emphasis was placed on the growth of social control over the populace by ecclesiastical and secular authorities. Parish priests and parochial organisations played a fundamental role in this control. Confraternities formed an integral part of the control system, given that they tended to be based in the local parish church. Confraternities were largely voluntary associations, designed primarily to prepare members for the afterlife. They were fully involved in the community's social, political and cultural life. Although numerous confraternities were founded prior to the Reformation, the rise of Protestantism provoked the establishment of many new ones.

Throughout the 16th century, the number of confraternities expanded significantly, in addition to diversifying their activities in response to various religious and socio-economic crises. Some were established with the intention of countering Protestantism; penitential confraternities cultivated a militant and crusading spirit, as evidenced by the confraternities that emerged during the French religious wars. Confraternities helped to reinforce a Catholic sense of identity – many were associated with particular saints and devotions. They ensured that social welfare was placed within a religious framework. While many confraternities allowed for a lay activism that was relatively independent of the clergy, in some cases the Church, and indeed religious orders, used these organisations to reinforce the Catholic faith.[21]

Doctrine and discipline

Control and reform of the laity was also facilitated by the work of the Inquisitions in Spain and Italy. Once the threat of Protestantism had subsided in these countries by the end of the 16th century, both Inquisitions directed their attention towards ordinary Christians. Instead of dealing with heterodoxy, the Inquisition increasingly focused on cases of morality, such as adultery and blasphemy. The reform of the laity had become a major focus of the Catholic Reformation. Prohibited from interpreting the Scriptures, the laity read devotional works, were taught about the centrality of the sacraments and that the only true access to God was via the mediation of the clergy.

In response to the emergence of Protestantism, Pius IV issued a Tridentine Profession of Faith in November 1564, which condensed the key doctrines outlined in Trent's decrees. The papacy called for the production of a catechism for those untrained in theology. The popes made full use of the German Jesuit Peter Canisius's catechism, which was published in 1555 as a *Summary of Christian Doctrine*. While this work was directed at university students, Canisius drew up more accessible catechisms for the laity in 1558 and 1566.

In due course, Pius IV commissioned theologians to produce the *Roman Catechism*, which was published in 1566 and directed towards priests. The Catholic Church did, however, recognise the centrality and importance of rituals, cults of saints and processions, and thus reform on a local level often reflected the demands of popular piety. Devotional practices also served to distinguish Catholics from Protestants, especially those focusing on the Catholic Eucharist, such as the feast of Corpus Christi, on veneration of the Virgin Mary and the saints. The Church sought to harness and control popular piety, while simultaneously trying to eradicate its superstitious elements. In similar fashion, the procedure for making saints was tightened up and after 1623 no more saints were canonised for the next 65 years.[22] Despite the apparent progress in the reform of local religion, Church authorities did not always succeed in stamping out superstitious practices and even pagan tendencies. Ultimately, both Protestant and Catholic territories experienced considerable difficulties in driving out pagan customs from the countryside.

The longer-term effectiveness of Tridentine reform

Tridentine reform did encounter problems. There was some regional opposition. It has been suggested that the Council of Trent established a too rigid, uniform approach to reform, which failed to accommodate local circumstances. Some have noted that Trent was too Rome-centred, with tensions existing between the Pope and territorial rulers. A major problem was that it took centuries rather than decades for Tridentine reform to be implemented; in that sense, Borromeo was the exception rather than the norm. Provincial councils and diocesan synods were not convened regularly throughout Europe. In the German lands, provincial councils met rarely. Although two important meetings were held at Salzburg in 1569 and 1573, not a single meeting was held at Mainz.

While bishops and priests were the principal targets of reform, Trent did not make a significant difference to the running of the *Curia*. Simon Ditchfield has emphasised what was omitted from the discussions at Trent, key issues that 'mattered to Catholics fighting on the front line of a confessionally divided Europe – communion in both kinds, a vernacular liturgy, clerical celibacy, and the veneration of saints', though the final point was discussed briefly at the end of the Council.[23] The Council devoted little attention to the association between the Church and the secular states, which was striking given that many European princes were empowered to make ecclesiastical appointments. The relationship between the papacy and bishops was also not given due consideration.[24] Missionary work beyond European frontiers was also neglected in the proceedings at Trent. Tridentine reform was partly resisted by the regular clergy due to their jurisdictional conflict with episcopal powers.

However, setting aside these significant criticisms, Trent set in motion a properly coordinated reform movement on an episcopal and on a parochial level, which was long overdue. Trent also represented a coherent theological response to Protestant attacks, thereby forcing Catholics into a more conservative mould. Though at times questioned, Trent reinforced papal authority. The example of Borromeo was copied in numerous dioceses throughout Western Europe, though rarely to the same degree of effectiveness.

Conclusion

The reform movements prior to 1545 illustrate that reform was possible, albeit undertaken in a largely spontaneous fashion and restricted to particular regions. The renewal of the Catholic Church before Trent was characterised by the establishment of new religious orders. The emergence of the Jesuits was integral to the later survival of Catholicism. The renewal of the Church was not without its more militant and aggressive dimension, as illustrated by the Spanish and Roman Inquisitions. All of these developments were in large part consolidated by the Council of Trent: from a doctrinal perspective, it set clear theological parameters between orthodoxy and heterodoxy; in disciplinary terms, it laid the foundations for the renewal of the Church at the episcopal and parochial levels.

Practice essay question

With reference to these sources and your understanding of the historical context, assess the value of these three sources to an historian studying the motives behind the Catholic Reformation.

Extract A: The Founding of the Jesuits, the Bull of Institution, 1540

Whoever shall desire to bear the arms of God under the banner of the Cross, and to serve the one God and the Roman Pontiff, his Vicar upon earth, in our Society, which we wish to be called the name of Jesus, having made a solemn vow of perpetual chastity, must purpose to become a member of a society principally instituted to work for the advancement of souls in Christian life and doctrine, and for the propagation of the faith by public preaching and the ministry of God's Word, by spiritual exercises and works of charity, and by hearing the confession of the faithful, aiming in all things at their spiritual consolation.[25]

Extract B: Council of Trent, Sixth session, decree concerning reform, Chapter IV

Bishops and other major prelates shall visit all Churches as often as this is necessary. Chapters of cathedral and of other major churches and the members thereof shall not by any exemptions, customs, judicial verdicts, oaths, agreements, which bind only the originators thereof and not also their successors, shield themselves so that they cannot even with Apostolic authority be visited, corrected and amended in accordance with the canonical statutes as often as shall be necessary by their own bishops and other major prelates, by themselves alone or with those whom they shall deem fit to accompany them.[26]

Extract C: Council of Trent, Thirteenth session, Canons on the Most Holy Sacrament of the Eucharist

Canon 1. If anyone denies that in the sacrament of the most Holy Eucharist are contained truly, really and substantially the body and blood together with the soul and divinity of our Lord Jesus Christ, and consequently the whole Christ, but says that He is in it only as in a sign, or figure or force, let him be anathema.

Canon 2. If anyone says that in the sacred and holy sacrament of the Eucharist the substance of the bread and wine remains conjointly with the body and blood of our Lord Jesus Christ, and denies that wonderful and singular change of the whole substance of the wine into the blood, the appearances only of bread and wine remaining, which change the Catholic Church most aptly calls transubstantiation, let him be anathema.

Canon 11. If anyone says that faith alone is a sufficient preparation for receiving the sacrament of the most Holy Eucharist, let him be anathema.[27]

Chapter summary

By the end of this chapter you should understand:

- the characteristics of the papal revival under Paul III and his successors, particularly Paul IV and Pius IV
- the spiritual regeneration created by the foundation of new religious orders, most notably the Jesuits
- the Catholic Church's concerted efforts at responding to the Protestant Reformation, as evidenced by the Roman Inquisition and by the theological decrees of the Council of Trent
- the Church's attempts to reform from within by placing particular emphasis on bishops and the impact that this had on society as a whole.

Endnotes

1   Eamon Duffy, *Saints & Sinners: A History of the Popes*. London and New Haven, Yale University Press, 1997, pp. 154–155.

2   John Olin, *The Catholic Reformation: Savonarola to Ignatius Loyola*. Fordham University Press, New York, 1992, p. 121.

3   P.G. Maxwell-Stuart, *Chronicle of the Popes*. London, Thames & Hudson, 2006, p. 177.

4   William Hudon, 'The Papacy in the Age of Reform, 1513–1644', in Kathleen Comerford and Hilmar Pabel (eds), *Early Modern Catholicism: Essays in Honour of John W. O'Malley, S.J*. University of Toronto Press, 2001, p. 51.

5   Robert Bireley, *The Refashioning of Catholicism, 1450–1700*. Macmillan, 1999, p. 45.

6   For an extract from this work, see Olin, *Catholic Reformation*, pp. 92–106.

7   Olin, *Catholic Reformation*, p. 182.

8   Simon Ditchfield, 'Catholic Reformation and Renewal', in Peter Marshall (ed.), *The Oxford Illustrated History of the Reformation*. Oxford University Press, 2015, p. 176.

9   Duffy, *Saints & Sinners*, p. 169.

10 John Patrick Donnelly, 'New Religious Orders for Men', in R. Po-Chia Hsia (ed.), *The Cambridge History of Christianity: Volume 6, Reform and Expansion, 1500–1660*. Cambridge University Press, 2007, p. 165.

11 John O'Malley, *The First Jesuits*. Cambridge, MA, Harvard University Press, 1993, p. 35.

12 Bireley, *Refashioning of Catholicism*, p. 33.

13 O'Malley, *First Jesuits*, p. 42.

14 Ditchfield, 'Catholic Reformation', p. 161.

15 R. Po-chia Hsia, *The World of Catholic Renewal, 1540–1770*. Cambridge University Press, 2005, p. 31.

16 Duffy, *Saints & Sinners*, p. 167.

17 Bireley, *Refashioning of Catholicism*, p. 49.

18 Duffy, *Saints & Sinners*, p. 167.

19 Bireley, *Refashioning of Catholicism*, p. 50.

20 Po-chia Hsia, *World of Catholic Renewal*, p. 14.

21 See, for example, Michael W. Maher, 'How the Jesuits used their Congregations to promote frequent communion', in John Patrick Donnelly and Michael W. Maher (eds), *Confraternities & Catholic Reform in Italy, France & Spain*. Kirksville, MO, Thomas Jefferson University Press, 1999, pp. 75–96.

22 Peter Burke, 'How to Become a Counter-Reformation Saint', David Luebke (ed.), *The Counter-Reformation*. Oxford, Blackwell Publishing, 1999, p. 131. See also Simon Ditchfield, 'Tridentine Worship and the Cult of Saints', in Po-Chia Hsia, *Cambridge History of Christianity*, pp. 201–224.

23 Ditchfield, 'Catholic Reformation', p. 170.

24 Robert Bireley, 'Redefining Catholicism: Trent and Beyond', in Po-Chia Hsia, *Cambridge History of Christianity*, p. 150.

25 Olin, *Catholic Reformation*, pp. 203–204.

26 H. J. Schroeder, O.P. (ed.), *Canons and Decrees of the Council of Trent*. Rockford, IL, Tan Books and Publishers, Inc., 1978, p. 49.

27 Schroeder, *Canons and Decrees*, pp. 79–80.

Glossary

Apocalyptic — relating to the end of the world, or pertaining to the Apocalypse, the Book of Revelation.

Apostolic action — refers to the practices of the Apostles, which set an example of spreading the Gospel message as part of an active ministry.

Biblia pauperum — tradition of picture Bibles. The Bibles placed the illustrations at the centre of the page, with only a brief text or sometimes no text at all.

Biblical exegesis — critical explanation or interpretation of the Bible.

Bull — document produced by, or on the authority of, the papacy.

Catechism — summary of key doctrines, often presented in accessible form for those untrained in theology.

Church Fathers — early Church theologians, some of whom were eminent teachers and influential bishops, such as St Augustine of Hippo and St Jerome.

Colloques — the regional organisation of the Calvinist Church in France, equivalent to a Catholic diocese.

Complutensian Bible — commissioned in the reign of Ferdinand and Isabella, the Complutensian Bible was completed in 1517 and the first edition was published in 1522 (at Complutense University, better known as Alcalá). It consisted of five volumes printed in their original languages with the Latin version (the Vulgate) in parallel columns.

Confraternities — Catholic voluntary associations of (mainly) lay people established for the promotion of piety and charitable works.

Consubstantiation — the Lutheran doctrine of the Real Presence, reflecting the belief that the bread and wine and body and blood of Christ coexisted exclusively during the communion service (following the Words of Institution).

Corpus Christi — a Catholic feast day celebrating the tradition and belief in the body and blood of Christ, and his Real Presence in the Eucharist.

Creedal statement — definitive statement of beliefs.

Exegesis — critical explanation or interpretation of a text.

Excommunication — act of religious censure by Church authorities, preventing individual from all participation in the Church's activities, especially access to the sacraments.

Fuggers — influential merchant banking family; important supporters of the Habsburgs.

Hagiography — book about the lives of saints. Protestant hagiographies looked at saintly lives, but presented a different slant, given that Protestants rejected the intercessory prayers to, and veneration of, saints.

Huguenot — a term used to describe French Calvinists.

Iconoclasm — wilful destruction of religious images and statues.

Justification — the act of declaring or making righteous in the sight of God.

Magisterial — relating to a magistrate or a person holding the office of a magistrate.

Omnipotence — reference to unlimited power of God.

Omnipresence — or ubiquity, the property of being present everywhere, another attribute of God.

Pharisee — member of an ancient Jewish sect that emphasised strict interpretation of the law.

Polemical debate — contentious argument that is intended to present a particular perspective via attacks on a contrary view.

Predestination — the doctrine that God has ordained all that will happen, especially regarding salvation.

Priesthood of all Believers — Luther's key doctrine that Christ has given believers direct access to God without the mediation of a priest. It represented the belief that God is equally accessible to all the faithful.

Primate
the chief bishop or archbishop of a province, such as the Archbishop of Toledo in Spain or the Archbishop of Canterbury in England.

Purgatory
a place between Heaven and Hell inhabited by the souls of sinners who are atoning for, or being cleansed of, their sins before going to Heaven.

Real Presence
the belief that the body and blood of Christ are truly present in the Eucharist.

Regular and contemplative orders
monastic orders that follow a strict adherence to a Rule ('regula' is a Rule in Latin), such as the Rule of St Benedict. Although they live in cloistered communities, certain monastic orders have greater access to the world than others. Some orders, such as the Carthusians and Cistercians, favour a complete withdrawal from the world for the sake of contemplation.

Religious guilds and fraternities
groups of individuals (such as merchants, artisans and other individuals from the ordinary classes of society) who were not necessarily part of the established religious, military or governmental hierarchies. These guilds or fraternities (sometimes known as sodalities) shared common secular, as well as religious goals.

Sanctification
the act or process of acquiring sanctity, of being made or becoming holy. Sanctification is the process by which the Holy Spirit makes us more like Christ, a development that is impossible without the redeeming work of Christ's suffering and death on the Cross. What divides Catholics and Protestants, and indeed is a matter of debate within Protestantism, is the extent of human intervention in this process.

Schmalkaldic League
a political and military alliance formed in 1531 to defend the Lutheran faith.

Scholastic theology
method of critical thought that dominated intellectual thought in late medieval universities. The scholastic approach is known for its dialectical method of argument, which represents a discourse between different points of view, with the objective of defining a truth by reasoned arguments.

Spiritual contemplation
spiritual contemplation represents prayer that is inspired by the Holy Spirit and has conformity with Christ as its objective.

Spirituali
a group of Catholic reformers, who were conservative in their understanding of the sacraments and Eucharist, but were sympathetic to Luther's doctrine of justification. By 1545, most of the spirituali had died or been largely discredited, especially during the pontificate of Pope Paul IV.

Systematic statement
characterised by the use of order and planning, methodical, and comprising a coherent system, such as the coherence of Calvin's religious teachings.

Transubstantiation
the Roman Catholic belief in the complete transformation of bread and wine to the body and blood of Christ in the Mass.

Tridentine
Of, or pertaining to, the Council of Trent.

Utraquism
from the Latin 'sub utraque specie', meaning in both kinds, representing the belief (held by the Hussites in particular) that the bread and wine should be administered to the laity.

Via mixta
represents a religious life that is between contemplation and action, incorporating elements of both.

Visitation
an official visit or inspection, especially by a bishop to parishes in his diocese.

Vulgate
the principal Latin text of the Bible, prepared mainly by St Jerome, revised in 1592, and adopted as the official version of the Roman Catholic Church.

Bibliography

General

Brady, Thomas, *German Histories in the Age of Reformations, 1400–1650*. Cambridge University Press, 2009.

Brady, Thomas, Heiko Oberman and James Tracy (eds), *Handbook of European History, 1400–1600*, Vol. II. Grand Rapids, MI, William B. Eerdmans, 1995.

Cameron, Euan, *The European Reformation*. Oxford University Press, 2012.

Dickens, A.G., *Reformation and Society in Sixteenth-Century Europe*. Thames & Hudson, London, 1970.

MacCulloch, Diarmaid, *Reformation: Europe's House Divided, 1490–1700*. London, Allen Lane, 2003.

Oberman, Heiko A., *Luther: Man between God the Devil*. London, Fontana Press, 1993.

Po-chia Hsia, R. (ed.), *The Cambridge History of Christianity, Vol. VI: Reform and Expansion, 1500–1660*. Cambridge University Press, 2007.

Marshall, Peter (ed.), *The Oxford Illustrated History of the Reformation*. Oxford University Press, 2015.

Pettegree, Andrew, *The Early Reformation in Europe*. Cambridge University Press, 1992.

Pettegree, Andrew (ed.), *The Reformation World*. London and New York, Routledge, 2000.

Scott Dixon, C. (ed.), *The German Reformation: The Essential Readings*. Oxford, Blackwell Publishers, 1999.

Scribner, Robert and Johnston, Pamela (eds), *The Reformation in Germany and Switzerland* (Cambridge University Press, 1993).

Rublack, Ulinka, *Reformation Europe*. Cambridge University Press, 2005.

Tracy, James, *Europe's Reformations, 1450–1650*. Oxford, Rowman & Littlefield Publishers, 1999.

Specific chapters

Chapter 1

Cameron, Euan, 'Dissent and Heresy', in R. Po-chia-Hsia (ed.), *A Companion to the Reformation World*. Oxford, Blackwell Publishing, 2004.

Huizinga, Johan, *The Autumn of the Middle Ages*. University of Chicago Press, 1996.

Larissa Taylor, 'Society and Piety', in R. Po-chia-Hsia (ed.), *A Companion to the Reformation World*. Oxford, Blackwell Publishing, 2004.

Rex, Richard, 'Humanism', in Pettegree, *Reformation World*.

Van Engen, John (ed.), *Devotio Moderna: Basic Writings*. New York, Paulist Press, 1988.

Chapter 2

Hamm, Berndt, 'What was the Reformation Doctrine of Justification', in C. Scott Dixon (ed.), *The German Reformation: The Essential Readings*

Oberman, Heiko, *Luther: Man between God and the Devil* (London, Fontana, 1993).

Truman, Carl, 'Luther and the Reformation in Germany', in Pettegree (ed.), *The Reformation World*

Chapter 3

Gordon, Bruce, 'Switzerland', in Pettegree (ed.), *The Early Reformation in Europe*.

Gregory, Brad, 'The Radical Reformation', in Marshall, *Oxford Illustrated History*.

Hendrix, Scott, 'Martin Luther, Reformer', in Po-chia Hsia (ed.), *The Cambridge History of Christianity, Vol. VI: Reform and Expansion, 1500–1660*.

Pettegree, Andrew, *Reformation and the Culture of Persuasion*. Cambridge University Press, 2005.

Pettegree, Andrew, 'Books, Pamphlets and Polemic', in Pettegree (ed.), *The Reformation World*.

Roper, Lyndal, 'Martin Luther', in Marshall (ed.), *The Oxford Illustrated History of the Reformation*.

Scott Dixon, C., 'The Princely Reformation in Germany', in Pettegree (ed.), *The Reformation World*.

Stayer, James, 'The German Peasants' War and the Rural Reformation', in Pettegree (ed.), *The Reformation World*. Stayer, James, 'The Radical Reformation', in Brady et al. *Handbook of European History*.

Taplin, Mark, 'Switzerland', in Pettegree (ed.), *The Reformation World*.

Truman, Carl, 'Luther and the Reformation in Germany', in Pettegree (ed.), *The Reformation World*.

Williams, George, *The Radical Reformation*. Kirksville, MO, Truman State University Press, 2000.

Chapter 4

Elton, G.R. (ed.), *The New Cambridge Modern History: Volume II, The Reformation*. Cambridge University Press, 1990.

Greengrass, Mark, *The European Reformation, c.1500–1618*. London and New York, Longman, 1998.

Chapter 5

Gordon, Bruce, *Calvin*. London and New Haven, Yale University Press, 2009.

Kingdon, Robert, 'The Calvinist Reformation in Geneva', in R. Po-Chia Hsia (ed.), *The Cambridge History of Christianity, Volume VI: Reform and Expansion, 1500–1660*.

McKim, Donald K. (ed.), *The Cambridge Companion to Calvin*. Cambridge University Press, 2004.

Murdock, Graeme, *Beyond Calvin: The Intellectual, Political and Cultural World of Europe's Reformed Churches*. London, Palgrave, 2004.

Prestwich, Menna (ed.), *International Calvinism, 1541–1715* (Oxford, Clarendon Press, 1986).

Chapter 6

Dickens, A.G., *The Counter-Reformation*. London, Thames & Hudson, 1992.

Evennett, H. Outram, *The Spirit of the Counter-Reformation*. Cambridge University Press, 1968.

Kelly, J.N.D., *The Oxford Dictionary of Popes*. Oxford University Press, 1986.

Luebke, David (ed.), *The Counter-Reformation*. Oxford, Blackwell Publishing, 1999.

Mullett, Michael, *The Catholic Reformation*. London, Routledge, 1999.

O'Malley, John, *Trent and all That*. Cambridge, MA, Harvard University Press, 2000.

Outram Evennett, H., *The Spirit of the Counter-Reformation* (Cambridge University Press, 1968).

Acknowledgements

The authors and publishers acknowledge the following sources of copyright material and are grateful for the permissions granted. While every effort has been made, it has not always been possible to identify the sources of all the material used, or to trace all copyright holders. If any omissions are brought to our notice, we will be happy to include the appropriate acknowledgements on reprinting.

The publisher would like to thank the following for permission to reproduce their photographs.

Cover image: P Deliss/Godong/Corbis. **Chapter 1 opener:** Peter Horree / Alamy. **Figure 1.2:** GraphicaArtis / Getty Images. **Figure 1.3:** DEA / G. DAGLI ORTI / Getty Images. **Figure 1.4:** Fine Art Images / Getty Images. **Chapter 2 opener:** INTERFOTO / Alamy. **Figure 2.2:** Lebrecht Music and Arts Photo Library / Alamy. **Figure 2.4:** INTERFOTO / Alamy. **Figure 2.5:** Private Collection / Bridgeman Images. **Figure 2.6:** The Art Archive / Alamy. **Figure 2.7:** The Art Archive / Alamy. **Chapter 3 opener:** Peter Righteous / Alamy. **Figure 3.1:** The Stapleton Collection / Bridgeman Images. **Figure 3.2:** The Art Archive / Alamy. **Figure 3.3:** akg-images. **Chapter 4 opener:** Interfoto / History. **Figure 4.1: Wiki. Figure 4.2:** Peter Righteous / Alamy. **Figure 4.3:** Historical image collection by Bildagentur-online / Alamy. **Chapter 5 opener:** The Art Archive / Alamy. **Figure 5.1:** Pictorial Press Ltd / Alamy. **Figure 5.4:** World History Archive / Alamy. **Chapter 6 opener:** The Art Archive / Alamy. **Figure 6.1:** World History Archive / Alamy. **Figure 6.2:** Mary Evans Picture Library / Alamy. **Figure 6.3:** DEA / VENERANDA BIBLIOTECA AMBROSIANA / Getty Images.

The publisher would like to thank the following for permission to reproduce extracts from their texts.

Extract Chapter 1: R.N. Swanson, Religion and Devotion in Europe, c.1215-c.1515, 1995, reprinted with permission of Cambridge University Press. **Extract Chapter 1:** From Reformation and Society in Sixteenth-Century Europe by A.G. Dickens © Thames & Hudson 1966 reproduced by kind permission of Thames & Hudson Ltd. London. **Extract Chapter 2:** Europe's Reformations, 1450-1650 by Tracy, James D. Reproduced with permission of Rowman and Littlefield Publishers, Incorporated in the format Republish in a book via Copyright Clearance Center. **Extract Chapter 2:** M. Mullett, Martin Luther's Ninety-Five Theses, History Today, September, Issue 46, reproduced with permission of History Today Ltd. **Extract Chapter 6:** E. Duffy, Saints and Sinners: A History of the Popes (Yale University Press, 1997), S4C.

Index

Lightning Source UK Ltd.
Milton Keynes UK
UKOW07f1905220216

268899UK00002B/4/P